Global Game, Local Arena

Global Game, Local Arena

Restructuring in Corner Brook, Newfoundland

Glen Norcliffe

ISER Books gratefully acknowledges the assistance of the Faculty of Arts, Memorial University of Newfoundland.

This book has been published with the help of a grant from the Canadian Federation for the Humanities and Social Sciences, through the Aid to Scholarly Publications Programme, using funds provided by the Social Sciences and Humanities Research Council of Canada.

Library and Archives Canada Cataloguing in Publication

Norcliffe, Glen
Global game, local arena : restructuring in Corner Brook, Newfoundland / Glen Norcliffe.

(Social and economic studies ; no. 70)
Includes bibliographical references and index.
ISBN 1-894725-03-4

1. Corner Brook (N.L.) – Economic conditions – 20th century. 2. Corner Brook Pulp and Paper – History. 3. Corner Brook (N.L.) – Social conditions – 20th century. I. Memorial University of Newfoundland. Institute of Social and Economic Research. II. Title. III. Series: Social and economic studies (St. John's, N.L.) ; no. 70.

HC118.C67N67 2005 306.3'09718 C2005-901505-5

Published by ISER Books - Faculty of Arts Publications
Institute of Social and Economic Research
Memorial University of Newfoundland
St. John's, NL A1C 5S7

Printed and bound in Canada

Contents

To Sophie and Angus

Preface

As a nine-year-old growing up near Liverpool in England, I became aware of the city of Corner Brook several years before I was awakened to the existence of Toronto and Montreal. The circumstance for this early discovery of Corner Brook was the showing at school of a film that had been procured by a friend's father employed at Bowater's factory in nearby Ellesmere Port. The year was 1952. I now realize, 50 years later, the significance of that film. It had been made to record the post-war expansion of Bowater's Corner Brook mill that made it the biggest newsprint mill in the world (by rated capacity). I would not have guessed then that 40 years later I would spend three summers at Corner Brook gathering information for this study.

My original intention, in writing this book, was to interpret changes in the mode of production practised in Corner Brook's large pulp and paper mill *following* its takeover by a Canadian multinational corporation in 1984, during a period of extensive modernization. I had hoped to deploy aspects of regulation theory, and particularly the transition from Fordist production to more flexible post-Fordist forms. It soon became apparent, however, that such a project was too circumscribed. I needed to situate the Corner Brook story in the much larger context of globalization, and it became necessary to examine a wider range of post-Fordist forms of production. In order to connect theoretical understandings of the global-local relationship and the empirical work I had embarked upon in Corner Brook in the early 1990s, I found it increasingly neccssary to push back my time horizons and enlarge the geographical context. Thus I ended up tracing the story of the mill from its colonial beginnings as a company town in the early part of the twentieth century and contextualizing its new spatialities at scales ranging from the local to the global.

State power working with capital was instrumental in launching the project to construct the mill, and has been decisive at several subsequent moments in the transformation of the mill to its present form, very much along the lines outlined by Henri Lefebvre in *The Production of Space* (1991). In this respect, little has changed since the plan to construct a mill was hatched in the early 1920s. British imperial interests joined up with local politicians and entrepreneurs, shook some money out of the pockets of British banks and the British government, and the project was launched. After changing ownership four times, the mill has been operating for nearly a quarter-century as a fully owned subsidiary of the Kruger Corporation of Montreal. During this period the mill has been extensively restructured, with the model of lean production best describing the pattern of change. From a geographical perspective, these changes did not end at the mill gate – they spread to the households of mill employees, to the larger community, and in certain respects were rescaled up to the global level.

In his 2002 book, *Making Native Space: Colonialism, Resistance and Reserves in British Columbia*, Cole Harris takes up a number of themes that resonate in the context of British Columbia. The title of this book might have been a play on Harris's title, such as: *Making Industrial Spaces: Colonialism, Restructuring, and Resistance*. Newfoundland's history is, of course, different from that of British Columbia, but both were marked by a colonial status that lingers yet in various post-colonial legacies. The industrial space of Corner Brook was remade in the image of globalization after 1984. Given the industrial sclerosis that enveloped the plant in the 1960s and 1970s, it is hardly surprising that aspects of the restructuring were contested. Active resistance in the workplace created industrial unrest in the early years of restructuring, whereas in more recent years I will argue that resistance has taken a more subtle form.

Acknowledgements

I gratefully acknowledge the financial support granted by the Social Sciences and Humanities Research Council of Canada for project number 410-91-1763 entitled “Place and Workplace: Geographical Studies of Industrial Restructuring and Social Change in Canadian Pulp and Paper Communities.” Principal investigators of this project were: Roger Hayter at Simon Fraser University; John Holmes at Queen’s University; Suzanne Mackenzie, formerly of Carleton University, who very sadly did not live to see the final parts of this project completed; Glen Norcliffe and Valerie Preston at York University; and Damaris Rose at the Institut National des Recherches Scientifiques in Montreal. I owe much to my co-researchers for the energy and creative insights they contributed to this team project.

The project’s research assistants in Corner Brook were Judy Bates, Maureen MacIsaac, and Justin Wyeth, who worked hard to meet a busy interview schedule. Subsequently, Cathy Kemp did a wonderful job of converting the taped interviews into transcripts. Judy Bates gave invaluable help in coding the transcripts and leading me through the intricacies of the NU*DIST program for ethnographic analysis. The principal, librarian, and faculty of Sir Wilfred Grenfell College (of the Memorial University of Newfoundland) in Corner Brook kindly made college facilities available to me. Dr. Ingrid Botting was most helpful in sending me an unpublished paper and excerpts from her Ph.D. thesis written at Memorial University.

I offer my sincere thanks to the management of the Corner Brook Pulp and Paper Company, to the executive of the locals of the (then) Canadian Papermakers’ Union, to employees and former employees of the Corner Brook Pulp and Paper Mill, and to their families for their generous help in providing information, data, and guidance in responding to the questionnaire survey and for participating in longer interviews. I particularly thank Shirley Kennedy for her insights. My return trips to Ontario laden with bottled moose, cods' tongues, partridgeberry jam, and bear steaks are indicative of the extraordinary hospitality of the residents of Corner Brook. The presidents and executives of union locals based at the mill were particularly helpful in encouraging their membership to participate in the research project. The management of the Corner Brook Pulp and Paper Company, and especially Doug Kendrick, were equally supportive in explaining to me the company's operating practices and providing other baseline information. Keith Newman, the research officer with the Communications, Energy and Paperworkers' Union in Montreal, also provided valuable background information.

At York University, Gladys Fung of Scott Library has gone to a great deal of trouble tracing material through the interlibrary loan system. Carolyn King and Carol Randall drafted excellent maps and diagrams. Kathy Armstrong's computer skills transformed my messy files into a neat manuscript. My wife, Mary, patiently read the manuscript text and suggested numerous improvements. During the long gestation period and subsequent production of this book, the staff at ISER Books have been supporters of the project. And in the final stages, Richard Tallman patiently copy-edited the entire manuscript. To all these people who have been so consistently helpful, my manifold thanks are due.

This book has been published with the help of a grant from the Canadian Federation for the Humanities and Social Sciences, through the Aid to Scholarly Publications Programme, using funds provided by the Social Sciences and Humanities Research Council of Canada.

This book is dedicated to my two grandchildren, Sophie and Angus, with the hope that their working lives will be blessed with the collegiality and friendship that I have enjoyed in such large measure for so many years at York University.

The Global-Local Nexus 1

Scattered across Canada's vast hinterland are hundreds of small towns engaged in harvesting and processing resources used to produce goods that are sold either in Canada's heartland or in export markets. On account of their sheer numbers, their substantial contribution to Canadian GDP, and their importance as a source of exports, resource towns remain an important and current theme in the nation's economic geography. Although they have often been dismissed as part of the *old economy*, in practice resource industries and the towns in which they are located have close ties to contemporary economic, social, political, and cultural changes; indeed, they have sometimes been impacted more heavily by free trade, flows of foreign direct investment, and various forms of deregulation than have metropolitan centres that are identified with the *new economy*. Thus, as Hayter, Barnes, and Bradshaw (2003) have proposed, resource peripheries also belong at the core of current theorizing in economic geography. Because resource towns are directly connected by trade to the global economy and by investment to international capital, they experience the roller-coaster existence that accompanies most instances of resource dependence. Not surprisingly, some of Canada's resource communities have prospered, some have been closed and become ghost towns, while others have passed through one or more phases of boom and bust as price fluctuations on world commodity markets have affected local production and local economies.

Precisely how many resource towns there are in Canada depends on the definition adopted, but according to Randall and Ironside (1996: 24) the Canadian Association of Single-Industry Towns reckoned that there were more than 1,000 such resource communities in 1987. They are, unquestionably, an important element in Canada's geography: without them, much of the nation's hinterland would remain unoccupied. Resource towns form part of Harold Innis's (1956) *staple economy* in which a community's economic fortunes are governed by demand for resource products in external markets. Innis's seminal contribution to Canadian economic history was to theorize how a distinctly Canadian version of staple-dependent economic development has unfolded, which is why Barnes (1993a, 1993b) proclaims Innis as a *local* hero. In Innis's view, staple-dependent communities often became trapped in their specializations, thereby failing to diversify their economic bases to any great extent. The capital equipment used in these resource industries was mostly supplied from abroad, the staples themselves were exported, and beyond some investment in necessary transport infrastructure, local development remained narrowly based on the particular resources available, plus a few service industries (Watkins, 1963, 1982). In addition, there were some spinoffs in management functions and financial services in Canadian metropolises (Careless, 1989)

Today, we should follow Britton (1996: 97) and talk of the *new staple economy*, with some changes in the mix of resources exported and more emphasis on processing and adding value to them, but resources still remain the foundation of many communities' hopes (Hamilton and Seyfrit, 1994). The connections between Canada's resource towns and the outside world have also subtly changed between the earlier colonial phase and the current global phase. In the earlier period of company towns, vertically integrated firms to a certain degree could insulate their towns from world commodity price fluctuations. These oligopolistic firms could pass on production cost increases; during economic downturns, they had no great incentive to lay off large numbers of workers since if they moved out of town it would be costly to recruit replacements when the firm next geared up for expansion. More recently, however, a whole series of institutional changes associated with the widespread adoption of neo-liberal agendas since the 1980s have connected resource towns to the vagaries of the global economy, in so doing re-scaling global processes to the local level where they have often triggered rounds of restructuring.[1] These changes include:

- tariff reductions under the General Agreement on Tariffs and Trade (GATT), its successor, the World Trade Organization (WTO), and the North American Free Trade Agreement (NAFTA);
- fewer restrictions on international capital flows;

- the vertical disintegration of many large integrated corporations;
- the transfer of company towns to public municipal status;
- accelerated corporate takeovers, de-acquisitions, and mergers;
- extensive restructuring.

Although many of these resource communities are small and remote, they are more susceptible to global upturns and downturns than Canada's largest cities, which are buffered from the biggest economic swings by their large administrative and service sectors. Hence the paradox that Canada's resource towns are more nakedly part of the global economy than are large metropolises such as Toronto and Vancouver, which are heralded as *world cities*.

RESOURCES AND GLOBALISM: EXAMINING THE GLOBAL THROUGH THE LOCAL

This study examines one of Canada's medium-sized resource towns – Corner Brook – which is situated on the west coast of Newfoundland. Like most single-industry towns, Corner Brook has experienced boom times and slumps, restructuring and layoffs, in-migration and out-migration, and high hopes followed by despondency about its future prospects.[2] In fact, the case of restructuring in Corner Brook is particularly appealing because it engages many of the themes of current interest to human geographers and, most centrally, debates about the relationship between local change and the global economy, about the character of economic restructuring, about the connections between economy and society, about the rescaling of economic processes to produce uneven patterns of development, and about the role of institutions and culture in economic change. Having been a company town set in a colonial outpost of the British Empire for the first quarter-century of its existence, Corner Brook has since evolved into a public town set in an integrated continental economy, while its status as a single-industry town has been qualified by its emerging role as the regional service centre for western Newfoundland. Significant restructuring has occurred in Corner Brook, although this has not been on a massive scale; technology in the mill has been progressively upgraded, and there have been job losses, so that labour and capital productivity have risen quite substantially. Some jobs have been outsourced, and the quality of the final product – newsprint – has been steadily improved. Job losses in the same period in other resource sectors, such as fishing, mining, and logging, have compounded these effects so that Corner Brook's rate of population decline in the past decade has been among the fastest of all Canada's census agglomerations. These have not, however, been headline-grabbing changes. But precisely because they have, for the most part, passed under the national radar, they can in some sense be viewed as typical: comparable changes have been occurring in hundreds of Canada's single-industry resource towns over the past two decades, again mostly unheralded. As we shall see, although these acts of restructuring from a distance may appear fairly routine, their impacts on individual households can be quite devastating, and collectively they raise disturbing questions about the long-term viability of Canada's entire mid-North.

The main objective of this book is to examine the tensions between globally driven pressures for industrial restructuring and the re-scaling of these pressures in the specific resource community of Corner Brook, a town that has been much affected by this process. The period of restructuring began with the purchase of the mill by a new owner in 1984 and continued on an incremental basis for the following 15 years. This was a period when the highly regulated international economy conceived at the Bretton Woods Conference of 1944, and managed along Keynesian principles until the 1970s, was being actively reshaped along neo-liberal lines (Brenner, 2004). The institutional framework for managing the global economy has been substantially revised in the recent neo-liberal era: trade has been liberalized, international capital flows have been largely deregulated, and the number and scope of transnational corporations have greatly expanded. The result, then, has been a major transformation of the global economy, which is reflected in several important shifts:

- a very large expansion of international trade and investment;
- the emergence of the triad trading blocks (NAFTA, the European Union, and Japan and the newly industrialized economies of East Asia);
- the growth of a small number of global cities, such as Tokyo, London, and New York, as centres of control of the global economy;
- a big increase in international subcontracting of production;
- increased international migration;

- the transformation of international agencies and institutions to facilitate this neo-liberal program (e.g., the creation of the World Trade Organization out of the less formally structured General Agreement on Tariffs and Trade).

At the same time, as Stephen Flusty (2004) points out, globalization has also entered into our daily lives in myriad ways that are not directly economic: we hear Congolese music on the CBC, we get e-mail from friends travelling far away, we see images of distant disasters in close to real time, and we encounter the sound of unfamiliar languages on the streets.

The "local" is a more elusive concept, not least because local interests are often promoted by operators working at much larger scales, for instance, when local representatives are able to influence policy at the federal level or within an international agency. In the present case, the term *local* evidently encompasses the city of Corner Brook and the surrounding region, but activities at the provincial scale within Newfoundland are commonly acts of local construction. The fact that a string of Newfoundland's leaders, including Prime Minister Richard Squires, and premiers Joseph Smallwood, Frank Moores, Clyde Wells, Brian Tobin, and the present premier, Danny Williams, have represented Corner Brook or its region at the provincial or federal level has helped place local concerns in the minds of many provincial politicians. Premier Smallwood, in particular, micromanaged the entire province, much like a town manager.[3] There have also been many occasions when entrepreneurs and administrators in New York, Ottawa, Montreal, and other cities have given priority to the narrow interests of particular localities such as Corner Brook rather than broad national or global interests.

Here I will focus on how these tendencies for global restructuring have had an impact at a very different scale – that of a small resource community. Of particular interest are the economic impacts of restructuring to lean production, their consequences for workers, workers' families, and the larger community, and the periodic acts of local resistance to such changes. The dialectical relationship between global and local interests has attracted the attention of a wide range of social scientists during the past 30 years, particularly in development studies where conflicts between outside forces such as transnational corporations and local groups such as peasant farmers have created a series of *causes célèbres*, as with the Chiapas rebellion in southern Mexico. During the 1970s, mainstream economic geography began to follow regional science in a search for universal laws to account for disparities in regional development. For a while this drew economic geography closer to the law-seeking practices of neo-classical economics than to the discursive approaches of political science and social anthropology. Subsequently, as Allan Scott (2000) explains in his masterly historical overview, mainstream human geography has shifted its ground to inhabit a series of *post*-prefixed territories – the postmodern, post-feminist, post-structural, and the post-colonial – where different actors are recognized as working out locally their competing interests, and where instrumental rationality is replaced by contingent explanations situated in place and time. Census tabulations and econometric models were either superseded or complemented, in this paradigm shift, by interviews, focus groups, actor network models, and other qualitative methodologies. Trevor Barnes (2001) characterizes the former as *epistemological theorizing* given to the search for universal laws that accurately mirror the world, and the latter as *hermeneutic theorizing* given to more pluralistic and discursive explanations, acknowledging reflexivity on the part of the researcher, and viewing the world as overdetermined and somewhat chaotic (Jessop, 1999).

The approach adopted here is broadly *post-structural* and *critical.* The aim is to probe beyond empirical and essentialist explanations of the observed changes in Corner Brook to identify the underlying social and political processes. It is taken as given that global processes are re-scaled in somewhat different ways by different local interests and power relations, divergent political arrangements, and contrasting local geographies, so the objective is not a universal model of restructuring in resource towns. Understandings are locally contingent. The evidence used here is partly quantitative (drawing on Statistics Canada data and a questionnaire survey) and partly qualitative (including local newspaper reports and ethnographic research involving extended personal interviews).

Over the years, promises of prosperity made by the promoters of resource development have been sufficiently enticing that proposals to create Canada's resource towns have rarely met with local resistance; indeed, if historical accounts are to be trusted, across the land the initial response from remote communities has been to welcome the opportunity to connect into world trade. The voices of the few opposed to the creation of new towns have usually been drowned out by the majority who favour civic boosterism, corporate expansion, and, above all, new jobs. Thus the plan to establish a new newsprint town in western Newfoundland in the early 1920s was greeted with approval in most parts of the island. The civil engineering project that was then launched was quite remarkable for its scale and speed of implementation, and in its context compares with some of Canada's most ambitious development schemes of the late twentieth century. In short shrift, a new company town was created on the shores of the Humber Arm consisting of a large pulp and paper mill, a deepwater port, workers' and management housing, social services, and a hydroelectric installation at Deer Lake.

A wave of industrial restructuring has affected many of Canada's resource towns in the past quarter-century. It has been a political project triggered mainly by the liberalization of international trade and capital flows, and by market deregulation designed to raise productivity in order to become competitive with industry leaders, whether these are located in Scandinavia, Japan, the United States, or elsewhere in Canada. Such restructuring is different from long-term changes due to technological progress: restructuring is associated with major qualitative and quantitative changes in the relations of production brought about by geographical switches in capital (Lovering, 1989). In the case of Corner Brook, restructuring was a consequence of the mill being opened to intensive international competition following its takeover by the Kruger Corporation, and being required to engage in an extensive modernization program financed partly by government and partly from the mill's own revenue stream. Restructuring is also geographically contingent, with the form it takes depending on local circumstances. As the witticism goes, corporations faced with the need to restructure may choose to *automate, emigrate, or evaporate.* In the case of Corner Brook, the choice was essentially to automate.

Swyngedouw (1996) and Cox (1997) identify 1972, after the U.S. dollar was de-linked from gold, as the year that marked the beginning of the dismantling of the institutional arrangements envisioned at the 1944 Bretton Woods Conference to regulate post-war global economic relations. Since the early 1970s, the progressive deregulation of the global economy has inaugurated an era of *competitive austerity* and rapid spatial adjustment (Albo, 1994). The concept of rapid spatial adjustment connects with Swyngedouw's (1992, 1997) use of the term 'glocalization' to describe the changes occurring in the global economy. There are two main elements of this process. First, major rounds of capital restructuring are initiated in each sector of the economy, often accompanied by takeovers, downsizing, and switches in markets as companies jockey to improve their competitive position. The precarious economic regime created by this uninhibited and aggressive movement of capital has been labelled *disorganized capital* by Lash and Urry (1987) due to the instability found in its circuits of capital, which are continually being renegotiated, leading to changeable patterns of corporate transactions, labour relations, and geographies of production. Second, a scalar shift follows from this as each firm translates its new local circumstances into global strategies, and in turn builds global circumstances into local strategies, with spatial adjustments that may include plant closures and openings, product changes, plant upgrading and downsizing, outsourcing, automation, and layoffs. There is, therefore, as Kelly (2000) reminds us, a continuous and reflexive interpenetration of the global and the local as restructuring occurs so that the global is to be understood as much by the way global processes trigger *local* economic transformations as by the changes wrought at the global level. Such changes, particularly negative ones, are contested by actors from the global down to the local. The precise form of restructuring is different in every community – each is a distinct arena in which the relations among global, national, regional, and local interests have to be worked out – the common thread being corporate pressure to be competitive in deregulated global markets (McQuaig, 1998). In turn, local changes feed back up to larger scales so that with restructuring there is a recurring interpenetration of the global and the local. This process, a form of *reflexivity*, is important to a post-structural understanding of economic change because it asserts that you cannot simply read off local consequences of restructuring from some master template: local outcomes are *constructed* through a subtle interaction of global and local interests.

There is extensive evidence of the incremental deregulation of the global economy during the past three decades as states and regions, as a requirement of signing various international agreements, have agreed to reduce protective barriers. In direct consequence of being exposed to new competitive pressures, a number of sectors and communities have petitioned governments to provide new forms of (often "temporary") assistance to counter global competition (which they invariably characterize as "unfair trade" in order to legitimate the intervention). Thus in 2002 the George W. Bush administration in the United States, whose election platform included the rhetoric of free trade and which has actively promoted the creation of a Free Trade Area of the Americas (FTAA), signed into law legislation protecting the U.S. softwood lumber, steel, and agricultural industries on the grounds that foreign governments were providing unfair subsidies. This contradiction was widely attributed to political motives, specifically the desire to win votes in swing states in which these industries are major employers. At a subnational scale, it is not uncommon to find states, provinces, and municipalities offering incentive packages and tax holidays to attract new investment.[4] In part this results from the *subsidiarity* practised by central governments anxious to reduce their expenditures by downloading social programs to lower levels of government. This raises an important and hotly debated issue: do local and provincial governments have much leverage in development, or are they now largely at the mercy of major corporate players in the global game? By offering substantial incentives, communities can sometimes attract direct investment, but can they mitigate the negative aspects of restructuring? For instance, do local communities have the capacity to contest restructuring, downsizing, layoffs, or plant closures? Can they shape these processes to match local preferences?

Commentators including Piore and Sabel (1984) and Saskia Sassen (1991) contend that global interests have awesome powers, not least because capital is so mobile. This discourse sees locational fluidity giving transnational corporations the power to relocate, switch production, contract with new suppliers, and lay off workers. It sees the hyper-mobility of capital leaving communities with few cards to play as global interests set community against community, extracting concessions, and then repeating the process in the next round of restructuring. Neo-liberals contend that capital mobility increases national competitiveness, even if social programs are squeezed in the process.

There is, however, an alternative discourse that Susan Clarke (1993) calls *the new localism.* Cox (1992, 1997) asks whether globalization and capital hyper-mobility are necessarily linked, coming to the conclusion that current debates about globalization "undermine the collective power of the working class" and the potential for worker resistance (Cox, 1997: 177). In her studies of restructuring in the Australian coal industry, Gibson (1992) argues that, contrary to conventional wisdom, there is considerable scope for local resistance to international capital. She recommends strategies for a new localism by engaging the state in constructing a program that promotes local interests and turns the rhetorical tide in favour of labour by resisting decertification, layoffs, rollbacks, and givebacks. The new localism argues that the state should be disconnected from global interests favouring intensified international competition and reconnected back to local priorities; the logic suggests that this matter is to be resolved in the fields of local politics, institutions, and regulation.[5] In addition, the literature on community economic development (CED) asserts that communities have considerable traction if they choose to grasp the possibilities available to them. Thus, in his study of community development in Newfoundland and Labrador, House (2003: 235) stresses the need "to institutionalize a partnership approach between government and community." Recent contributors to the debate on CED, including Dhesi (2000), Simon (2001), and Kenny (2002), stress the importance to local development of social capital built by "interested and resourceful individuals." Bates and Norcliffe (2005) in their study of the impacts of restructuring on the region surrounding Corner Brook argue, however, that the controversial concept of social capital – which is apparently in good supply given the region's well-developed family and social networks, associational life, and high levels of trust – is not in itself sufficient to advance community economic development. What is lacking are the institutional structures needed to mobilize social capital.[6]

Within Canada, recent deregulatory acts have tended to sharpen global-local differences. By various acts of deregulation, including joining NAFTA, being a signatory to the GATT's Uruguay Round and (since 1995) to the World Trade Organization, permitting freer international flows of capital, and adopting a floating exchange rate, the state has promoted globalization. In an earlier era when many resource towns were company towns, municipal and corporate interests were identical: what was good for the corporation was good for the town. But in the age of neo-liberalism, community aspirations and those of the proprietary transnational companies have diverged quite dramatically, thereby creating possibilities for conflict.[7] The corporations argue that, since newsprint mills face stiff competition from foreign producers when selling their products in distant markets, their need to remain competitive in the global economy has to take precedence over local interests, even at the expense of jobs and quality of life. If the mill shuts, everyone suffers. As international trade has been progressively deregulated, so actors in the global economy have increasingly pleaded the case for remaining competitive. These strategies, commonly given the label *lean production*, include:

- automation so that machines increasingly dictate the pace of work and employment is uncoupled from production;
- shrinking the labour force, which puts downward pressure on wages;
- requiring greater labour flexibility of those still employed;

- subcontracting various activities to low-wage suppliers to squeeze costs;
- focusing on producing core products and discontinuing subsidiary activities;
- developing new higher value-added products;
- using resource inputs more efficiently;
- partial and complete closure of older production facilities, and opening new facilities.

In most cases, such forms of restructuring have had negative local and regional impacts by requiring concessions from the workforce, their families, and the community. Some of these impacts are short-term, but others do enduring harm. Corporations insist that in the long run restructuring usually helps the continued existence of the plant. It is no surprise, then, that these globally driven restructuring strategies have sometimes been locally contested. In turn, these contests have influenced the way economic geographers look at restructuring.

In her assessment of the contribution of economic geographers to an understanding of globalization, Susan Roberts (1995) (see Leyshon, 1997) makes three criticisms. First, from a structuralist viewpoint, she argues that it is important to go beyond the empirical observation and measurement of changes to identify and excavate the underlying processes at work. Second, she sees a need for analyses of globalization to address political, social, and cultural factors as well as economic factors.[8] And third, she advocates a more critical analysis that does not simply accept globalization as an inevitable step in the march of economic modernization. The relation of each of these three criticisms to this study of Corner Brook needs some elaboration.

Roberts's first criticism concerns the empirical orientation of many studies of globalization. Since the ideas developed here grow out of a case study, it is impossible to avoid presenting quite a lot of empirical material, especially as key sources of information include a questionnaire survey and interviews with mill management, employees, and their families. The aim, however, is to use these empirical data to develop a grounded interpretation of how restructuring has occurred in Corner Brook. I argue that globalization of the newsprint industry involves more than organizations and networks operating at the global level. As Kelly (2000) demonstrates for Cavite in the Philippines, globalization also finds expression at the local level through the activities of local actors, local interests, and local processes of economic and social change.

Second, the interpretation consciously includes non-economic factors. Political and institutional factors have been crucial to the development of the pulp and paper industry in Corner Brook from the very beginning. The approach in Chapter 2 is historical, interpreting the history of the company (and post-company) town up to 1983. Chapter 3 deals with the political and social debates that surrounded the purchase of the mill in 1984 by the Montreal-based Kruger Corporation. Chapter 4 is mainly economic but also has a political dimension, in that it uses the blueprint of lean production to interpret changes to production at the mill since it was purchased. Although Chapter 5 examines the economic activity of work, many social insights were provided by the employees who were interviewed. Chapter 6, which examines the impact of restructuring on families and on the community, focuses explicitly on social and cultural issues. The concluding chapter returns to the central theme of global-local tensions, arguing that institutions are important to our understanding of the local impacts of global change.

THEORETICAL POSITIONS

The critical perspective adopted in this book relates to the position of Trevor Barnes (1996: 250) when he writes of universal explanations in economic geography:

> there is neither a single point of inquiry, nor a single logic, spatial or otherwise. The best we can hope for are shards and fragments; there is not one economic geography, but many economic geographies, not one complete story but a set of fragmented stories.

In the late 1990s, mainstream thinking in economic geography began to question our ability to provide formulaic and universal explanations of economic activity, substituting more fragmentary *constructivist* understandings that Barnes connects to various "post-prefixed" theories (e.g., postmodernist, post-structuralist) and a number of other related critical frameworks. These draw particularly on the philosophical works of Richard Rorty and French theorists such as Michel Foucault and Jacques Derrida, who argue that our understandings of the world do not constitute objective knowledge but are constructions based on our individual experiences and on the fluidity of meaning of words. In short, knowledge is often subjective: our understanding of the world mirrors what we already know and how we interpret texts on globalization. It follows that we need to be critical when making our assessments for fear that we end up seeing what we want to see. The global game is evidently played out in a different way in each arena, thus requiring a critical perspective that rejects formulaic explanations and interrogates explanations at all levels. This makes explanation a much more subjective and introspective process than we might have suspected, hence the importance of avoiding explanations that reflect our own inclinations. Nor should we view the world purely in ideographic terms where every event is accounted for by a unique set of factors. A critical approach leaves us somewhere in between, with partial understandings (the shards and fragments) that refuse to fit neatly together in one universal jigsaw puzzle, although they do connect sets of events. It is here that geographical perspectives become particularly valuable because these fragments make most sense when viewed in their geographical context. Quite simply, they are locally contingent, and that contingency revolves around local geographies and histories. The process of globalization is worked out in a different way in each community because a unique set of circumstances is always to be found at the local level. What this implies is that we may achieve 'middle-order' explanations (to use Michael Storper's term) that are less than universal but have some degree of generality. Clearly implicit in such a position is the possibility of constructing local strategies to combat global pressures.

Regulation, Institutions, and Local Development

In searching for a foundation on which to conceptualize the *recent* social and economic changes seen in Corner Brook, several contributions were considered. Harold Innis's staple theory provides a comprehensive historical understanding of the development of Canada's resource economy and of how the economic projects of the British Empire were re-scaled to numerous communities, which became trapped into particular resource activities (see, e.g., Innis, 1954, 1956; Drache, 1995). But his theory is addressed to the circumstances that existed from the colonial period until the mid-twentieth century. It did not describe (nor could it be expected to) the technological and institutional changes associated with the shift to lean production that occurred half a century after his death, when neo-liberals were engaged in a sustained attack on the Keynesian social democratic constructions of the post-war "Fordist" era. Innis's theory in some regards connects well with the ideas developed here – for instance, his *staple trap* has much in common with the institutionalists' *regional lock-in* and *path dependence* (discussed below). Thus the present study, while acknowledging a debt to Innis, seeks to extend his institutional framework to current circumstances, placing more emphasis on the social ramifications of economic change.

A related framework that draws on Innis's ideas is proposed in Rex Lucas's *Minetown, Milltown, Railtown*, published in 1971. Lucas's model suggests an economic progression in single-industry towns, with four stages: construction of the community; recruitment of citizens and workforce; transition to stability; and maturity. Bradbury and St. Martin (1983) have added a fifth stage: winding down – as has happened in a significant number of mining towns (see Neil et al., 1992). Lucas's model does capture the early stages of Corner Brook's development, discussed in Chapter 2, but the main interest of this study falls into what Lucas calls "maturity" (which has connotations of a stable economy that is fully developed). In practice, since achieving "maturity" Corner Brook has been caught up in a round of restructuring that has changed the entire mode of production at the newsprint mill, as well as its social correlates. Lucas's model has much in common with Walt Rostow's *Stages of Economic Growth* (1960), and can be criticized on the same grounds. Both are inductive and somewhat deterministic models that generalize what has happened, but they do not excavate the underlying structural processes, particularly the restructuring of international capital. They both posit a final stable stage (high mass consumption/maturity) with the implicit modernist assumption that there is then an end to history. Like Innis's work, Lucas's model predates the recent era of globalization and the transition to lean production. It also presumes universal processes, in contrast to the post-structural approach adopted here, which suggests that these larger processes are worked out locally to produce a range of different outcomes. Most evidently, single-industry towns based on non-renewable resources can be expected eventually to be wound down when the resource is exhausted, whereas towns based on renewable resources are likely to undergo periodic rounds of restructuring as sunk capital is worn out, provided that the resource is managed on a sustainable basis.

Several of the themes developed in Innis's and Lucas's studies were incorporated into Patricia Marchak's landmark book, *Green Gold*, published in 1983 at a time when British Columbia's forest industries were in crisis following the deterioration of their softwood lumber and newsprint export markets as a result of the severe recession of 1980-82. Marchak takes her analysis much deeper than Lucas by introducing a carefully constructed sociological analysis of the impacts of recession on households and on communities. Her discussions of class, of patterns of employment and unemployment, and of women's work – both formal and informal – were highly innovative. She went beyond examining the economic impacts of perturbations in world commodity markets on resource communities to assess the human impact. Marchak presents case studies of Mackenzie, an *instant town* located north of Prince George, and of Terrace, an old logging town located close to the port of Prince Rupert. Marchak's three major themes, capital, labour, and communities, will be taken up in this study. But the context of Corner Brook in the 1980s and 1990s differs from that described by Marchak in several important respects. Above all, Marchak described an economy being squeezed by recession and the decline of the U.S. construction industry in the late 1970s, whereas in Corner Brook the main pressure to restructure came from the opening of the industry to global competition and the urgent need to raise productivity. For Corner Brook, restructuring took place in a period of fairly robust demand for newsprint, though with a significant recession in the early 1990s. The recessions of the 1970s and early 1980s had initiated a wave of restructuring in the forest product industries of British Columbia at a time when the Corner Brook mill had barely started to come to grips with its outdated pulping and papermaking equipment. B.C.'s forest industries also differ from those of Newfoundland due to the quality of the wood. B.C.'s superior timber – especially old-growth timber – is suitable for construction and for making a variety of high value-added wood products; only cut ends, damaged wood, and poorer-quality logs are used for pulping. Newfoundland's wood is of low grade and, apart from minor local use for domestic construction, its only commercial use is for pulping. The social context of Newfoundland also differs markedly from that of British Columbia. In B.C. the workforce in most towns was recruited from distant places and included many immigrants. The labour force of Newfoundland's mills was recruited largely in local outports from families who had settled as fisherfolk several generations earlier and therefore had extensive local family networks and a long tradition of connecting with the local resource base (Botting, 2003).

During the 1980s and 1990s a group of geographers based in British Columbia published a major series of studies of B.C.'s forest industries, drawing particularly on the insights of contemporary labour theory. Among the important contributions are those of Roger Hayter, Trevor Barnes, Gunter Grass, Scott Prudham, and Greg Halseth.[9] The central post-Fordist concept adopted in most of these studies is the notion of *flexibility*, a concept that certainly informs part of the changes that occurred in Corner Brook post-1984, especially in the logging industry; these changes are examined in some detail in Chapters 3 and 4. But in the present context, work flexibility is seen as part of the larger story of lean production, with flexibility an important strand of the story. As already suggested, the geographical contingency that goes with post-structural accounts leads one to expect this kind of difference of emphasis. B.C.'s diverse forest industry includes several processes and products – such as sawmilling, short runs of customized specialty papers, plywood and strandboard, and the manufacture of windows, doors, and prefabricated houses – that are not continuous process activities, so that a wider range of flexible strategies are available when restructuring occurs. Pulp and newsprint making, in contrast, are inherently inflexible, the primary goal of the makers being to run their behemoth paper machines 24 hours a day, as close as possible to 365 days a year as maintenance work and statutory holidays permit, employing the smallest number of workers consistent with producing high-quality paper. Labour flexibility does, of course, appear in newsprint mills in the form of a numerically variable secondary labour force, overtime, subcontractors managing parts of the fibre supply system, cross-trading, and several other strategies that are significant elements of newsprint making. But here they are viewed as strands of an even larger strategy of lean production.

Allen and Henry (1997) question whether flexibility alone, although evidently important to an understanding of contemporary industrial geography, provides a comprehensive explanation of many of the new forms of industrial production. Can flexibility be better understood as a corollary to the shift to lean production, which in turn is a response to rising levels of risk in contemporary industry? Prudham (2002) makes a connection between the risky nature of late capitalism and flexibility. In a similar argument, Allen and Henry (1997) view flexibility as a derivative of more fundamental processes connected to the increasing risks inherent in the globalization of capitalist enterprise. Very often work has become more precarious so that insecurity, not flexibility, is the most urgent characteristic of work. Allen and Henry also have reservations about the use of flexibility as a reductive category subsuming quite different aspects of labour adaptation such as multiple tasking, part-time work, contract and temporary work, job insecurity, and job instability. They argue that each of these forms of flexibility needs to be understood in terms of local and specific changes in labour relations.

The form of post-Fordist adjustment has varied not only geographically, but also by industry. For instance, Prudham (2002) has examined the adaptation of the logging industry in Oregon to downsizing and the shift to subcontracting by independent contractors.

Such flexible arrangements allow producers to escape the rigidities of collective bargains, but Prudham notes that although the argument for recognizing flexible production systems in the era of late capitalism is useful, it does not provide a sufficient explanation of what has happened in Oregon. He suggests that the decision to "buy" rather than "make" (Coase, 1937), that is, to purchase an input from a supplier rather than produce the good or service within the firm, is also governed by the element of risk inherent in nature-based activities such as agriculture and forestry. The vagaries of nature, of the weather, of outbreaks of pests and fires, and the inherent difficulty of predicting yields with such "inconstant geographies" make subcontracting an attractive strategy because it transfers much of the risk to the "gyppo" or family-based independent loggers. The logging industry therefore lends itself to flexible production much more than the newsprint industry does.

The most recent major study of B.C.'s forest industries is Maureen Reed's milestone study, *Taking Stands: Gender and the Sustainability of Rural Communities* (2003). Reed's focus is on the impact of restructuring of the forest industry on northern Vancouver Island, where changes have pitted environmental activists against others engaged in resource extraction. She recognizes that globalization and restructuring have disconnected employment from production such that there can be widespread job losses, even as production continues, making communities and households engaged in the forest industry particularly vulnerable. But, Reed finds, when it comes to the central debates over resource exploitation and the environment, women's multiple layering and social contingencies prevent them from being placed in simplistic *pro* and *anti* categories. Their position on the key environmental issue is complex and depends on a range of considerations including livelihood, community, family, household, and education. She concludes that planning for this region should seek to establish a dialogue between competing factions within the communities to create a form of participatory citizenship that recognizes different human needs in particular geographical settings. Reed's work focuses primarily on women's activism, whereas this study is concerned initially with changes within the mill – which is overwhelmingly a male work world. Her study will be taken up again in Chapter 6 when the impacts of changes within the mill on the larger community are considered.

Two bodies of theory seem well suited to describing the recent economic and social changes in Canada's resource hinterland, namely "real regulation" and the closely related institutional approach. Both approaches throw light on restructuring at Corner Brook. Since the days of Adam Smith, mainstream classical and neo-classical economists have emphasized the price system as central to their utilitarian explanations. A major challenge to this position came from Thorstein Veblen (1857-1929), who was the founder of institutional economics. It is to Veblen that we owe the term *conspicuous consumption* – buying goods for their status value even if they are not very useful. This concept forms part of his theory of the leisure class. Veblen also wrote on business enterprise and on the institutions that manage society, including government and its many agencies, thereby anticipating the later works by J.K. Galbraith on technocracy. The central point, for Veblen, was the importance of institutions to the entire economic system. He saw institutions such as government, firms, banks, the judiciary, non-governmental organizations (NGOs), unions, communities, and social institutions (e.g., schools and colleges, churches) all playing a role in the growth and operation of economic systems.

Geographers paid little attention to Veblen's ideas for much of the twentieth century, although his ideas were a central influence on Harold Innis's staple theory of Canadian economic development and on his studies of communications and empire published in the 1920s, 1930s, and 1940s. By the 1980s geographers had begun to take an interest in related ideas proposed by the French regulation school, focusing less on the abstractions that intrigued the French theorists and more on the practical nuts and bolts of regulation. For instance, studies of west coast forests by Prudham (2002) and Halseth (1999b) make explicit reference to regulation concepts, noting a switch from Fordist to flexible production. Institutions are important to both of the major components of the regulation approach, namely the *mode of production* and the *mode of social regulation*, particularly if one adopts the perspective of geographers and other social scientists by focusing on the local specifics of a place. By the 1990s, this line of research had commanded considerable interest among geographers, who labelled this shift in emphasis the *institutional turn* (Martin, 2000). Although this perspective shares much with the regulation approach, the institutionalists have a stronger concern for cultural influences, which, as Nigel Thrift (2002) notes, explicitly add a local dimension to interpretations.

As originally formulated by a group of French political theorists led by Michel Aglietta, Alain Lipietz, and Robert Boyer, regulation theory was a rather abstract set of ideas that drew on the work of the Italian Marxist philosopher, Antonio Gramsci.[10] It spoke of overarching regimes of accumulation consisting of the mode of production and the mode of social regulation by which a regime reproduces itself. Such a regime is formed when "co-stabilization" occurs between a mode of production and the system of social regulation that sustains it. Fordism is the regime of accumulation that has been most widely discussed; indeed, Lipietz (1986) claims that regulation theory became preoccupied with Fordism. Rather little has been written from a regulationist perspective on artisanal production, while the nature of post-Fordist regimes of accumulation is still hotly disputed (see, for instance, Boyer, 1986; Brenner and Glick, 1991; Boyer and Drache, 1996). Gramsci traced the roots of Fordism to the melding of Henry Ford's form of mass production based on the moving assembly line with the mass consumption society. Regulationists suggest that the Fordist regime of accumulation became established in Western industrialized nations after World War II as co-stabilization occurred between national systems of vertically integrated mass production and Keynesian methods of interventionist economic management (Dunford, 1990). A number of geographers have taken up these ideas, notably Gordon Clark, Jamie Peck, and Adam Tickell, although their interpretation has been more practical and less abstract than those of the original regulation theorists, mainly because geographers talked of regulation grounded in specific places and governed by explicit sets of rules and regulations. Thus Clark (1992) has used the term "real regulation" to capture this group of tangible powers and to distinguish them from more abstract approaches. For similar reasons Jamie Peck, in *Work-Place* (1996), argues that place has a key influence on the regulation of work.

In regulationist terms, Canadian paper mills operated a local version of Fordism, especially from World War II through to the late 1970s. Specifically, whereas in many countries Fordism had been created as part of a post-war class compromise between labour and capital, in Canada a variation known as *permeable Fordism* was put in place (Jenson, 1989, 1990). Canada's permeable Fordism originated in the United States but was modified in crossing the border: here it was directed more to the project of nation-building, particularly through the economic redistribution of social programs and equalization payments to make federalism work. The European version of Fordism put emphasis on fostering class harmony; the Canadian version emphasized regional harmony. In the years after 1945, permeable Fordism has also involved American industry aggressively engaging in continental economic integration by investing in Canadian firms, by exporting resource products back to the United States, and by capturing segments of the Canadian consumer goods market. Meanwhile, in Privy Council Order 1003 of 1944, Canada imitated the U.S. Wagner Act by assigning labour relations to private collective bargaining (Albo, 1994); this was formalized in the 1948 Industrial Relations and Disputes Investigation Act requiring decentralized plant-by-plant contract negotiations.

Discussions of Fordism are very relevant to Canada's newsprint mills, which, internally, operate quite like a car plant. Wood, pulp, and paper flow along a continuous production line operating 24 hours a day. There is a complex technical division of labour, set out in collective agreements, with each worker specializing in one small step in this long chain of production. The large productivity gains and lower newsprint prices achieved by this system of mass production have been matched by a system of mass consumption based on the large market of customers in America and Europe who purchase increasingly voluminous newspapers on a daily basis. Simultaneously, the large volumes of fibre needed by Fordist newsprint plants created environmental problems due to unsustainable logging, pollution while transporting logs to mills, and large volumes of airborne and waterborne emissions and contamination around the mills themselves.

Negotiations over working conditions between the management and unions at Corner Brook have for long been regulated by provincial and federal labour laws. From the outset, the mill had an *internal labour market*: most of the ancillary activities – logging, hauling wood to the mill, installing machinery, repairs, maintenance, and shipping – were performed by employees of the mill, and promotion took place with internal career ladders, and not by external competition. Fordism was an *intensive* system of production. Thus increases in production at the paper mill were achieved by installing new pulping equipment or an improved paper machine that was wider, ran faster, and produced better-quality paper, or by reorganizing patterns of work to increase output. Production could thus be increased by intensifying the use of capital and raising labour productivity. In the years after the opening of Corner Brook's mill in 1925, new technologies and changes in work practices were introduced on many occasions to intensify production. This Fordist mode of production was accompanied by a complementary system of social regulation. Workers' benefits and incomes grew, an apprenticeship system trained a younger generation of workers, and sons and grandsons worked the machines their forefathers had installed. The company store provided many of the needs of an employee's family, and management and foremen were provided with company housing. There were, of course, occasional confrontations, but they scarcely deserved to be called crises.

Piore and Sabel (1984) suggest that Fordism reached its limits sometime in the early 1970s, after which date the regime of accumulation began to crumble. There followed a decade of high inflation coupled with stagnation as inflationary wage demands were not matched by corresponding increases in productivity. Workers refused to moderate their demands, and their resistance to adopting new forms of work and greater flexibility were seen as contributory factors in the demise of Fordist production. This was a period of strong unions that were willing and often able to resist corporations. Producers began to cast around for alternative ways of producing goods and services, collectively labelled post-Fordist. Among competing post-Fordism modes of production, flexible production has been most frequently cited in the literature, although the position taken here is that "life after Ford" has taken a number of different routes, including lean production.

The program of restructuring at Corner Brook since 1984 has been attributed to the need to re-establish the mill's profitability in an increasingly competitive global economy by replacing the aging Fordist mode of production with a leaner way of making paper and profit. This program of restructuring coincided, at the federal level, with the implementation of a series of neo-liberal policies by the Progressive Conservative governments of the 1980s and early 1990s and the Liberal governments of the 1990s. Here the arguments of Tickell and Peck (1995) come into play, since the net effect of the widespread adoption of neo-liberal policies in the last two decades has been to destabilize local systems of production, not just in Corner Brook but across many parts of the globe.

Adam Tickell argues that the regulation approach, in general, has made five enduring contributions to geography that make it a useful framework for interpreting many aspects of the recent history in Corner Brook.[11]

(1) It provides a believable description of economic development over time, and particularly the alternation of relatively stable periods when a regime of accumulation operates fairly smoothly with occasional periods of turbulence and systemic restructuring. Between 1949 and 1984 the Corner Brook mill did not undergo large-scale reorganization: the paper machines had minor upgrades: some thermo-mechanical pulping was introduced; logs were still transported to the mill by a variety of methods; and the mill did nearly all its own installation and repairs. Systems of apprenticeship and summer employment in the mill allowed the workforce to

reproduce itself. During this post-war period often associated with the ascendancy of Fordism, the mill's mode of production remained comparatively stable. Since then, there has been substantial change, largely aimed at introducing aspects of lean production and increasingly technical work that requires the recruitment of a highly skilled workforce and quite frequent training programs.

(2) Unlike neo-classical and neo-Schumpeterian theory, regulation theory assigns an important role to institutions, both governmental and non-governmental, in stabilizing capitalism and regulating its various manifestations. Governmental institutions have been particularly important to Corner Brook. The British government provided the subsidy that contributed to the mill's initial construction, and the colonial government through the Bowater Act of 1938 awarded the Bowater Company extensive forest tracts in the Gander basin that resulted in the mill's expansion immediately after World War II. The Federal/Provincial Modernization Agreement of 1984 underwrote a significant part of the cost of upgrading the mill, while the environmental compliance schedule initiated in 1987 was the rubric under which many of the changes in the 1990s were introduced. Cultural institutions local to Newfoundland, including outport fishing communities, the cabin, ice fishing, and the system of moose licensing, have contributed in more subtle ways to such matters as shift work, vacations, family recreation patterns, and activities of the mill's retirees.

(3) Regulationists take social relations into account in their discourse of economic development. Social relations, including class, gender, ethnicity, family size, local customs, and cultural mores, are all recognized as affecting how society reproduces itself. For two generations the mill's labour force was reproduced largely within family networks. Today, with greater skill requirements for most jobs, educational networks have become more important. And as some workers have been shifted into contingent work, their families have been affected, with wives entering the labour force, taking up full-time as opposed to part-time jobs, and changing the division of domestic work.

(4) The regulation method has acquired a geographical sensitivity by incorporating national and regional variations in the way that production is organized. Thus, although a global dimension is seen to influence some aspects of regimes, they are locally formed. Newfoundland's mills, for instance, lagged behind the mills of Sweden, or indeed those of British Columbia, in initiating the recent round of restructuring.

(5) This approach is not economistic but it addresses the whole economy, including production and consumption, economy and society, politics and institutions, formal laws and informal practices, locally embedded culture and imported contemporary shifts in cultural practices. The diverse corollaries of restructuring in Corner Brook are found to range from direct impacts on patterns of work, to lifestyle changes that reconnect with the surrounding region, to the Kruger Corporation promoting education programs at local institutions of higher education.

These insights into the processes of economic change learned from the regulation approach have to be set against a series of quite trenchant criticisms. First, the theory is quite mute on the precise mechanics whereby conflicts between labour and capital are resolved to stabilize a regime of accumulation. Indeed, some accounts of regulation theory amount to a form of technological determinism (Marden, 1992), with machine production being inexorably succeeded by Fordism, which in turn is destined for replacement by flexible accumulation, and so on; the processes that drive this progression remain hidden in a black box. By focusing at the micro level and by tracking negotiations to restructure the mill over a critical 10-year period, we can pinpoint how the changes made at Corner Brook were achieved and how they impacted on the community.

Second, although regulation theory correctly assigns an important role to institutions in the regulation of economies, its advocates are rather reticent when it comes to the specifics. What are the various roles of government? How do non-governmental institutions interact with labour and capital? How important are locally embedded practices? This study seeks to identify the role played by institutions in the restructuring of the Corner Brook mill, drawing on evidence provided in interviews with key participants and a detailed analysis of local newspaper archives.

Third, while regulationists have followed other social sciences in identifying local culture as an important variable reacting to global forces, the connections between local culture and the wider regime of accumulation are asserted rather than demonstrated. Given the geographical mobility of international capital, do local interests have much leverage any more? By conducting an ethnographic study in Corner Brook based on 30 extended interviews, I have been able to identify some of the important aspects of local culture.

Finally, regulation theory is written mainly to describe the nation-state, with most empirical studies (beginning with Aglietta's of the United States) examining economic change within specific countries. The theory says much less about changes at the international scale; indeed, globalization is often treated as if it were an exogenous variable. Likewise, economists and political scientists working on aspects of regulation have said less about its workings at a local level, yet it seems inevitable, as geographers keep stressing, that regimes grow from local beginnings: after all, Henry Ford's moving assembly line began operating in one place, Highland Park, Michigan, in 1913. Since recent studies of restructuring in the Canadian newsprint industry show that the form it has taken depends on local circumstances (e.g., Hayter, 1997; Rose and Villemaire, 1997),[12] there is every reason to begin by examining local changes before trying to build towards an understanding of larger regimes.

In short, geographers' understanding of regulation has been more concrete than that of the French regulationists. Clark (1992) and Peck and Tickell (1995) view regulation as a social practice occurring within defined local, regional, or national spaces. Place-based experiences of restructuring constitute geographical shards that refuse to fit neatly together into universally applicable laws. Explanation of restructuring therefore requires a specifically local understanding. The nation-state and even larger organizations such as NAFTA and the WTO have set an international frame of regulation, but "real regulation" (to use Clark's preferred term) also involves the interplay of these global processes with the local state, with local social practices in many domains of human activity, with local institutions, and with the constraints of fixed capital sunk in myriad local structures including factories, schools, hospitals, churches, shops, houses, roads, and sewers.

As already noted, the geographer's approach to regulation took a subtle turn in the mid-1990s by making an explicit connection with institutions. Rooted in Veblen's institutional economics, the institutionalist approach emphasizes the rules, procedures, and conventions that govern social relations. It was also much influenced by a key contribution from anthropology – Karl Polanyi's *The Great Transformation* (1957 [1944]). Polanyi observed that in many non-Western societies the production and consumption of goods are often enmeshed in social relations, as opposed to market relations, which include various reciprocal obligations such as gift-giving and ostentatious rituals such as potlatch ceremonies. Granovetter (1985) pointed out that social conventions and institutional practices are not restricted to Polanyi's traditional societies – they are pervasive in contemporary economic life. For instance, in the context of Newfoundland's attempts to adapt to the knowledge-based economy under Premiers Wells and Tobin, Tomblin (2002) argues that reformers have failed to take into account the role of institutions that continue to determine political and policy outcomes. Subsequently, the notion of embedded social relations has been generalized even further, to include impacts of many aspects of economic life. Martin (2000: 85) suggests that we can now talk of at least four forms of embeddedness:

- social embeddedness, as described by Granovetter;
- political embeddedness, with different jurisdictions having very different rules that govern our practices;
- cognitive embeddedness, where ways of doing things are learned within the framework of enduring social systems;
- cultural embeddedness, where economic actions are embedded in cultural systems such as paid maternity leaves, settling debts before the New Year, and primogeniture.

Embeddedness can, in a sense, become habit forming, so that a region becomes somewhat locked in to a set of activities. Wine growing in Canada's Niagara region, for instance, is supported by research stations, seasonal migrant labour coming year after year from Mexico and the Caribbean, skilled local labour, specialist subcontracting firms, a tourist industry promoting visits to wineries, and various co-operative agencies helping to produce and market the wines. Very similar is Douglass North's (1990) concept of *path dependence*, where patterns of community development are sustained by local norms and networks of civic engagement. The *thickness* of such supportive institutions helps to account for the resilience of a local economy in the face of various kinds of challenges (Amin and Thrift, 1994). This is closely related to *regional lock-in*, where a sense of regional economic solidarity may help a region to resist externally imposed change (Martin, 2000), but this can go further to create *institutional hysteresis*, a form of chronic embeddedness, Setterfield (1997) suggests, that is capable of blocking needed economic renewal. Institutions appear time and again in this chronicle, beginning (in Chapter 2) with the practices of a company town and continuing through to the numerous community practices discussed in later chapters that connect the residents of Corner Brook with the land and the sea and to weekending at cabins, visiting ancestral outports, and engaging in locally rooted cultural activities in town.

FROM FORDISM TO LEAN PRODUCTION

The wave of restructuring observed in many industrialized countries in the 1970s and 1980s marked the break between what regulationists call the Fordist regime and the post-Fordist regime that followed.[13] The post-war boom was associated with mass-produced automobiles, and other consumer goods such as refrigerators and televisions, made in factories that adopted Fordist methods of mass production, typically with a moving production line, interchangeable parts, an internal labour market, an elaborate division of labour, and a unionized workforce, and it was sustained by a matching Keynesian mode of social regulation. Commentators suggest that, with the exhaustion of the main possibilities of the Fordist system of mass production after 1970, we entered a prolonged era of stagflation and then restructuring to launch the post-Fordist era. During the post-Fordist era, producers of goods and services have been searching for an alternative mode of production that is internally coherent and capable of increasing the profitability of firms. The speed at which firms have restructured and adopted new modes of production depends on a number of factors, including the age of sunk capital. Doreen Massey (1995) notes that investment tends to be laid down at particular times in particular places, ranging from Manchester's cotton industry in the early 1800s to Silicon Valley in the 1980s and 1990s, to produce spatial divisions of labour. She draws on the metaphor of sedimentary layers of investment to describe this process, using it to explain why waves of restructuring occur as this fixed capital wears out at about the same time in a given region.

The transition from Fordism to post-Fordism throws some light on the broad pattern of restructuring at the Corner Brook mill in the period since Kruger purchased it in 1984. There is, of course, a need to recognize the shorter waves of the business cycle that run from 7 to 10 years. During the recessions of the 1970s and early 1980s, commodity prices fell, and Bowater suffered financial losses and retrenched by closing down production lines and laying off workers. When demand picked up and newsprint prices increased, the reverse happened – production lines restarted and workers were recalled. Rather different were the changes initiated in 1984 (and described in Chapters 3 and 4), which were not cyclical but were irreversible shifts in the way newsprint was made. Both in Corner Brook and elsewhere in Canada, we find that during the crises of the 1980s and 1990s the red ink appearing on the balance sheets of many Canadian newsprint firms triggered rounds of vigorous restructuring (Holmes and Hayter, 1993; Rose and Villemaire 1997).

There has been considerable debate over how production was restructured when Fordism ceased providing significant new competitive efficiencies. In essence, four alternative new forms of production have been identified in the literature.[14]

1. *Neo-Fordism* (or *neo-Taylorism*, since this strategy essentially follows the principles of Frederick Winslow Taylor) relocates rigid mass-production methods into low-wage environments – whether right-to-work states in the southern U.S., maquiladora zones in Mexico, or free trade zones in newly industrializing countries – as part of a new global division of labour. At the level of the plant, the geographically fixed inputs of the Canadian newsprint industry make this option very costly, but at the level of the firm, some companies have indeed shifted production to locations with lower labour or input costs.
2. *Neo-artisanal production* breaks down large-scale production into regional groupings of small connected workshops in which workers have some control over the execution of their work and the products they make (Eberts and Norcliffe, 1998; Henry et al., 1996; Norcliffe and Eberts, 1999). Since the technology of newsprint production still favours very large machines, this form of horizontal and vertical disintegration has not played a major part in restructuring the pulp and paper industry, although it has occurred in a small way at its margins.
3. *Flexible mass production* has been widely touted as the main successor to Fordism. Although several features of flexibility are in evidence at Corner Brook, particularly in some of the mill's work practices, the main thrust of technological innovation and changed supply and marketing arrangements has been to cut costs and raise labour productivity; these changes have not greatly altered the mill's flexibility, nor has this been the mill owner's overriding priority. In fact, increases in flexibility have been an ancillary part of the mill owner's drive for lean production.
4. *Lean production* requires a firm to focus on its most profitable activities, automate wherever possible, and maximize its capital and labour productivity in those activities. Lean production has been promoted by two main forces. First, many industries have been caught up in the globalization of production. This helps explain why Bowater's, for instance, abandoned production at Corner Brook and switched to a new global production strategy that favoured the southeastern United States. It also provides the rationale for Kruger's insistence that they had to become competitive with low-cost producers located in low-wage regions outside Canada, as well as state-of the art producers located inside Canada. Moreover, as Holmes and Hayter (1993) show, during the 1980s Scandinavian and U.S. newsprint firms had

already achieved considerably higher productivity levels than Canadian producers. Kruger's highest priority was to re-establish the global competitiveness of the Corner Brook mill. Changes in world demand for paper, including a shift to thinner and brighter newsprint suitable for colour printing, also made it essential to raise the quality of the mill's product.

The shift to lean production has also been advanced by the need to meet progressively stiffer environmental regulations, both within Canada (Sinclair, 1991) and in some of the major foreign markets served by the Corner Brook mill. The costly investments in pollution abatement programs required by these regulations have also, serendipitously, increased mill efficiency. Kruger worked out an environmental compliance program with the Newfoundland provincial government that was signed in March 1987 after a year and a half of negotiations. The arrangement set out to reduce three forms of pollution: airborne particulate (especially soot and fly-ash); suspended solids (in water); and sulphur dioxide emissions.[15] This schedule was subsequently renegotiated several times as the cost of the program escalated, forcing Kruger to evaluate a number of alternative strategies. Later, the federal Pulp and Paper Effluent Regulations (1992), which set limits for the toxicity, biochemical oxygen demand, and dissolved solids in discharge from pulp and paper mills, led to a new round of technical change at the mill aimed mainly at installing a secondary water treatment plant. Rules setting a minimum recycled content in newsprint in several American states have also fostered lean production at the Corner Brook mill.

The term "lean production" was coined by the International Motor Vehicle Program (based at the Massachusetts Institute of Technology) during the late 1980s and became an organizing theme in the book resulting from that research project, *The Machine That Changed the World* (Womack et al., 1990). The roots of lean production date back, however, to the techniques pioneered by Taiichi Ohno of Toyota Motors in the early 1950s. Eiji Toyoda (of the founding family of the Toyota Motor Company) had visited Ford's Rouge River plant in 1950 with a view to copying Ford's methods in the hope of reviving the fortunes of his family's struggling company. In discussions back home with Ohno, who was Toyota's chief production engineer, Toyoda concluded that he simply did not have the capital resources to imitate Ford's methods. Instead of copying Ford by building hundreds of dies to stamp out large numbers of car parts, he developed a remarkable *quick-change system* whereby production workers changed one dye for another in a stamping machine to produce relatively small batches of stampings with minimal inventory. His workers agreed to do this kind of flexible work with a variety of task assignments, to accept frequent skill upgrading, and to work in teams in return for a guarantee of lifetime employment. Quality at Toyota rose dramatically, and the need for rework, i.e., fixing imperfect new components and parts so that they meet specifications, almost disappeared. Ohno then replaced linear (Fordist) machine arrangements with U-shaped and square machine formations so that workers trained with multiple (polyvalent) skills could tend several different machines all placed close to each other (Kenney and Florida, 1993: 37-9). When linked with just-in-time (JIT) delivery of parts, Ohno's system achieved substantial increases in productivity. Ohnoism assumes the rapid development of new products, low inventories, *kanban* (card) ordering systems among neighbouring work units using JIT deliveries, and efficient staffing. But it also required a particular type of labour force willing to accept this demanding form of work: the absence, in Japan, of strong craft unions greatly facilitated Ohno's experiments. Thus, Ohnoism developed in a particular historical and geographical context, and it was compatible with the existing culture of production and institutional arrangements in Japan.

Lean production was introduced to North America via Japanese automobile transplants, the first of which began operating in 1982 (ibid., ch. 4). From the outset these transplants incorporated teamwork, JIT delivery systems, work rotation, workers trained with multiple skills, and minimal job classifications. The success of these Japanese transplants in producing high-quality cars at competitive prices led American manufacturers to imitate them.

According to Womack et al. (1990) lean production is justified by its ability to respond flexibly to changing consumer demands, by its higher productivity, by the more satisfying work it creates, and by the push it requires for continuous improvement in all aspects of production. This rather favourable assessment of lean production rendered by MIT's International Motor Vehicle Program has, however, been hotly disputed on several grounds. First, there is little to support the suggestion that work under lean production is more satisfying. Wood (1993: 2) summarizes lean production as:

> a system which applies to the whole process of production from design to sales and distribution . . . it involves a reduction in the use of indirect labour, a breakdown of functional management and job de-

marcations, close long-term supplier relations and total quality management so, for example, repair lines no longer are necessary.

By this characterization, the claim that lean production enriches jobs seems unconvincing. Workers' tasks may become more varied, but they are no more creative. Indeed, lean production does not mark the end of Fordism but its continuation by other means. This matches the conclusion of Williams et al. (1992) in their essay "Against lean production," where they note that Ford's Highland Park and Toyota City had much in common. By extension, the advantages of lean production have not been universally accepted by workers in the system. From a Swedish perspective Berggren (1993) questions the success of Japanese auto transplants located in the United States. He contends that the relentless work regime is causing growing worker resistance, the short product cycles are a drain on human and natural resources, and frequent JIT deliveries result in substantial negative externalities in the form of traffic congestion and pollution. The undesirable aspects of lean production led Berggren to conclude that other forms of production will eventually emerge. Indeed Toyota, Nissan, and Volvo have already begun to experiment with "worker-friendly production." In addition, some of the claims made for lean production are suspect. Williams et al. (1992), who deride lean production as the apotheosis of the business school's infatuation with Japan, demonstrate that Toyota's claim to produce cars with "half the human effort" is greatly exaggerated and that lower labour costs in the Japanese auto industry have more to do with the very low wages paid by suppliers operating in offshore sweatshops than with automation and superior management.

The most trenchant critique and re-evaluation of lean production was developed by the late Bennett Harrison (1994) in his book *Lean and Mean*, particularly in the way he generalized the concept across a wide range of manufacturing industries. Harrison's approach is therefore readily transferable to the pulp and paper industry, and serves as a framework for the discussion of lean production at Corner Brook in Chapter 4. The very linking of "lean" with "mean" by Harrison indicates how far some commentators have shifted the concept from the positive connotation originally given it by Womack, Jones, and Roos. Harrison (1994: 8-12) identifies several basic building blocks that account for the recent recovery of the big-firm sector, each connected with leaner forms of production. These are:

1. Adopting computerized manufacturing and management information systems, which promote tighter co-ordination of

production and enhance product quality and productivity, while reducing set-up times and the size of the labour force. Jobs are lost, while the remaining workers are under constant pressure to produce more.

2. Concentrating in-house operations on activities central to the firm's existence – its core competencies – by paring the mix of activities. This reduces the diversity of work and leaves fewer niches of non-standard work to relieve the monotony.
3. Farming out (distancing) non-essential operations to rings of lower-wage suppliers (including exploitative workshops in authoritarian low-wage countries).
4. Shrinking the workforce by declaring redundancies, and introducing segmentation with (i) a functionally flexible core workforce and having on call (but not necessarily maintaining) (ii) a numerically flexible secondary workforce that has irregular patterns of work.
5. Eliciting the collaboration of the core workforce in the mission of the firm.
6. Building strategic alliances among groups of large firms and the first ring of smaller firms supplying parts and services. These suppliers work to tight deadlines and face regular price squeezes.

In the language of regulation theory, lean production represents a mode of production: it is a guiding principle that influences all aspects of the production process. But it is also a discourse – a story about how things should be done inside the contemporary factory. The same point is often made about globalization, which is viewed in business school logic as a desirable – even inevitable – economic process breathing new life into the competitive process, while in more skeptical circles globalization is understood discursively as a narrative in need of critical assessment (Norcliffe, 2001). Understood as a discourse, lean production becomes more like Raymond Williams's "structure of feeling," in which it is embedded not only in economic logic but also in social and cultural considerations, so that means of communication also become means of production (Williams, 1980: 50-63).

CORNER BROOK

Having stressed that the impact of global processes is contingent upon local geographical circumstances, it is important to provide a brief sketch of Corner Brook so that readers not familiar with the town and the surrounding region have an understanding of its geography. What follows is quite idiosyncratic and, as an outsider, I recognize that my knowledge of the region is far from complete, but my interviews with a large cross-section of residents lead me to believe that what follows highlights many of the town's main characteristics.

From high on the flank of the mountain that rises to the east of Corner Brook, the view looking westward is of a spectacular urban setting. The city itself, with a 2001 population of just over 20,000, occupies a huge natural amphitheatre situated on the south shore of the Humber Arm. A sparse network of roads, both major and minor, connect Corner Brook to fishing villages strung along the north and south shores of the Humber Arm, to the small towns of Pasadena and Deer Lake built inland in the Humber Valley, to the town (and former U.S. air base) of Stephenville to the south, and to numerous smaller settlements (see Figure 1). The geographical setting of Corner Brook therefore helped it to become the main regional service centre in western Newfoundland.

Indeed, at first glance one might assume that Corner Brook's development can be explained largely in local terms. Cars and pickup trucks, some travelling from more than a hundred miles up the Great Northern Peninsula, bring families into the main shopping centre to make their weekly purchases. A cluster of car dealers and rental car firms strung along the old Trans-Canada Highway serve customers drawn from much of the western part of the province. Western Memorial Hospital, the province's only teaching hospital outside St. John's, also serves much of western Newfoundland. Further down the hill stand Corner Brook's two institutions of higher education, Sir Wilfred Grenfell College – a satellite campus of the Memorial University of Newfoundland – and the West Viking Institute of Technology, both of which serve western Newfoundland, and Labrador. Close to these colleges are the criminal law courts for the western region, the city library, the sports complex, and the regional cultural centre. The antenna of CBC's radio transmitter indicates Corner Brook's role as a regional broadcasting centre, while nearer the harbour two more shopping malls, car dealerships, hotels, and the Anglican and Catholic cathedrals also connect this city with its region. Evidence of the city's role as a regional service centre is everywhere.

Surrounding Corner Brook is the city's immediate hinterland. To the west, the Humber Arm sweeps out in a long curve some 40 kilometres to the Gulf of St. Lawrence; it is a deep navigable fjord

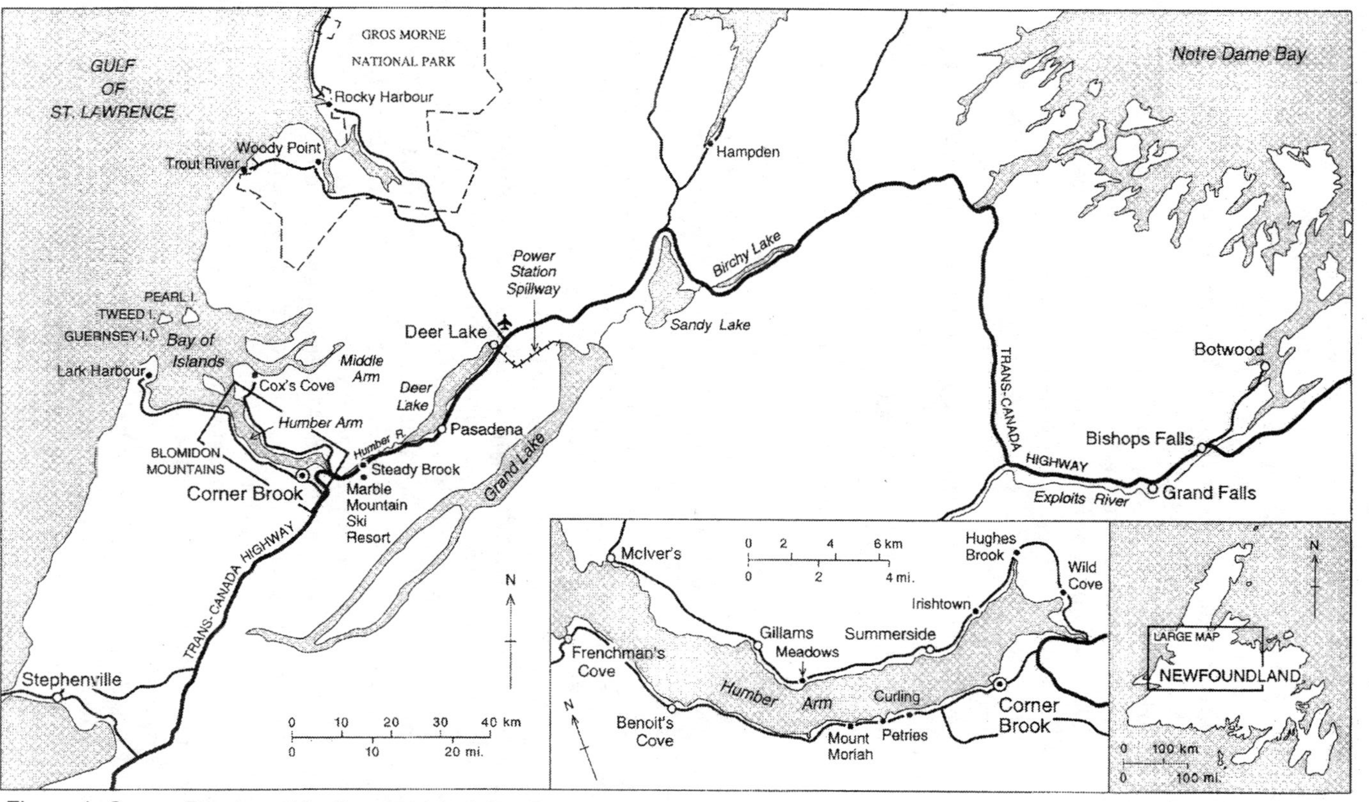

Figure 1 Corner Brook and its Geographical Context

gouged out by ice (see Figure 1). Although it is hemmed in by steep slopes in many places, on the flatter spots of land small fishing villages were built – Irishtown, Petries, Summerside, Meadows, Gillams, McIver's, Frenchman's Cove, Benoit's Cove, Mount Moriah, and Curling – names redolent of distant places and early European settlers. A mere 40 years ago, these outports were accessed only by the motorboat that each day took mail, goods, and passengers up and down the Arm, stopping in turn at each settlement. For three months each winter when the Arm was frozen, these small communities were periodically cut off by major snowstorms.

On the south side of the Humber Arm, the Blomidon Mountains run steeply down to the shores, their north-facing slopes snow-covered well into "June month." On the north side, but at a greater distance, stand the Gros Morne Mountains, which have been classified by UNESCO as a World Heritage site, such are the extraordinary formations found in this geological cauldron. Further west, three steep-sided islands – Guernsey, Tweed, and Pearl Island – rise abruptly out of the Gulf of St. Lawrence and guard the entrance to the Bay of Islands. To their south nestles Lark Harbour at the end of the road along the south shore of the Arm that was completed only in the 1960s. The road threading its way along the opposite shore swings sharply northward from McIver's over a high ridge to another outport, Cox's Cove, located on the shore of the Middle Arm. On evenings and weekends, vehicles head into town with their passengers bound for the downtown cinemas, bars, and clubs. Others are returning from visits to family and friends living in the outports or from a few days of hunting and fishing at the family cabin.

During the last 75 years, Corner Brook has built up a complex web of economic and social relations with a hinterland that comprises much of western Newfoundland and, for certain functions, Labrador, too. As a regional service centre, Corner Brook has acquired substantial *material assets* and *relational assets*, to use Michael Storper's (1997) terms. Material assets are tangible and include many of the elements already noted – the commercial centres, educational and medical institutions, industrial plants, libraries and law courts, places of entertainment, and urban transport infrastructure – that help produce the goods and services sought by consumers living in the city's extensive hinterland. Relational assets are intangible but are nevertheless of great importance in Newfoundland's tightly bonded society, where connections to place, family, and friends remain vitally important to daily life. These assets depend very much on institutions, conventions, and practices learned over a long period. Thus the teenage children of a large out-of-town family may take lodgings with a cousin living in Corner Brook to attend high school and college; a group of school friends may reunite each year when they return to camp at the same trout pond; a knitter, working at home, might sell her products to the same dealer with a tourist outlet beside the Trans-Canada Highway season after season; a small logger would habitually obtain his annual licence to cut firewood at the provincial office in Corner Brook; a hunter would pursue moose with his long-standing hunting partner; and a family living in town could return to their ancestral outport to wile away several weeks each summer. Transactions of material goods occur in social networks built over long periods around people and institutions. The stability and long duration of these relations are a major asset to a regional centre because they do not need to be laboriously renegotiated each time a transaction takes place.

One might easily assume that due to its geographical centrality, Corner Brook was developed primarily as the regional service centre for western Newfoundland. But this is not the case. Corner Brook was built as a paper town and its role as a regional service centre developed slowly, mainly in the years after World War II. The original set of material and relational assets linked Corner Brook partly with the woods supplying the mill, but mainly with the global economy, making the city as much the handmaid of international capital as it is the offspring of local geography (Andrews et al., 2000). Today, at frequent intervals, tractor trailers loaded with eight-foot-long logs cut over a huge area in central and western Newfoundland turn off the Trans-Canada Highway and ease down the steep grade of the Lewin Parkway in low gear, heading for the newsprint mill. Every day or two, cargo vessels glide up the Humber Arm to moor at the mill's dock. The newsprint mill itself sits at the very apex of the semicircular bowl in which the city of Corner Brook was built. Thus, despite the apparent centrality of regional services to the city's economy, the newsprint mill, both physically and symbolically, occupies a pivotal role because Corner Brook was and is a paper town.

Corner Brook was created in the colonial era on a site previously occupied by a sawmill and a small residential community. It was built by British interests as a company town between 1923 and 1925, grew spasmodically on the roller coaster of the booms and slumps of the newsprint industry, and reached its pinnacle shortly after World War II as home to the world's most productive newsprint mill. In the decades that followed, as deregulation made newsprint production increasingly competitive on a global scale, the mill began to suffer industrial sclerosis until, by 1983, it came close to being permanently closed. The Corner Brook mill was then purchased by a Canadian multinational company that set in motion a project to restructure its operations. A much leaner model of industrial production was then set in place, although vestiges of the earlier colonial model still survive to this day, mixing in traces of a post-colonial economic geography.

The region surrounding Corner Brook has also experienced hard economic times in the past two decades. The most decisive setback was the closure of the groundfish fishery in the Gulf of St. Lawrence and on the South Shore in 1994 (the northern cod fishery had been closed by the then Minister of Fisheries, John Crosbie, in 1992). These closures hit hard in outports with fish-packing plants when men working on the offshore trawlers and women working in the fish plants lost their jobs. Fortunately, the inshore fishery, especially the crab and lobster fisheries, has generally thrived since then, and several other species, such as lumpfish, have found a new market, and this has alleviated some of the problems. Nevertheless, as Sinclair et al. (1999) have shown, many outports have had to reconstruct their social lives since the imposition of the cod moratorium, with both men and women having to rework their identities and roles within the family and the community (Sinclair and Felt, 1992; Power, 2005). These are, as Felt and Sinclair (1995) put it, communities living on the edge.

Inland, the logging industry has also suffered from job losses due to mechanization, although the expansion of silviculture has offset some of these job losses. There have also been conflicts between environmentalists and tourist promoters wishing to preserve the best remaining old-growth forest areas, such as the Main River watershed, and the newsprint industry interests wishing to log these lands to overcome potential fibre shortages (Janes-Hodder and Sinclair, 2003). Bates (1997) has examined the rise of home-based work in the Corner Brook region as a response to the economic hardships faced by its residents, finding that many of the jobs so created are quite marginal. In sum, the restructuring both of the town's leading industry and of the main activities of the surrounding countryside has obliged residents of Corner Brook to make adjustments at the household and community levels. In 1990, Fairley et al. found evidence of resistance in many Atlantic Canada communities to the restructuring then underway and demonstrated that a number of places had successfully reinvented themselves. Community economic development initiatives in the Corner Brook region have so far had limited success, however, and not for lack of social capital but, it would appear, because there are no strong institutional structures to mobilize this social capital. The demographic evidence to be presented in the final chapter suggests that many of the younger generation in Corner Brook are responding by leaving the region, while those who stay have found subtle ways of resisting the pressures of globalization.

This book examines and interprets the phase of restructuring that began in Corner Brook in 1984 and continues to this day. The interpretation is not situated in a grand narrative that packages the growth of Corner Brook in a single rational and seamless story; on the contrary, it is more like the presentation of evidence from an archaeological site that required careful excavation. This interpretation of restructuring in Corner Brook will therefore be guided by the 'constructivist' agenda (Leyshon, 1997), which, while it denies the operation of a preordained and totally rational economic order, does not accept that restructuring is a random process either. As Nigel Thrift (1996) argues, some order is specific to time and place; locally we are not obliged to "shut up and dance" to the tune of an all-knowing global Pied Piper. Key elements in the construction of local economies are the existing institutional relations, the rules and regulations that frame activities, local and provincial politics, local cultures of work and play, and the capital that is sunk in local production, transport, housing, and social infrastructure. The initial construction of the company town of Corner Brook and its evolution as a post-company town from 1955 up to 1984 therefore become important to the analysis that follows, and are described in the next chapter.

The Company Town 2

The literature on company towns mainly examines the histories of individual towns, although Robinson's (1962) and Lucas's (1971) studies bring an understanding of the larger processes at work. The opening section of this chapter seeks to expand on that understanding by describing some of the institutional arrangements of company towns. The sections that follow present an account of the origins of Corner Brook as a company town, its construction, and the crisis of ownership that followed soon after. Various sources, but mainly the stories of interviewees, are then used to develop a picture of life in a company town. The chapter concludes with a brief account of the transformation of the town to public status and of the events leading up to Bowater's decision to sell the mill in 1984.

THE INSTITUTIONAL ARRANGEMENTS OF A COMPANY TOWN

A company town is a very distinctive institution. It has a corporate identity, with its citizens beholden to the parent company either as employees, as dependants of employees, or as service providers located in town at the pleasure of the company. Residents gain certain advantages by living in such a town, including jobs, housing, fire and police protection, and (often) health services and schools, but they lose certain rights of citizenship, including the freedoms of a local democracy, and they are ultimately obligated to the company, or to its representative, the town manager. Historically, unforgiving regimes could sometimes be found in company towns, giving rise to such melancholic song lines as "I owe my soul to the company store." Even today, reports come from developing countries with authoritarian regimes of exploitative treatment of individuals living in company towns (Deyo, 1981). But in other instances the company has been a benign influence, with the town's residents enjoying a number of perquisites.

The town manager enjoys unusual powers. Since the company town is a private space, the manager has powers of exclusion and expulsion, can set rents and prices for goods and services provided by the town or sold by the company store, can curtail or increase the range of social services offered, and can summarily reallocate such things as company houses and land for parks. These arbitrary powers are not subject to appeal unless they breach public laws. This is not to suggest that there is a tendency for town managers to act like malevolent dictators; most have an interest in preserving harmonious relations – indeed, their actions are often quite benevolent – but they nevertheless have extensive residual powers that are not subject to the normal democratic process.

The vast majority of company towns are built around the exploitation of a single resource at a single site, whether a mine, a factory, a mill, a trading post, or a plantation. They are, therefore, normally a feature of the staple (resource) economy, although some in developing countries are factory towns. Typically, there is a tendency to vertical integration of production within company towns: due to their physical isolation and the exclusionary nature of private space, the companies tend to do their own installation, maintenance, transport, and packaging, and they may even fabricate some of their own capital equipment.

If the company that owns a town is a multinational firm, then the welfare of its residents is necessarily linked to the international economy by its corporate ownership. Such links include: various investments and debt instruments held by foreign banks, corporations, and shareholders; input and output transactions with foreign subsidiaries; management control; expatriate workers sent from an overseas headquarters; and direct and indirect purchases and sales. Even when a company town is domestically owned, it is difficult to insulate its products from foreign competition. Thus the pulse of the global economy beats strongly in most company towns. Corner Brook is a case in point; it was created by British interests in the 1920s and has remained linked to the international economy ever since. The founding of this company town transformed western Newfoundland from a remote resource frontier populated by numerous small fishing villages and a handful of sawmills into an industrial region dependent on global newsprint markets. The fortunes of Corner Brook have been determined since that time largely by people in distant places.

The institutional arrangements of company towns are quite distinctive in a number of ways. They are private spaces. This means that, although the democratic processes of federal and provincial governments apply, the normal municipal activities of electing a town council that levies local taxes and provides various local services are absent. Local democratic institutions are supplanted by the administrative arm of the corporation, which typically offers the same range of social services as an elected council and school board. Citizens are not in a position to remove city administrators from office by democratic means because the administrators hold office at the pleasure of the corporation. On the other hand, the corporation may exercise the ultimate sanction of expelling a citizen from its privately held space. Thus the range of democratic freedoms available to residents of a company town is limited.

Economically, company towns internalize markets in several significant ways, notably with respect to labour, housing, and retailing. The existence of internal labour markets has long been recognized (Doeringer and Piore, 1971), whereas much less has been written about the internalization of retailing and housing markets. Osterman (1984) has examined in depth the main features of internal labour markets, which include the following:

- Labour is fragmented into segments, each of which functions quasi-independently.
- Employees find it difficult to move from one segment into another.
- Job promotion takes place within the firm, so that only persons already employed by a firm within the given segment may apply for a vacancy.
- Wages are determined by labour contracts, not by bargaining on the open market.
- Seniority rules rather than human capital and skills determine who is eligible to apply for a job posting.
- Employees remain employed in an internal labour market for long periods so that their earnings become increasingly related to their position on the wage ladder rather than to their productivity or human capital.
- Firms may locate in isolated places so that training and skill formation are also internalized, often by establishing apprenticeship programs.

The net effect of the creation of an internal labour market in a company town is to separate jobs into a primary (corporate) segment with well-paid jobs, which is very difficult to enter (except as a young recruit), and one or more secondary sectors with poorly paid and insecure jobs.

The internalization of markets in company towns is not limited to jobs: very often the corporation provides houses for its workers. The net effect in such situations is that the supply of houses is controlled by the company, which, if it chooses, can sell property at quite arbitrary prices. Some companies have sold off company housing to sitting tenants at quite low prices in order to liquidate assets, especially if the company has long-term plans to wind down its interest in the town. In other cases the ability to promise houses for workers is an effective recruiting strategy. Where companies have sold off their housing stock, local housing markets have often become quite speculative as buyers and sellers seek a price equilibrium.

Company stores have sometimes achieved legendary status by selling their employees overpriced goods needed by their families, in effect quickly repatriating their employee's wages. It was not uncommon for companies to pay workers partly with store tokens or by simply adding credit to their account at the company store. It seems likely that the appearance of "shadow towns" just beyond the city limits of company towns was an attempt to break the monopoly of the company store. Beyond the reach of the company, these stores traded at market prices and sold goods such as liquor and tobacco that were often not available at the company store.

ORIGINS OF THE COMPANY TOWN OF CORNER BROOK

John Cabot's voyage of 1497 from Bristol to Newfoundland inaugurated 500 years of resource exploitation in Newfoundland. Fish, fur, fowl, whales, and wood were treated as free resources to be caught, harvested, processed, and exported to foreign markets (Hiller, 1982). Thus the international economy in its mercantile form penetrated Newfoundland very early on and set in motion a resource cycle that culminated with the extinction (or near-extinction) of several species of whale and the spearbill (great auk), and of Newfoundland's indigenous peoples – the Beothuk (Mannion, 1977; Marshall, 1996). More recently, resource exploitation has generated increasing concern about the supply of wood fibre to the pulp and paper industry (Janes-Hodder and Sinclair, 2003) and, since its closure in 1994, for the future of the offshore fishery, this being the very resource that had attracted Cabot in the first place (Norcliffe, 1999).

How did this ruthless cycle of resource depletion occur? In explanation, Graham and St. Martin (1990) stress how the inherent variability of most renewable resources makes it difficult to distinguish between a cyclical decline in yields attributable to natural swings and resource collapse due to overexploitation. Ludwig et al. (1993: 17) demonstrate that "large levels of natural [resource] variability mask the effects of overexploitation. Initial overexploitation is not detectable until it is severe and often irreversible." In other words, the stock levels of many resources are subject to large natural fluctuations so that a decline due to mismanagement is likely to be detected too late to prevent permanent damage. In fact, improved harvesting technologies may result in increasing catches or harvests even as a resource is in catastrophic decline – as happened with the Newfoundland cod fishery. Coupled with the historically free access to many of Newfoundland's resources and the large profits made through successful exploitation, it is hardly surprising to discover that foreign capital took considerable interest in Newfoundland's more abundant resources, especially fish, wood, minerals, and oil.

For four centuries following Cabot's voyage, the island supported a fishing economy (Head, 1976; Rowe, 1980). By 1900, the colony's population of 215,000 was dispersed in hundreds of fishing outports where self-provisioning and reciprocity were central to the way of life. Indeed, it was only when fish were sold to merchants and when supplies were purchased from the factor's store that cash might enter into a household's reckoning (Mannion, 1977). Fishing remained the island's economic mainstay into the twentieth century, although the beginnings of a wood industry were in place by 1910, when nearly 200 small sawmills were in operation (Hiller, 1982) and many fishermen worked seasonally in the forests. Young men and women faced the choice of following their parents into fishing and working in the woods during the winter months, or migrating elsewhere. The colony's finances were chronically weak, and sometimes so precarious that it became necessary to petition the British government for financial assistance (Chadwick, 1967). At the turn of the twentieth century, the most expedient way for the cash-strapped administration to open up the forest and mineral resources of the interior was to grant companies access to resources on Crown lands on condition that they build the infrastructure needed to open up the interior, thereby creating de facto partnerships of public and private capital (Hiller, 1982; Horwood, 1986). Newfoundland's colonial governors were well placed to broker such partnerships.

Prior to 1832 Newfoundland had been administered by a governor who exercised absolute power in the name of the British sovereign, under the rather distant supervision of the government of the day at Westminster (Head, 1976). Governors were drawn either from the upper ranks of the British civil service or from the ruling class, and could be relied on to nurture British commercial interests in their day-to-day management of the colony's affairs. An unwieldy system of representative government operated from 1832 until 1855, in which year the introduction of the system known as *responsible government* gave residents of the new Dominion of Newfoundland a greater say in their affairs (Smith, 1901). This system consisted of an elected House of Assembly and a Legislative Council appointed by the Governor on the recommendation of the Prime Minister (Hiller and Neary, 1980). In theory, responsible government meant what it says, since in addition to electing members of the House of Assembly, the executive branch of government was also made answerable to the people of Newfoundland (Parker, 1950). In practice, the Governor continued to wield considerable power, and any legislation passed by the House of Assembly was signed into law by the Governor only after he had transmitted it to London for approval by the British government (Chadwick, 1967).[1] Governors also continued to exercise their influence behind the scenes to promote British corporate interests, particularly in gaining access to Newfoundland's resources.

In the latter part of the nineteenth century efforts were made to diversify the island's economy so as to reduce its dependence on fishing, and to improve the Dominion's shaky public finances (Horwood, 1986). As already noted, the forest and mineral resources of the interior appeared to offer the most feasible route to economic diversification, but in the absence of roads connecting the settled parts of the island the Newfoundland interior remained largely inaccessible, except on foot (Hiller, 1982). Thus, the first step to developing forest industries was to build a narrow-gauge railway across the island in the years after 1898 (Rowe, 1980). From St. John's, the main rail line was built westward from the head of one major bay overland to the next major bay along the north coast of the island, then it swung inland up the valley of the Exploits River and over the height of land to drop into the Humber Valley and down to the coast, where it weaved in and out along the island's west coast to Port-aux-Basques with its ferry connection to Cape Breton Island in Nova Scotia (Figure 2). Lacking the capital to pay for this railway construction project and unable to attract the necessary funding, the Newfoundland government resorted to granting large tracts of

Crown land to the developer, the Reid Newfoundland Company, in lieu of cash. Robert Reid, the principal of the Reid Newfoundland Company, was a director of the Canadian Pacific Railway and the Bank of Montreal (Hiller, 1982; Rowe, 1980). Public resources were therefore privatized to stimulate more resource-based development. It was anticipated that the sale of timber from these lots (which became known as Reid lots) would generate the cash flow Reid needed to sustain railway construction.

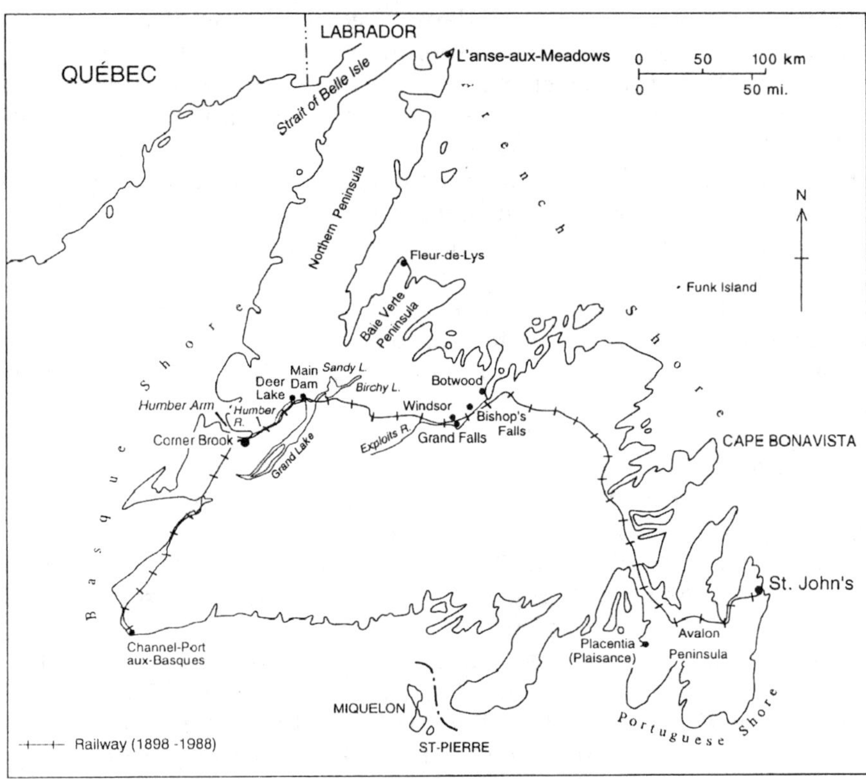

Figure 2: The Newfoundland Railway

Reid's immediate hope of recouping the capital outlay rested mainly on cutting and exporting white pine, which at that time was much in demand for ships' spars (Gray, 1981). Unfortunately for Reid, however, much of Newfoundland's pine turned out to be diseased and of low quality, so the railway company was forced to fall back on the plentiful stands of balsam fir and black spruce, which could be used for pulp and for low-grade sawn timber used in local construction, but little else (Hayden, 1986, 1988; Gray, 1981). Meantime, the Dominion government continued to view the forest resources as the best hope of diversifying the island's economy out of fishing. Thus a community of interest slowly developed among the Reid Company, the Newfoundland government led by Premier Robert Bond, and the island's residents, who were anxious to see the job base expand and diversify.[2] Between 1909 and 1914, five small pulp mills were opened along the railway, although only one of these – the mill at Grand Falls – was to survive and grow.

The corporatist policies pursued by the Newfoundland government to foster railway construction were also used to promote the building of pulp and paper mills (Pound and Harmsworth, 1960). Alfred and Harold Harmsworth (later Lord Northcliffe and Lord Rothermere, respectively) visited Newfoundland in 1902 searching for a site to build a newsprint mill that would supply the *Daily Mail* and other Harmsworth newspapers published in London, England (Botting, 2003). Subsequent negotiations with the Newfoundland government resulted in the Harmsworths' new subsidiary company based in Newfoundland gaining the rights to cut pulpwood on about three-quarters of a million acres of leased Crown land, as well as permission to generate power at the excellent hydroelectric power sites on the Exploits River at Grand Falls and Bishop's Falls (Botting, 2003).[3] The following year, in partnership with the Reid Newfoundland Company, Harmsworth created the Anglo-Newfoundland Development Company (AND), which built a mill and a company town at Grand Falls. Part of the deal was that the colonial government recognized AND's freehold over approximately one million acres of forest land that had originally been granted to the Reid Company in payment for constructing the Newfoundland railway. By this act, the Newfoundland government transferred extensive resource assets to this British company at very low cost, including about two million acres on freehold and leasehold forest land (see Figure 3) and the right to generate electric power privately at very low cost (Pound and Harmsworth, 1960).[4] Thus from its beginning Newfoundland's newsprint industry was an appendage to the colonial economy created by offering substantial public incentives to British corporations. The Harmsworths, for their part, are described by Botting (2003: 6) as "embodying the spirit of guilt-free imperialist Britain."

In several respects, Grand Falls served as a model for the subsequent development of Corner Brook. In particular, both were the creation of international capital attracted by public subsidies (Hiller, 1990). This is not to imply that Corner Brook is therefore a carbon copy of the founding mill; on the contrary, much happened between the opening at Grand Falls in 1909 and the commencement of work at Corner Brook in 1923. But equally, since both were company towns built and owned by overseas companies, there were some strong similarities. In both cases, the Newfoundland government transferred considerable resource assets to British companies at very low cost, including virtually free timber resources on freehold and leasehold land and hydroelectric power generating rights. In both cases, too, the influx of foreign capital took place with virtually no resistance from local people – indeed, there was a strong shared interest, at this stage, between international capital and local resi-

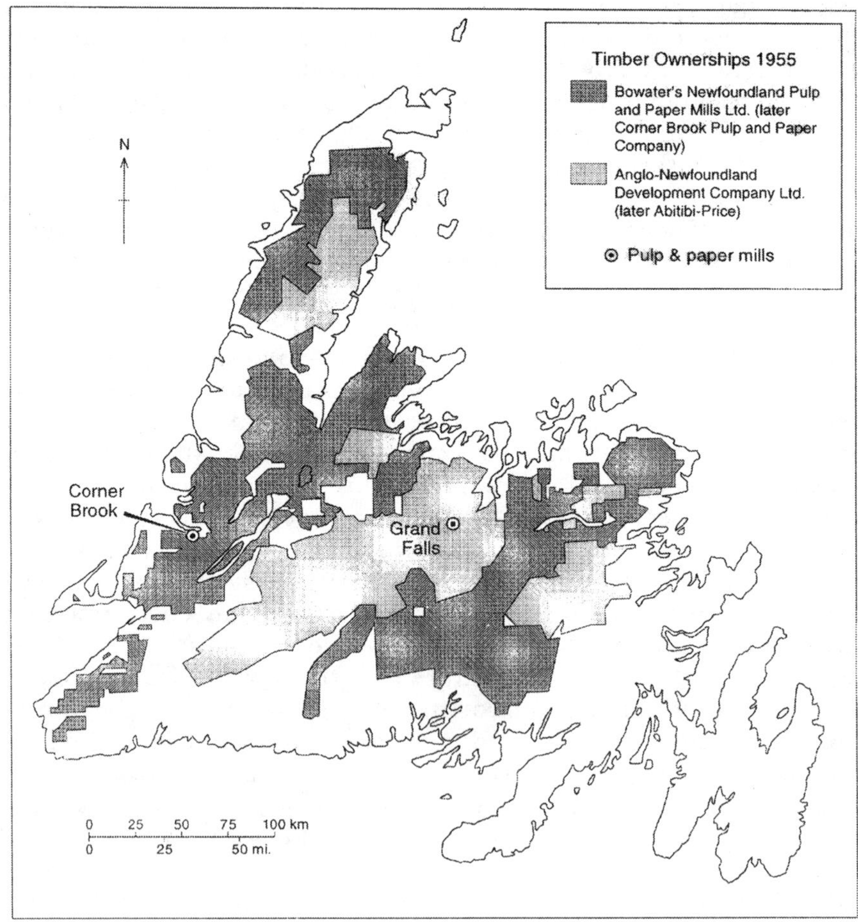

Figure 3: Timber Rights in Newfoundland, 1955

dents. The Harmsworths wanted an alternative to Scandinavian newsprint for their newspapers, the Newfoundland government was anxious to diversify the Dominion's economy, and parents living in outports were eager to see new job opportunities created for their children, especially if they offered an alternative to the hazardous life of fishing. This was a pattern of regulated development to be repeated through much of the twentieth century. As Hiller (1990: 3) puts it:

> Since neither firm [at Grand Falls and at Corner Brook] was indigenous to Newfoundland, profits were largely exported. Thus what had occurred was the development of an enclave industry at very considerable cost in terms of control over resources and obtaining an adequate governmental return.

The Grand Falls newsprint mill was opened by AND in 1909, making it Newfoundland's first paper mill. It was located beside the power site at Grand Falls due to the big loss of power then experienced when electricity was transmitted long distances. Being situated some 35 kilometres inland, the mill had to transport newsprint by rail to the port of Botwood for export. Around the mill AND built a company town, including offices, a company store, and housing for managers. A fascinating urban dialectic then commenced with the unplanned development, just outside the Grand Falls city limits, of the non-company town of Windsor, which became home for many of the mill's workers and the place where drinking and more raucous activities went on. In 1923, AND took over the pulp mill at nearby Bishop's Falls, and since then has used both sites to generate most of its electricity requirements.[5] The Anglo-Newfoundland Development Company operated the mill for over half a century, expanding operations on several occasions; in fact, by 1925, when the Corner Brook mill was opened, a sixth paper machine had been commissioned at Grand Falls (Pound and Harmsworth, 1960).

CONSTRUCTING THE COMPANY TOWN

The success of the Grand Falls paper mill, particularly during the Great War of 1914-18 when newsprint prices were high, led the Dominion government to resuscitate the idea of constructing a second newsprint mill in the western part of the island where substantial wood resources remained untapped. The obvious location was somewhere beside the Humber River or the Humber Arm, along which logs could be run. But where, exactly? One possibility was at Deer Lake, where, with a large investment in engineering, a major power installation could be created. Such a location at a power site would mirror the situation at Grand Falls. A second possibility was a site beside the Humber River, with its potential for running logs. The third alternative was a coastal site that would facilitate shipping, the logical point being somewhere close to the railway that had been built along the south shore of the Humber Arm between Humbermouth and Curling in 1898. By 1921 Corner Brook had a population of 411, Curling, 569, and Humbermouth, 389, so the three neighbouring communities, with a combined population exceeding 1,300, constituted the largest settlement in the area (Horwood, 1986).

The recession that followed the Great War cooled interest in this project, but the election of Richard Squires as Prime Minister of Newfoundland in 1919 put in place a keen advocate of building a second newsprint mill on the west coast (Hiller, 1990). Given the risks involved, Squires felt that financial incentives were an imperative, so he set about persuading the British government's Trade Facilities Board to underwrite a bond issue to finance the launching of the paper mill project.[6] Horwood (1986: 28-9) and Hiller (1990) describe the convoluted negotiations that Squires then conducted to promote the construction of the mill complex by the Newfoundland Power and Paper Company. Four key actors were involved in the agreement: Armstrong Whitworth, a large British engineering and armaments firm; Eric Bowater, the manager of a small British family firm that marketed paper; the Reid Newfoundland Company; and, of course, Richard Squires.

Armstrong Whitworth would build the mill, supply the equipment for the power station at Deer Lake, and become the major partner in the operating company. With the Great War over and demand for naval ships and armaments much reduced, this firm was looking for civil engineering projects to occupy its workforce. Armstrong Whitworth had flourished building engineering projects in many parts of the British Empire and thus the plan for Corner Brook was, from the firm's point of view, another link between "industry and empire."

Eric Bowater, who managed his family's company that marketed paper manufactured at other mills, was at that time in discussion with Armstrong Whitworth with a view to constructing a Bowater paper mill. Bowater was made a director of Newfoundland Power and Paper and given responsibility to market the mill's paper, mainly in the United States. Subsequently he became a pivotal figure in the development of Corner Brook.

The Reid Newfoundland Company, which was in financial difficulty (Hiller, 1990), held a minority interest in Newfoundland Power and Paper, and provided the power site and freehold forest limits amounting to some 1.6 million acres (640,000 hectares).

Richard Squires, leader of a Liberal-Union coalition government, brokered the entire deal, although he was hostile to the Reids and to the Humber project until he saw it as a "surefire" election issue for the 1923 election (Hiller, 1990). He persuaded the British Treasury to guarantee a £2 million debenture at 5 per cent secured by a first mortgage (this was later increased when the project ran into financial difficulties), while the Newfoundland government guaranteed a further £2 million second debenture, these being crucial to launching the costly and risky project;[7] he approved major changes to the island's hydrology by building a dam 75 feet high and 800 feet long at Main Dam, thus flooding land to unite Birchy Lake, Sandy Lake, and Grand Lake into one large body of water and reversing the flow of water towards a spillway that flowed down to a large power plant at Deer Lake; he promised extensive timber cutting rights to the new company; and he made complicated deals with Reid that included purchasing the loss-making Newfoundland Railway. Subsequently, Squires was charged with corruption over some of these deals, and though an official inquiry found evidence of extensive graft in his government, the charges were eventually dropped (Horwood, 1986). Hiller (1990) argues that, overall, Squires's actions were both wise and positive.

The construction of the Corner Brook mill and Deer Lake power station complex was one of the most remarkable feats of civil engineering ever witnessed in Newfoundland, and is an achievement comparable to the more recent Churchill Falls and Hibernia projects. This is not just because it was a large project, or because it was built in a remote region that experiences very hard winters, or because of the total absence of a local workforce with previous experience in constructing large civil projects or with papermaking and electrical skills. The speed at which the whole project went ahead was equally impressive. The Deer Lake power station required damming three lakes, building a 15-kilometre spillway to the height of land over Deer Lake, and constructing the power station itself, which was connected by a 66,000-volt transmission line to Corner Brook, 60 kilometres away (see Figure 4).

Even larger was the civil engineering project required in Corner Brook. The mill site was reclaimed from marshland and the shallow waters of the Humber Arm near the mouth of Corner Brook by dumping nearly half a million cubic yards of rock. This created the 20-hectare mill site with deepwater berths for ships on its water side. The mill constructed on this platform of rock consisted of a

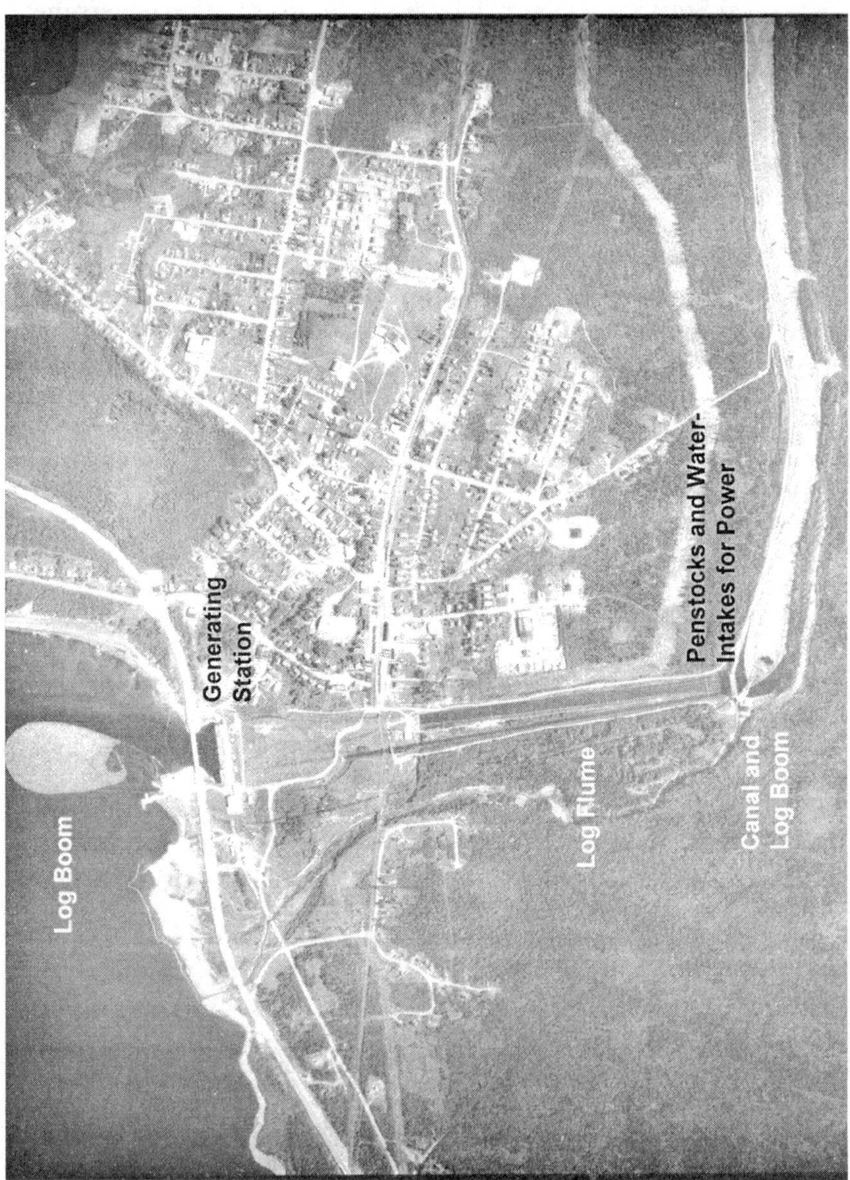

Figure 4: Aerial photograph of the Deer Lake spillway and power station (17 September 1968)

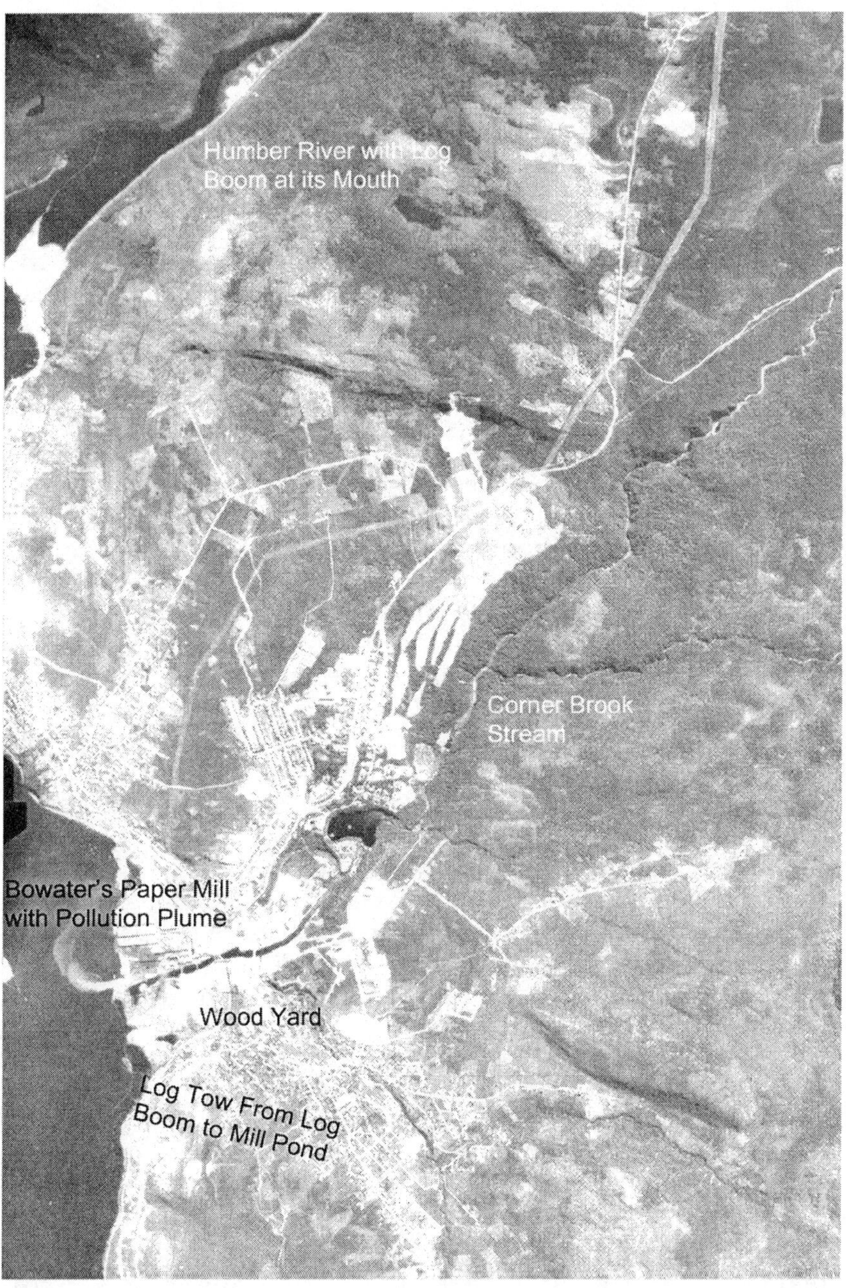

Figure 5: Townsite, the company mill town, aerial photograph (14 August 1950)

woodyard, ground wood and sulphite pulp mills serving four paper machines, and three warehouses capable of storing nearly six months of mill production in case shipping was blocked by ice for long periods. Beside the woodyard was a mill pond into which logs could be floated. Newfoundland Power and Paper also ordered two cargo vessels specially built to transport rolls of paper without damaging them (Horwood, 1986).

In addition, there was a town to build. The detailed plan of the company town, called Townsite, was prepared in 1922 by Thomas Adams, a British planner who was active in the New Towns Movement (Adams, 1932; Wonders, 1954). Adams and his colleagues had secured a number of similar contracts on Canada's resource frontier, where they designed towns based in British conceptions of good planning – which did not necessarily correspond with the rigours of Canadian winters, nor did it account for the social melting pot that occurred among migrants to these new communities (Saarinen, 1979). These planned company towns followed a standard model, where status in the company hierarchy, class, and social standing had a major influence on where a family lived (Fortier, 1996). Townsite was a garden city inhabited by mill management and foremen and provided with schools, churches, sewers, a water supply system, the company store, and the Glynmill Inn, which served as quarters for visiting engineers, management, and government officials (see Figure 5).

This series of engineering projects was pushed ahead at remarkable speed despite an inexperienced workforce. There were considerable risks for those involved, and much waste, thereby pushing up costs substantially (Horwood, 1986). Quite a number of accidents occurred, some recorded in histories of the period and some still carried in the collective memory of successive generations. One interviewee employed at the mill recalled the injury his father suffered:

> He had an accident there. He ruptured himself pretty bad and he never went back to the mill after. That was during the construction of the mill. They were driving piles, apparently, and he slipped and fell on a pile. Actually he never had an operation for it either, he went through all his life like that. But he was in on the construction of the mill.

Following the precedent of the AND mill at Grand Falls, the Newfoundland government granted Newfoundland Power and Paper Company at Corner Brook access to extensive natural resources at minimal cost in order to promote the building project (although in this case the power site was 60 kilometres away at Deer Lake). Horwood (ibid., 35) reports that in 1925, when the Corner Brook mill opened, it had cutting rights to a million acres (400,000 hectares) of forest in the Humber Basin, and close to another million acres near the rail line beyond the Basin (in Figure 3, most of the dark shaded lands stretching northeast and southwest from Corner Brook). Of these 2 million acres, about 37 per cent are productive forest. The local state therefore played a key role, as facilitator, as grantor of extensive resource rights, as guarantor of loans, as negotiator with private capital, and as legislator confirming the informal agreements.

The company town of Townsite, as it was known, was also home to the mill's management. It was built on the flatter land created by quarrying material needed to fill the nearby mill site beside the harbour. Its planned streets and gabled houses gave it a distinctive character (Wonders, 1954). As at Grand Falls, the promise of regular work brought in a wave of migrants from fishing villages around the Bay of Islands, from Bonne Bay, and from outports across Newfoundland. They had to be housed, but since company housing in Townsite was reserved, most of these migrants either bought plots of land or squatted on parcels from Curling to Humbermouth. Botting (2000) has found that the company towns of Grand Falls and Corner Brook also attracted a substantial number of young single women to work as domestic servants. Some men who came without their families, or who were single, lived in bunkhouses without running water and sanitation built near the mill. One retired mill worker recalls the shanties that were occupied by some workers:

> People from the outer Bay of Islands, Frenchman's Cove and Benoit's Cove, they would build small living quarters and then they'd come up and live all along the track just close to the mill. They couldn't get home every night because there was no way to get home. . . . Most of them didn't stay the wintertime because these people worked on the shipping and the shipping shut down in the wintertime and the paper was shipped out of Port aux Basques.

The largest number of recruits to the mill's workforce settled on the west bank of Corner Brook, outside the town limits of Townsite, in an area known as Corner Brook West that became the antithesis of the company town. Townsite had the company store, Corner Brook West had the Lebanese trading stores where credit was available when cash ran out; Townsite had the banks and the churches, whereas its unplanned sister town had the bars and the brothels; and while sobriety reigned with the clerical, managerial, and professional classes in their corporate enclave, the settlement to the west pulsed with the rhythms of everyday life.

The layout of the Corner Brook mill at the time of its opening is not much changed today (Figure 6). The woodyard often held huge quantities of logs in case of supply problems, particularly during seasonal fluxes when logging roads turned to quagmire. A mill employee with long service who once worked on the tugboats recalls how these logs were brought to the mill. Most of them were floated in log runs down the Humber River: "we were going around weaving the wood into the big log booms . . . we used to haul the wood to the mill in tugboats, and we'd float it into the mill pond." Jack ladders would then pull the four-foot-long "junks" out of the water and cranes would stack them in the mill yard. In addition, an ocean-going tug, the *Balsam Lake*, brought log tows down the coast from the Northern Peninsula, and the railway was used to transport logs either directly to the mill yard or to a point beside the mouth of the Humber River where they were pushed into the river and towed to the mill yard. Sitting in the yard for up to a year, the logs could become hard and dry, making pulping difficult. First the bark was removed and then they were pulped using one of two processes. The groundwood mill consisted of a tower into which four-foot-long logs were placed in magazines. A former worker recalls this process, which was one of the most gruelling jobs at the mill:

> Five years as a casual in the groundwood mill. I was loading magazines – holes in the floor going down to the [grind]stones below. As the weight goes on the stones the logs are ground up. You used to have to keep it filled up. It was . . . fairly physical. But they were a lot bigger logs than what they get coming down there now.

Revolving grindstones at the bottom of the hopper physically ground the logs into a short-fibre pulp, which, by itself, had insufficient tear-strength for newsprint but was satisfactory when mixed with long-fibre chemical pulp.

Chemical pulping with the sulphite process made use of limestone quarried at Steady Brook, inland from Corner Brook. This began with another arduous job: the quarried stone, sometimes in pieces weighing up to 100 pounds, was shovelled into boxes that held about a ton at a time, and the boxes were wheeled onto an elevator that took them to the top of stone towers where they were emptied into hoppers. A retired worker recalls:

> I used to shovel 30 tons of rock, what they called rock limestone, five days a week. Some days we worked four hours' overtime, probably two or three days a week. I was only 20 years old then, I was in good shape. . . . We shovelled every day, and if it rained you didn't go in out of the rain, you stayed out in the rain and shovelled. . . . Winter! You stayed out in the wintertime and it was blowing and

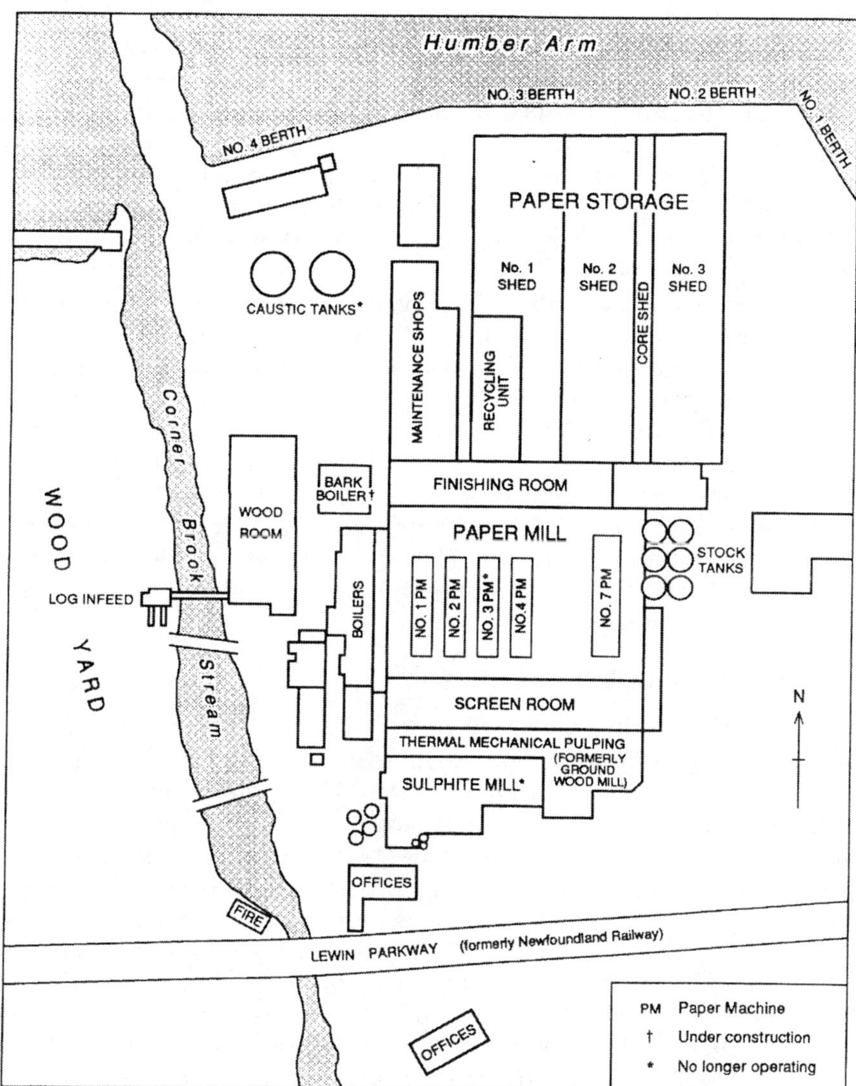

Figure 6: Layout of thc Corner Brook Pulp and Paper Mill

> snowing and you just had a piece over your head like that. It was a canopy but everything was open.

Sulphur was burned at the bottom of the towers and the gas this gave off was blown up through the stones, while water was sprinkled down from above. The resulting compound ate the stone away, forming an acid suitable for pulping logs. The logs for chemical pulping were reduced to wood chips that were fed into huge pressurized digesters full of acid and boiled at about 120 pounds per square inch pressure for 6-9 hours. Boiling in acid separates the cellulose fibres from the lignin that binds them together. These long fibres were then mixed with the short fibres of groundwood pulp and screened to remove bits of bark and chip before being fed down the pulp lines to the paper machines.

The lines from the pulp mill served four paper machines, each 234 inches wide and a football pitch long. The pulp fed into a paper machine contains over 90 per cent water and ends as newsprint with around 8 per cent water content. In between it passes over a wire mesh (with the Fourdrinier single-wire process) that permits water to drain out, through hot presses that remove more water, into a dryer to remove more moisture, then through calenders that give the paper a smoother surface for printing, and finally it is wound into a huge roll on a winder. In the finishing room, paper rolls are rewound and cut to customers' specifications, wrapped, and put in a warehouse ready for shipping.

CRISIS AND CHANGES OF OWNERSHIP

The production of the mill's first batch of newsprint on 8 July 1925 was marked by a banquet and ball – attended by Newfoundland's finest – held in Number One Paper Shed.[8] The completion of this major construction project in two years was a remarkable achievement. But there was a large associated cost, partly in accidents due to lapses in safety, partly in the premium prices and overtime paid to get quick results, but mainly in the cost of training a large and inexperienced workforce. Newfoundland Power and Paper had recruited some qualified tradesmen, construction foremen, and mill workers, but most of the workforce on the construction crews were totally unskilled labourers from fishing outports – they learned on the job. With the construction complete, many of these workmen were recruited to the workforce of the paper mill. A slow and painful learning process then began for both the management and the workers. The paper machines ran slower than anticipated, yet even so there were frequent tears and breakdowns. Inexperienced crews found it difficult to maintain consistently good paper quality. Cash flow was below expectations, and the company had to service a huge debt incurred during construction (the cost of construction had been severely underestimated). After a year Newfoundland Power and Paper was still barely covering its operating costs (mostly wages), never mind servicing its debt of $39 million, and bankruptcy seemed imminent (Hiller, 1990).

In a decisive act of regulation the Newfoundland government stepped in and sought out a new owner – not for the last time, as will become apparent in the next chapter. A buyer was found in International Power and Paper (IP&P) of New York, which paid the banks $2.5 million cash and converted the rest of the company's debt into preference shares. Thus the workings of global finance were evident even at this early stage as the mill's ownership switched from Britain to the United States. To smooth this transition of ownership, the government made various guarantees, in return gaining the right to appoint directors to the board. The new owners then settled down to make paper by working the bugs out of the continuous flow mode of production. One by one the problems were ironed out, and electricity generating capacity at Deer Lake was increased. It is important to stress that the Dominion government played an essential regulatory role in resolving this start-up crisis by mediating with international capital.

The mill's labour force entered into this program of regulation by organizing. Horwood (1986: 43) notes that the International Union of Papermakers, which was already established at Grand Falls, began to organize as an exclusive craft union at Corner Brook in 1925, and within a year all the papermakers were recruited. In 1926, the International Union of Pulp, Sulphite and Papermill Workers began to organize the rest of the mill's labour force as Local 64. This was evidently done to create a united voice for the interests of labour. The lack of reported conflict during these early days between management and labour suggests that a local regime of production was indeed in the making. Until the 1930s the unions were not formally recognized, nor were contractual collective agreements in force. But there were informal annual meetings at which wage scales were discussed and set, apparently without rancour.

Within a few years the mill became one of the more productive in North America. IP&P installed two additional small paper machines (numbers 5 and 6), one making wrapping paper, the other pulp, while the four existing paper machines were speeded up. These gains in efficiency allowed the mill to weather the first years of the Great Depression of the 1930s better than most (Forsey, 1935), but the mill ran at a loss from 1933 through 1937 (Hiller, 1990). For the loggers supplying the mill's wood supply, the early years of the Depression were marked by appalling hardship, declining wages (to well below poverty levels), and, eventually, collective action. Gillespie's (1986) illustrated essay gives some sense of the desperate plight the loggers faced. Paid on a piece rate system, they received between $1.30 and $1.50 per cord of wood, which took most of a day to cut. Working 12 hours a day, six days a week, they might gross between $40 and $50 dollars a month, from which was deducted their food and lodging at the logging camps, to leave a net income closer to $20. Gillespie (1986: 58) estimates loggers' net pay at this time was 11½ cents an hour compared to 30-35 cents an hour for workers inside the Corner Brook mill. Pay, food, and living conditions at the camps were so bad that in 1934 the Commission of Government appointed Gordon Bradley, a lawyer and former opposition leader in the House of Assembly, to investigate the plight of the loggers. His investigation discovered conditions so scandalous that his report was suppressed, but members of the Commission of Government did extract from the two newsprint companies a promise to pay loggers a minimum net wage of $25 a month as a condition of keeping the report under wraps (Neary, 1985).

Despite operating profitably in the early years of the Depression (AND at Grand Falls made a profit of over $1 million in 1933), the paper mills lowered the price paid to loggers for a cord of cut wood. In response the loggers began to organize, but with 12,000 loggers spread over numerous tiny camps, this was difficult. Eventually, in 1936, the organizing drive led by John Thompson was completed, and the constitution of the Newfoundland Lumbermen's Association was registered in St. John's (Gillespie, 1986). At the end of winter logging, in early 1937, the NLA demanded from AND union recognition and improved pay for loggers, and threatened to block the spring log drive if this was not done. Within two days an agreement was reached, and the price paid per cord was increased from the $1.00-$1.30 range to $2.00 to $2.50, or almost double. Armed with this agreement, Thompson and the Newfoundland Lumbermen's Association next went to Corner Brook to seek a similar settlement with International Power and Paper. There were negotiations, but no agreement, so again a confrontation developed between international capital and local labour. Gillespie (1986: 61) describes the scene:

> On May 17, 700 men left their camps and headed into Deer Lake and Corner Brook. Some wanted to close the flume at the Deer Lake power plant, a move that would have cut power to the mill and the

> entire town of Corner Brook. Always respectful of the law, Thompson, with the help of the local magistrate, talked the loggers out of that plan. When negotiations dragged on for more than a week, they acted without Thompson's permission. [A mob surrounded and threatened to beat up IP&P's woods manager, but were eventually dissuaded by the police.]
>
> It was only a temporary respite. That evening about 200 loggers gathered on the intake to the Corner Brook mill and threatened to shut it if an agreement wasn't reached right away. The police intervened again, but this time the men refused to back down. At 11:30 the next morning Thompson had an agreement similar to the agreement with AND.

In this case, forceful local resistance sustained by widespread local support did force foreign owners to make substantial concessions to the loggers. The crisis of the 1930s was a period when established local working practices were challenged, not least because so many people who had migrated from Newfoundland to other parts of North America had lost their jobs during the Depression and had chosen to return home in the hope of at least being better fed. In such hard times, the determination to resist foreign corporate interests was strong. From a regulationist perspective, this period may be seen as the beginning of the collapse of the paternalistic mode of corporate production within company towns, and its replacement, in the years after the war, by a more open, international, and competitive mode of social regulation.

The pulp and paper industry was not the only activity squeezed by the Depression. Faced with crushing debts, responsible government in Newfoundland was suspended by the British government following a lengthy inquiry. The elected National Assembly was dissolved and Newfoundland reverted to Crown colony status with a Commission of Government, which took office in February 1934, consisting of the Governor, three Newfoundland commissioners, and three commissioners appointed by the Crown (Parker, 1950).

At the Corner Brook mill, the inventory of unsold paper became huge as the world economy slid into recession. Work was cut to five, then four, and at one stage to two days a week, although the mill never closed completely. But the mill lost money for five consecutive years and International Power and Paper began to look for a possible purchaser. At this point, the firm of Bowater-Lloyd came into play. For some years Eric Bowater had been considering the possibility of opening a newsprint mill or a pulp mill in North America in order to diversify the wood supply of his British paper mills, which at that time depended largely on Scandinavian pulp (Reader, 1981). This became a priority as the looming menace of war in Europe threatened his Scandinavian supply lines. Accordingly, in 1937 Bowater took an option on the Reid Newfoundland Company's forest lands in the Gander Valley in the east of Newfoundland (these appear in Figure 3 as the darker shaded lands south and east of Grand Falls). In return, he made a commitment to the Commission of Government to construct a pulpwood mill in the Gander Valley. Before constructing the pulp mill, he first obtained interim permission to export pulpwood. In the same year Eric Bowater received a cable from IP&P in New York indicating that the company was interested in selling the Corner Brook mill. Bowater had been a director of the original company and also handled the mill's paper sales, so he had an excellent understanding of the prospects. The mill matched Bowater's goals to expand into North America perfectly, and he followed up on the offer.

Once again the Newfoundland government entered into the negotiations, offering Bowater access to the colony's resources to secure the deal. A specific act of the Commission of Government, the Bowater Act of 1938, confirmed Bowater's rights by succession to the freehold timber limits of 640,000 hectares that formerly belonged to Reid Newfoundland, to timber cutting rights on 1.7 million hectares of Crown land leased for 99 years, and to the right to generate electric power at Deer Lake (Horwood, 1986). Bowater even managed to hold on to his new timber cutting rights in eastern Newfoundland intended for the putative pulp mill on the Gander River. This he had achieved simply by promising to increase pulp production at Corner Brook by 30,000 tons a year, although this arrangement was vigorously criticized as a government sellout by easterners anxious to see a pulp mill built at their end of the island that would create local jobs. The unelected Newfoundland Commission of Government simply ignored the objections. Bowater raised the $5 million purchase price by borrowing the sum from the Bank of Montreal, then having Bowater-Lloyd of St. John's issue a debenture for the same amount, guaranteed by the Bowater Companies in England. Bowater's Newfoundland Paper Mills took over the Corner Brook mill on 18 August 1938. Figure 3, which plots the timber holdings (in 1955, but hardly changed since 1938) of the AND mill at Grand Falls and the Bowater mill at Corner Brook, shows the curious geography that resulted; Bowater's bloc of forest land in eastern Newfoundland created an inefficient ownership pattern with Bowater timber being, in effect, hauled past the doors of the AND mill at Grand Falls to a distant site in the west of the island.[9] Until the Newfoundland government repurchased all the island's forest lands in the late 1990s, the illogical pattern of timber limits of these two mills served as a historical reminder of the intention, in the late 1930s, to construct a pulp mill on the Gander River.

Bowater had the good fortune to see the mill make substantial profits for the next 11 years. A mill expansion program was begun at Corner Brook, although the war intervened before it was fully underway. Most of the mill's workforce switched from a two-shift system with 11- or 13-hour shifts to three shifts of eight hours each. The mill continued to close on Sundays, which was a repair day (only in 1966 did the mill switch to seven-day operation). New management took over and safety standards were raised, new lumber camps were built, and hundreds of trees were planted to beautify Townsite. The mill began to run at a profit and continued to do so through the war years (ibid.).

Bowater's plan to expand the mill came to fruition after the war. Approval to install a seventh paper machine, giving the mill the largest rated capacity in the world, was granted in 1946. An interesting decision was made, one consistent with the Fordist principal of internalizing work in the firm: the company's tradesmen would install the machine themselves (ibid.). With hindsight, this appears to have been a bad decision on two counts. First, it took a long time to do and cost more than expected (installation costs ranging from $7 million to $12 million are cited). And second, the machine didn't work consistently well. Different explanations have been offered for this. A retired papermaker stated:

> What they were saying at that time is that they couldn't get the speed on the machine, and when they could get the speed . . . she would vibrate and this would cause a sheet to break in the dryer or at the dry end. They blamed this, I think, as if the machine itself was out of line, or she had settled.

The recollections of a retired mechanic who had helped to install the machine offered another explanation:

> This machine they were building was a Beloit machine . . . it was supposed to be the biggest and fastest in the world at the time. Bowater never paid five cents for that machine. She was an experimental machine, first big paper machine in the world. . . . It cost them $12 million [to install], and it was only going to be $1 million when they started off.

Current management disagrees with both of these versions, claiming that the problem was due to lack of experience in installing a prototype machine. In any case, bugs were slowly ironed out and soon the mill set daily world records for paper production, although annual records took longer to achieve due to the machine's unreliability.

The installation of number 7 paper machine was accompanied by the addition of two new pulp lines, this time using thermal-mechanical pulping (TMP) so that three different methods of pulping logs were then in use. In many ways this period represented the mill's zenith, with a production record set at Corner Brook in 1952, and record corporate profits, too. It was during this period, in 1949, that Newfoundland voted to join Canada as the tenth province (Parker, 1950). Newfoundland's newly elected government, led by Joseph Smallwood, proceeded to close down dozens of small outports and relocate their populations to larger settlements situated, where possible, close to the abandoned outports (Iverson and Matthews, 1968). Some, however, found work at the expanding Corner Brook mill so that abandoned outports are now remembered only by the elderly – including many retired mill workers living in Corner Brook.

LIFE IN A COMPANY TOWN

From its founding in the early 1920s through to its incorporation in the amalgamated city of Corner Brook in 1956, Townsite was a company town in the full sense of the term.[10] There was not just an internal labour market within the mill but also, within the town, an internal housing market and an internal retail market. Initially, the company owned most of the real estate and provided all the services – water, sewers, housing, education, and hospitals. This housing stock was enlarged in 1947-49 as prefabricated houses were imported from England and erected in an extension of Townsite built to coincide with the expansion of the mill and the installation of number 7 paper machine. Employees were paid partly in coupons that were redeemable at the company store. The company supplied coal, sold milk from the company farm, and owned the local newspaper, which allowed it to manage the news. The company owned the houses in Townsite and tenants had rent deducted from their wages at the mill. A retired employee recalls:

> They got paid cash but you could get some coupons if you wanted them. We used to go to the company store and even the local dairy farmer. We used to get milk because if you were an employee of the mill or family, you got milk cheaper . . . the employees at the mill seemed to be more looked after. You lived in a company house. This was a company house and everything was done. They even came in the fall of the year and put your storm windows on and come up in the spring and take them off.

No taxes were paid because there was no municipal government to spend them. The town was run by a manager, employed by the company, who was not subject to the kind of democratic accountability that applies in a normal municipality. The town manager reported to the general manager of the mill, who supervised his activities. Mill work and town work at times merged: one fire brigade served both, and in a crisis such as a heavy snowstorm or floods, the mill's maintenance workers might be called out to help.

The bond between company and town was strongest during the Bowater period. Sir Eric seems to have had a personal affection for the town, due partly to his family living there during the war, safe from German bombing, and partly to the fact that in Corner Brook the entrepreneur had his greatest success: this was his crowning achievement (Reader, 1981). He acted out the role of seigneur. An elderly, retired mill employee recalls:

> I can remember him coming over, he used to come around September month and he'd be ramrod straight and everybody thought he was almost God. Well, this was his town, his people, and people respected him and he treated people well.

A retired boatman recalls that Sir Eric sometimes invited his business friends to visit Corner Brook for some fishing and hunting.

> I had him [Sir Eric] out in the passenger boat lots of times – the *Blarney* it was called. I used to take all the big shots out in the Bay. Fishing, yes . . . Bowater was heaven to work for. . . . You worked harder with Bowater, but every man enjoyed it.

Bowater originally lived in Townsite but then built a substantial hunting lodge at Strawberry Hill, outside town, where he entertained a string of guests when he visited Corner Brook. Among many employees there was a perception of an enduring connection between mill and town. His acts, such as his gift to the town in 1957 of the Lady Margaret Bowater Park, helped cement this bond. As one former worker explained:

> Bowater was a pleasant company. I mean they were English people. They had their strict rules and regulations, but I remember up there in the feeders they used to polish all the brass and everything. Every bit of brass was shining. It's not the same [now].

At the start of World War II, Bowater promised that all the men who volunteered for war service would be found a job on their return, and eventually this was done. The mill manager, Monty Lewin, also helped organize the Veterans' Housing Co-operative to build houses for those returning to mill jobs. Several interviewees commented on the more relaxed atmosphere of the company town era. A job was for life even though there may be temporary layoffs during downturns; a feeling of job security was often mentioned in interviews. But a few reflected on the long-term implications of things becoming too relaxed, suggesting that practices such as doing "thank-you jobs" (i.e., non-company jobs) on work time in the mill's shops helped account both for Bowater's later difficulties and for the necessity of the lean work practices introduced by the subsequent mill owner.

If the above comments give the impression that the Bowater era was universally seen as the halcyon days, then this impression must be corrected. Several interviewees felt that Bowater's primary goal was to make the most of the region's resources for the least cost. Reflecting this viewpoint are comments like "Bowaters were here just to get the best of it," "if Sir Eric Bowater was alive today the place probably wouldn't be alive," and "all the money [the company] made through there, it never went back into this mill." A long-time employee expressed the following view:

> Bowater never done anything for us either when it came to that stuff. They went out in the woods and they raped – whatever you call it . . . well, they took the government for everything they could, they couldn't get any more money from the government. That's why they pulled out.

The reminiscences of older and retired workers are of a company town serving a Fordist newsprint operation, with its own internal labour market and a plant that was highly self-sufficient as far as operations and repairs went. The remoteness of Corner Brook, and the lengthy periods in winter when it was effectively cut off, gave the owners extra incentive to make the mill self-reliant. Work at the mill also became a family affair. Third-generation employees are now on the mill's payroll, and when several generations of uncles and brothers are taken into account, some large extended families can still be found working within its walls.[11] These conditions engendered a sense of stability that allowed the semblance of a regime of accumulation to take shape, at least within the circumscribed world of the company town. There were minor perturbations – strikes and temporary layoffs – but the broad pattern of operation agreed upon among the owner, the Newfoundland government, and the workers held sway for nearly half a century.

BOWATER BOWS OUT

The beginning of the end of the company town era began in 1942 when Corner Brook West applied to the Commission of Government in St. John's for permission to incorporate and to elect a town council. Curling followed suit in 1947, as did Corner Brook East in 1948 (Horwood, 1986). In 1951, Corner Brook East was permitted to expand its boundaries to absorb Humbermouth and Brake's Cove. Townsite remained a company town, with a town council presided over by the mill's general manager, as Newfoundland voted by a whisker in the second referendum of 1949 to become Canada's tenth province. But the writing was on the wall. Indeed, in 1948 Bowater had begun to sell off non-mill assets such as the Glynmill Inn, the local newspaper (the *Western Star*), the Corner Brook Store, Crown Laundry and Dry Cleaning, and the western terminals in order to concentrate on the core activity of papermaking. Bowater also sold off the company's housing stock. A retiree recalls:

> In 1958 they decided they would sell their homes to anybody who lived in them. . . . Everybody who was living [in Townsite] had an opportunity to buy their homes. They didn't have to but they gives you the opportunity. It was a very good opportunity because a home like this here went for $2,500.

The demise of Townsite as a company town followed on a vote taken in 1955 on the amalgamation of Corner Brook West, Corner Brook East, Curling, and Townsite into one city. Strongly supported in a public referendum, the deed was achieved by a formal act of the Newfoundland provincial legislature. Premier Smallwood then set about establishing the new city as the main regional service centre of western Newfoundland by investing in hospitals, education, housing, roads, and government and community services. The population of the city peaked at 27,116 in 1966 and has declined by several hundred in each five-year census since then. Nevertheless, the city of Corner Brook, with a population that had declined to 22,410 by the time of the 1991 census (and barely 20,000 in 2001), remained in an important way a "post-company town."[12] To this day, the mill does not pay municipal taxes, but instead pays a contribution of its own choice towards the running of the town; indeed, this was one of the conditions set by Bowater when it made the town public, which was renewed by Kruger as part of its purchase agreement.

By the mid-1950s a perceptible decline in the centrality of Corner Brook to Bowater's corporate strategy was becoming apparent as construction began on a new mill at Calhoun, Tennessee, financed in part by profits made at other mills, including the one at Corner Brook.[13] Improvements were still made to the Corner Brook plant, but it was no longer a state-of-the-art mill as it slowly slipped from its position as a world leader. A major fire at the mill in April 1957 was a serious setback, badly damaging paper machines 1, 2, 3, and 4; it took nearly 13 months to get the mill back to full production. Significantly, the Bowater Company used the $4 million insurance settlement to repair the original four paper machines dating to 1924 rather than purchase a new machine embodying the latest technology.

The unexpected death of Sir Eric Bowater of cancer in 1962 marked a decisive point in the history of the town. Sir Eric seems to have had a personal commitment to the well-being of Corner Brook. His successors in the management of Bowater had no such ties, and soon came to the opinion that the southern United States, where pulpwood species grow to maturity in around 30 years (compared to 60 years in Newfoundland), was the best location to concentrate production. But they could not simply pull up their roots in Corner Brook: they had sunk a large amount of capital in the mill operations, and it was still profitable at times when world newsprint prices were high.

The years from 1968 to 1971 were a time of rising unemployment, recession, and depressed world newsprint prices. The mill was periodically closed, and despite attempts to sell newsprint in Britain (due to weak demand in the American market) inventory was still large and growing. In October 1971 Bowater's decided to close down number 7 paper machine, which 20 years earlier had been the most productive paper machine in the world, and contemplated closing the entire mill. Politically, the timing could not have been worse: a provincial election was in progress, and Premier Smallwood's Liberal Party was in trouble. It was a measure of the regulatory powers of the government and the highly interventionist practices of Joey Smallwood that he flew to Corner Brook and drew up papers giving the government an option to buy the mill – in effect, to nationalize the mill – with a view to selling it back to the private sector when a buyer could be found (Lang and Mintz, 1979). To avoid the possibility of being nationalized, Bowater kept number 7 paper machine operating until December, which was after the late October election date. The Liberal Party lost the October 1971 election by one seat but, despite not having a majority in the legislature, Smallwood refused for three months to resign as Premier. When he eventually resigned, the Conservatives assumed office and immediately called another election, which they won with a landslide victory. The new government allowed the option to buy the mill to lapse. The new Conservative Premier, Frank Moores, went on record stating that he wished to avoid the interventionist policies of his predecessor.

Bowater's management struggled on although the mill continued to experience large losses through 1972, by which time the paper machines had been upgraded to make the whiter and lighter-grade paper increasingly demanded by newspapers. From then on Bowater began to run the mill as a cash cow, with much of the profit made in good years funnelled into Bowater projects elsewhere, notably in the southern United States. Modest upgrades were made at the mill, including two more TMP lines in 1976 and the introduction of machines to monitor the quality of newsprint coming off the paper lines. Phasing out of the old groundwood pulp mill began, and paper machines 5 and 6 were permanently closed. With world prices for newsprint remaining high through the rest of the 1970s, the mill once again became profitable, but only a fraction of the profits were used to upgrade the mill's equipment. Also, the mill still had a huge workforce, approaching 2,000, although some reductions in the workforce were instituted. One worker recalls that when he started at the mill in the mid-1960s there were 24 men employed on the crew repairing seven operating paper machines, whereas by the time Bowater sold the mill this had shrunk to a crew of 12 maintaining four paper machines (by 1994, Kruger had shrunk this to five permanent workers). Looking back, a long-time employee thought: "It's hard to understand how they made money with all the men down there. When I worked in the pipe shop there was 31 people, now they're down to 11 or 12."

The business cycle cranked on, and by the start of the 1980s world demand for newsprint again went into decline and market prices fell. By 1983, Bowater had closed down number 7 paper machine once more and laid off one-third of the mill's workforce. It was not widely known, but since 1981 Bowater had been trying privately and discreetly to find a buyer for the mill. In August 1983 the company went public, having first informed the government of Newfoundland if a buyer could not be found by the end of the year it would close the mill down. After 45 years, Bowater was pulling out: the newsprint mill at Corner Brook had become marginal to the company's new global strategy and would be sold.

The deterioration of the mill was no secret to mill employees. Through the 1970s and early 1980s they had seen restructuring occur in many other Canadian paper mills, with the local form of restructuring being quite diverse and contingent (as post-structuralists would argue) on local and provincial circumstances. Restructuring strategies depended on corporate priorities, on the condition of the capital sunk in the mill, on local labour markets, on the cost of power, and on fibre supply (see Hayter, 1997, and Rose and Villemaire, 1997, for two quite contrasting examples). Provincial governments often affected these decisions, having a decisive influence over resource management under the terms of the British North America Act. Available options included replacing groundwood pulp with TMP and CTMP (chemical-thermal-mechanical pulping) and decommissioning dozens of vintage paper machines, replacing them with a few modern machines that produced more paper of better quality (Hayter, 1997). Some firms chose less costly strategies by upgrading older paper machines, which, rather like warships, may be refitted several times during their working life. Such refits might include switching the wet end from single-wire to twin-wire technology, installing new dryers and calender stacks, and upgrading the dry end and winder. Many mills switched completely to TMP and CTMP. By 1983, the workers at the Bowater mill were sufficiently worried about their future that they discussed the idea of taking a pay cut in return for a commitment from Bowater to make a major investment in upgrading the mill. These discussions came to nothing. However, the city council and the provincial government leaned on Bowater's management and extracted from them the concession that they would extend the sale-or-closure deadline by one year to the end of 1984. The project to find a purchaser for the mill was then launched in earnest, but a glance at changes underway across Canada suggested that the old ways of making paper with a large workforce secure in their jobs, a self-contained mill with an internal labour market, rigid patterns of work laid out in lengthy labour contracts, and powerful unions were likely to be replaced by a rather different regime of production. Such changes had to be negotiated in 1984, and given the long tradition of papermaking at Corner Brook, a battle royal could be expected over the form they would take.

CONCLUSION

Right from its beginnings in 1923, the company town of Corner Brook and its newsprint mill were a creation of the international economy. Like the Harmsworths at Grand Falls, Armstrong Whitworth at Corner Brook seized all the advantages the colonial system offered. It was not just the mill, the docks, and the power station at Deer Lake, but also the section of the present town called Townsite that came under the direct control of foreign capital, and remained so until the amalgamated city of Corner Brook was established in 1956. The full story of the negotiations and deals that lay behind the setting up of Newfoundland's pulp and paper industry and the company towns of Grand Falls and Townsite is far more tortuous and complex than what has been presented here. Hiller (1982, 1990) has unravelled most of the details with clinical precision to reveal a political and frequently mercenary story of backbiting and intrigue. What is clear is that very few of the key players were native to Newfoundland. They were mostly political appointees of the London government, owners and agents of the corporations based in England and central Canada, and their buddies acting as intermediaries. For such hardened players, the concerns of the average Newfoundlander hardly appeared on their radar. Local politicians, in contrast, did have to address these local concerns – at least until the Commission of Government took over in 1933 – but they had few trumps up their sleeve in dealings with the big players, and it shows. In effect, they parted with Newfoundland's forest resources to politically well-connected imperial companies at a bargain price. As Hiller (1990: 3) notes, AND held 99-year leases on 3,670 square miles of timber at a rental of only $2 per square mile, and was exempted from paying stumpage fees on pulpwood. To a degree, the company town of Corner Brook functioned as a state within a state, since it was an international enclave with significant autonomous powers. Its citizens were granted a limited form of citizenship. Only after its incorporation in 1956 was the city itself not under the direct supervision of international capital, after which time the local citizens began to elect their own independent representatives to the city council. But even then, Corner Brook retained enough company town characteristics that it might still be called a "post-company town."

A company engaged in continuous mass production represents a special and in some ways an archetypical Canadian version of the Fordist mode of production. Normally, Fordism involves continuous mass production based on an internal labour market, but in the case of a company town, the housing and retail markets, education, newspapers, utilities, and medical care may also be internalized. This was certainly the pattern at Corner Brook. In this sense, internalization took place in company towns not just at the level of the plant but over the whole territory under the control of the company, and thus included most of the urban functions operating within that territory. The version of Fordism developed at Corner Brook, and in many other foreign-owned company towns in Canada, has been termed *permeable* because levels of production and management operations were often controlled from outside Canada (Jenson, 1989, 1990). This variant of Fordism is especially susceptible to the endless rounds of restructuring by international capital.

In the 1950s this high level of internalization began to dissolve in Corner Brook as Bowater began to shed the various urban functions – education, hospitals, local newspaper, housing, stores, and hotels – that were peripheral to its main function of making paper. The merger of Townsite into the city of Corner Brook marked the formal end of the company town. In the process, citizens assumed greater control over their own destiny by creating a forum outside the firm where local interests could be expressed. But the paper mill itself continued to operate along Fordist lines much longer. It retained an internal labour market with well-defined career ladders; it did most of its own maintenance and installation; it managed its own subsidiary activities such as logging, transporting wood to the mill, and shipping newsprint to foreign markets. The literature suggests that in other paper mills, by the late 1970s the Fordist mode of production was under attack (Holmes and Hayter, 1993). By that date, some Canadian newsprint mills had begun to negotiate new labour contracts requiring greater labour flexibility; productivity incentives were built into wage settlements, and ancillary activities were subcontracted via competitive bidding. Thus local production practices were exposed to foreign (especially Japanese) management ideas, but the mill at Corner Brook lumbered on into the 1980s little changed. With the death of Sir Eric Bowater, and worldwide reorganization underway in the pulp and paper industry, Corner Brook was simply no longer one of Bowater's priorities. It seems likely that by the early 1980s, Bowater's head office would not have regretted seeing the mill close, but failing that, they were not prepared to expend much capital and managerial effort in restructuring the mill along more flexible lines. This meant that when the crunch came in 1984, whoever purchased the mill would introduce a more drastic set of changes to mill operations than might have been the case if Bowater had begun to implement more radical modernization a decade or more earlier. The year 1984, therefore, was of great significance to this paper town: very different modes of production, and of social regulation, were about to be established locally as trends evident internationally in the newsprint industry were rescaled to the local setting of Corner Brook. They would, however, be locally resisted. In addition, many provincial institutions had a vested interest in the outcome to these struggles.

A New Industrial Era? 3

The withdrawal of Bowater from Corner Brook in 1984 marked the end of an industrial era. The company town had been formally wound up for over two decades, but the culture of the company town and its institutional arrangements had been deeply embedded in mill operations and worker culture so that many of the associated practices – above all, the internal labour market – remained intact. By contrast, in the world beyond Corner Brook a profound restructuring of pulp and paper production (e.g., Hayter, 1997; Rose and Villemaire, 1997) and of logging (e.g., Prudham, 2002) was well unerway; it was accompanied by big changes in technology, work practices, markets, ownership, and products (Holmes and Hayter, 1993; Mackenzie and Norcliffe, 1997). As the weeks of 1984 filed by and the tense negotiations to sell the mill ground on, it became clear that more than ownership was at stake. The underlying issue for the putative purchaser was industrial sclerosis: would the mill make a decisive shift away from the long-established Fordist system of mass production towards a new and as yet not clearly defined system of lean production? Such a shift would require the mill's workforce to abandon many of the institutional arrangements of the Bowater era, arrangements that were palpably cherished by the mill's labour force. And could the Newfoundland government be persuaded to take the workers' position and prop up the existing system of production?

In practice the changes implemented at Corner Brook saw a private multinational company, and not the state, become the most important actor. The corporation in question argued, moreover, that in the name of global capitalism and the imperative of keeping abreast with foreign competitors, it was essential to pursue deregulation and a laissez-faire agenda by restructuring the mill's operating practices. The state, however, did play a very active role in mediating between players at the global game and actors in the local arena. The Newfoundland government took on this role precisely because both local and global positions were re-scaled to become pressing provincial issues: to attract global investment and promote economic development, the provincial government had to appear friendly to business; but to keep local voters content, the province had to salvage jobs and promise a rosy future. In other words, the economic and technological trends of the 1970s and 1980s made the prospective purchaser determined to abandon many of the mill's Fordist ways of doing things. However, the workforce resisted such changes, and since they represented a powerful political force in Newfoundland's parliamentary democracy, they were a local voice not to be ignored. The provincial government therefore became a formal regulator, in the sense that governmental powers were used in various ways to complete the sale of the mill. Regulation was also on the agenda in the more abstract sense used by regulation theorists: a search was underway for something much broader – a new and leaner mode of production and its associated institutional arrangements that would characterize the mill's pattern of operation for years to come. Neither the Kruger Corporation (the likely purchaser) nor the mill's joint unions' negotiating committee was willing to give ground in the negotiations to restructure the mill. The Newfoundland government sought to achieve a settlement acceptable to both opposing parties.

The exploration of this theme will take the form of a discourse on the institutional arrangements at play in Corner Brook at this crucial juncture. Four main themes are examined. First, the question of *in situ* restructuring will be considered; the paper industry was not one that could simply pull up its stakes and move elsewhere, so if changes were to be made they would have to be made in Corner Brook. The second theme is to identify the broad outlines of the new, leaner way of producing newsprint that was being adopted by the pulp and paper industry worldwide during this period. Third, emphasis is put on the social and cultural practices associated with the accommodation (regulationists call it *co-stabilization*) between global forces of production and local forces of social reproduction that occurred as the turbulence of 1984 gave way to a new compromise. This in turn leads to the fourth theme, an aspect much stressed by legal positivists, namely the role of the state and particularly the legislative framework that it has created. But first, there is a need for a brief chronicle of the events leading up to the mill's sale.

REAL REGULATION AT CORNER BROOK

In late October 1983 the mill owner, the Bowater Corporation, publicly announced a divestiture plan: if the mill was not sold by the end of 1984, it would be closed down. The negotiations that then began, and which eventually came down to the wire in December 1984, were focused, in the most general sense, on the way the mill's future operations would be regulated. The negotiations therefore provide some important insights into the process of social regulation. Two crucial factors were operating. First, the mill represented a considerable sum of sunk capital (Clark and Wrigley, 1995, 1997), notwithstanding the poor state of its aging equipment. The precise value of the mill's total assets, including the power plant, wharves, ships, and forest tenure and the human capital invested in the mill's skilled workforce, would depend very much on what the highest bidder might offer; figures between $50 million and $100 million were not out of line. Moreover, local and provincial circumstances made the mill's continuing operation a high priority. Even with the diversification of Corner Brook's economy in the years following Newfoundland's entry into Confederation, Bowater remained by far the largest private employer, with direct employment in the mill and wood operations then approaching 2,000, an annual wage bill of close to $40 million, and local annual expenditures of about $30 million. In addition, the mill generated activity in the city's port. Thus the mill was still the main pillar of the town's economic base and its closure would reverberate through every branch of the local service economy. Provincially, it was a major employer in Canada's poorest province, which had an unadjusted unemployment rate in January 1984 of 21.7 per cent (compared to the national rate of 12.4 per cent).[1] Hence, a mass layoff would only worsen an already grave employment situation. A province such as Newfoundland simply could not allow its forest, hydroelectric, and skilled labour resources to go to waste.

Second, the mill's operations were situated in a complex web of social arrangements that correspond with Michael Storper's (1997) analysis of relational assets. The mill had extensive timber limits – its supply hinterland – where logging by the company and its subcontractors was the economic mainstay. The mill's workforce, the best paid in the region, supported the town's retailing, clubs, schools, churches, and other social activities, and they were active in local politics. The mill itself formed part of a long commodity chain that began in the woods and then involved transporting logs to the mill, processing the wood into paper, shipping newsprint to newspaper printing works, and ending up as daily newspapers on breakfast tables in Europe and the Americas (Leslie and Reimer, 1999; Raikes et al., 2000). The institutional arrangements in place at every stage in this chain were, in practice, a great asset, even though some of them were destined to be renegotiated. Thus, from a social and economic perspective, the need for local interest groups to achieve a regulated solution to the immediate crisis of 1984 was a matter of pressing urgency.

However much it was expected, Bowater's announcement on 31 October 1983 of its intention to sell the mill raised the level of anxiety both in Corner Brook and in St. John's, the seat of Newfoundland's provincial legislature.[2] Since it was obvious that the mill would not easily be sold, a local advisory committee was quickly formed with a membership drawn from members of the mill's unions, the city council, and the local chamber of commerce. This committee had no budget and no statutory powers; its role was to lobby for the community's interest. In practice, the committee was immediately bypassed by the main players – the potential buyers and the provincial government – and it played an insignificant role in the subsequent negotiations. Meanwhile, in the provincial capital, the Conservative government of Brian Peckford had been re-elected in 1982 on a platform that promised, among other things, an end to large public subsidies for development projects. Competitiveness within a free-market economy was the Peckford government's preferred way to improve Newfoundland's fortunes.[3]

By January 1984 the Liberal provincial opposition was exploiting an advantageous political situation. They could support the sale of the mill, but failing that they proposed its purchase by a Crown corporation, knowing full well that the former would be difficult and that the latter, although it had popular support, would almost certainly end up requiring the large public subsidies the Conservative government sought to avoid.[4] Thus, in mid-January 1984 the Conservatives felt obliged for political reasons to reject publicly the Crown corporation solution, citing various examples of financial ineptitude by the Smallwood Liberal government, including: the contractual sale of power from the Churchill Falls project to Hydro-Québec at fixed low prices for an absurdly long period of 65 years; the loss of about $300 million in selling the ill-conceived Stephenville linerboard plant to Abitibi-Price; and the costly failure of the Come-by-Chance oil refinery. But the Peckford government knew full well that if a buyer were to be found for the mill, some form of incentive would almost certainly be needed to increase the attractiveness of the package and to set in motion an urgently needed modernization program. In practice, the Peckford government was offering incentives within a week.

Given the urgency of the problem, on 18 January the provincial government and Bowater signed a "joint offering memorandum" in which they agreed to collaborate in the sale of the mill. This memorandum, which was circulated to a long list of possible buyers, included a promise by the government of short-term money to assist in the modernization of the plant. This memorandum also had the effect of excluding the local advisory committee in Corner Brook from direct involvement in the negotiations: henceforth the committee would only receive information that the provincial government chose to pass on.

Discussions continued through the early part of the year with a number of interested parties. They were sufficiently advanced that the government set a deadline of 16 April for the submission of proposals to purchase the mill, including the Deer Lake power plant that supplies the mill, and large tracts of owned and leased forest land. The government made it clear that negotiations would be conducted in confidence. Thus, only on 9 June were the names of three of the five bidders publicly identified by the provincial Forestry Minister, Charles Power. The two parties not named appear to have been asset strippers, who wished to use the mill as a tax write-off. The three named bidders were:

- Atlantis Corporation, a St. John's-based consortium of venture capitalists who had no experience in the industry. Their bid was $12 million higher than that of the eventual successful bidder, the Kruger Company of Montreal.
- Humber Newsprint consisted of a group of entrepreneurs, including former management of the mill, formed solely to bid on the Corner Brook mill.
- Kruger Corporation, a private family company but nevertheless a multinational, is one of Canada's larger papermaking companies, with a track record of taking over older mills and successfully modernizing them. Kruger's head office is in Montreal.

As a private company, Kruger never revealed the sum it paid for the mill, but it was the low bidder and was clear about wanting government assistance to modernize the mill. Kruger, however, was the most credible bidder: the company had experience in operating three paper and board mills in Quebec; it had a marketing network in place in Canada, the United States, and Britain; it had successfully modernized the older mills it had acquired at Bromptonville in 1950, and at Trois-Rivières in 1973; and it had the financial resources needed to tackle the large task of modernization.[5]

Intense negotiations were clearly underway through May, June, and July. At one point in late July it was rumoured that Atlantis was the preferred buyer since they had bid the highest amount and sought no provincial financial support. In early August, Dennison Mines (one of Canada's largest mining conglomerates) briefly appeared as a possible suitor. Then, on 17 August came the announcement that the federal government had entered the negotiations: the federal and Newfoundland governments had signed a crucial agreement in July under the federal Pulp and Paper Modernization Program whereby the federal government would pay the larger part (80 per cent) of a subsidy to modernize pulp and paper mills in Newfoundland.

By late August two contenders remained in the negotiations. The Atlantis Corporation had engaged technical experts from Finland's pulp and paper industry to add credibility to its bid. Kruger, in turn, stressed its experience in the industry and its willingness to enter into a long-term modernization plan for the mill, provided that appropriate subsidies could be negotiated. The latter argument proved to be the most persuasive, and on 14 September a tentative agreement was announced selling the mill to Kruger. The agreement was signed on 18 September at a press conference that started two hours late as Bowater, Kruger, and the provincial government bargained down to the wire. This was the first public evidence that Kruger intended to negotiate a tough deal. The tentative sale would become final in 60 days, provided a series of nine conditions were met.[6] Among these, the two key conditions were, first, that Kruger insisted its negotiations with the various mill unions had to be satisfactorily concluded, and second, an agreement had be to reached with the federal and provincial governments to provide a modernization subsidy.[7] (The Conservative government of Brian Mulroney had been sworn in at Ottawa the previous day, and this was expected to result in a much better working relationship between the federal government in Ottawa and the provincial government of Newfoundland.)

Intimations of the difficulty of the negotiations to follow came right away when the mill's joint unions' chairman warned that the deal was not sewn up. A chill was felt as rumours circulated that between 250 and 1,000 workers would be laid off. The opening stance of the Canadian Paperworkers Union (CPU) was reinforced by the national president, James Buchanan, who announced that the union would make no concessions to the new purchaser.[8] A week later, negotiators for the Carpenters and Joiners of America (representing about 900 loggers) walked out of negotiations with Kruger. The local president of the loggers' union, Gonzo Gillingham, accused Kruger of wanting to set the clock back 30 years by proposing to contract out all its wood operations, in so doing eliminating union members' seniority and vacation rights and squeezing wage rates and health and welfare benefits. Kruger responded by stating that its position was inflexible, and its negotiating team flew back to Montreal on 12 October. The essence of Kruger's position was that the mill could not become viable unless productivity levels were raised to approach those of state-of-the-art mills in Canada and other newsprint-producing countries (Smith et al., 1995).

The provincial government could not allow the negotiations to fail; locally, the political and economic repercussions would be too great. Thus, on 16 October the provincial Labour Minister, Jerry Dinn, announced that the government's top priority was to bring the loggers' union and Kruger back to the negotiating table. Two days later Kruger made its "final" contract proposals, simultaneously outlining ambitious plans for the mill that prescribed precisely the long-term investment program the provincial government was looking for. The company would spend $198 million over five years to modernize not only the four operating paper machines, but also the larger number 7 machine that Bowater had decommissioned. This tantalizing scenario would become a reality only if the mill and logging employees co-operated with Kruger.

The unions responded by recommending to their membership that they reject the offer. By 22 October, the situation had become so critical Premier Peckford warned the mill workforce that if the unions and Kruger could not reach an agreement by the 60-day deadline of 28 October, the mill would probably close. Kruger was now the only viable bidder, and was in a strong bargaining position. Yet on 23 October the five mill unions did reject Kruger's "final" offer of 18 October, for reasons explained to Kruger but not made public. To break this impasse, the provincial government insisted that negotiations would continue. Kruger's "final" offer became an interim one, and the company set a 48-hour deadline for an agreement to be reached, after which it would withdraw from the mill purchase.

The front-page headline of the *Western Star* on 25 October 1984 read "Kruger withdraws offer to buy mill." Four days before the final deadline Kruger's negotiators had pulled out and again flown back to Montreal because "the unions were not taking the talks seriously." This *coup de grâce* left the provincial government and the unions swinging in the wind. Premier Peckford had to become directly involved to restart the negotiations, but it was now clear that

Kruger was in a position to extract maximum concessions from the government and the unions. Kruger returned only in response to a direct personal intervention by the Premier and on condition of a news blackout. Final negotiations began on 28 October and went on almost continuously until 4 a.m. on 31 October, when negotiators for the mill workers reached an agreement they felt they could recommend to their membership. Dexter Fudge, the union chief negotiator, made it clear that every one of the six unions would have to accept the agreement for it to hold. Voting was to take place very quickly. CPU Local 64, the key local, accepted the agreement by a narrow margin (56 per cent) and by the following day the other five unions had followed suit. The next day it was announced that agreement had been reached in negotiations with the loggers' union, and this, too, was subsequently accepted by their membership.

It appeared that three formalities remained: the sale needed the approval of Investment Canada since Bowater was a foreign corporation; Kruger and the two levels of government had to sign a modernization agreement; and the same three parties had to formalize an agreement on the funding of modernization. However, in practice two Acts still had to be passed by the Newfoundland legislature, one of which remains a contentious piece of labour legislation while the other awarded to Kruger resources that may be comparable in value to any of the largesse dispensed by the Smallwood government.

Bill 52 was "An Act to Ratify, Confirm and Adopt Certain Agreements Entered into between the Government of the Province, Kruger Inc. and other Parties Respecting the Future Operation and Modernization of the Corner Brook Newsprint Mill" (the Kruger Act). Among its more important sections was the transfer from Bowater to Kruger of the assets of the Deer Lake Power Company (which provided the mill with most of its electric power needs). Also transferred from Bowater to Kruger were 1.7 million hectares of Crown land leased to Bowater for 99 years in 1938 and 640,000 hectares of freehold that began as Reid lots granted to the Newfoundland Railway in return for its construction. Three other important concessions were: a financial guarantee by the provincial government for $30 million of the $80 million term loan Kruger took out to purchase the mill (secured by the Deer Lake power plant, valued at much more than $30 million); a $40 million grant under the Pulp and Paper Modernization Agreement (this covered 20 per cent of the capital costs of modernization, set at $200 million, with the federal government providing 80 per cent of the grant and the provincial government the remainder); and third, a loan of up to $11 million covering 20 per cent of any modernization costs in excess of $200 million. Bill 52 was pushed through the legislature with indecent haste. Indeed, its first reading contained little specific information because the negotiations that the Act sought to ratify were still underway and were expected to take another month to complete! Moreover, chapter 30 of the Statutes of Newfoundland reporting the ratification of Bill 52 contains little more information – the agreement (deposited with the Clerk of the Executive Council) was to remain confidential at the insistence of Kruger. The government's Kruger Agreements Act was nevertheless accepted by the Liberal opposition and given assent on 19 December 1984.

Bill 37, an Act to Amend the Labour Standards Act, was far more contentious. The source of the problem was that when Bowater had shut down paper machine Number 7 in April 1983, it had laid off 300 employees. These employees had been given 16 weeks' notice, as required by the Labour Standards Act. However, that notice had not included the required 12-week period of full employment because low world demand for newsprint had led Bowater to close the whole mill down for several weeks in the early months of 1983. This made Bowater liable for $6.7 million in back wages. The significance of this liability only became apparent in November when the main agreements had been signed. On 19 November, Bowater offered the affected employees half a million dollars in settlement of this grievance and then paid it "voluntarily" a week later. However, the union did not drop its claim to full compensation for its members. On 2 December, the Peckford government introduced an amendment to the Labour Standards Act stating that only one to two weeks' notice was required for a layoff (depending on length of service), and *this provision was to be retroactive to 1 August 1978.* The Liberal opposition fought this, attempting a filibuster that was stopped by a closure motion limiting MLAs to speeches of 30 minutes. The bill received assent on 19 December. As early as 3 December, Kruger had made it clear that it was not prepared to inherit Bowater's liability for $6.7 million and would withdraw from the agreement if this obligation was not removed. To finalize the agreement, then, the Peckford government had to move quickly to solve the problem. The constitutionality of this Act was never challenged in the courts.

There remained one other issue. Since Corner Brook had been founded as a company town, the original mill company did not pay municipal taxes to itself. When the four municipalities – Corner Brook West, Corner Brook East, Curling, and Townsite – were amalgamated to form the city of Corner Brook in 1956, Bowater retained this exemption, instead paying a grant of its own choice in lieu of taxes. Thus in 1983 Bowater paid a grant of $475,000, or less than half of the estimated taxes of $1 million. By 2004 this had risen to $1,070,000. Kruger refused to give up this tax exemption, despite a formal vote by the city council requesting that the new mill owner become a fully contributing corporate citizen.

IN SITU RESTRUCTURING

Most commentators attribute the wave of industrial restructuring that was underway in the 1980s and early 1990s to exhaustion of the technical possibilities of the Fordist mode of production and to a resulting decline in the rate of profit.[9] For reasons explained below, I would also add the deregulation of international trade and investment as a major contributory factor. In particular, many national economies had been opened to greater international competition by the reduction of tariff and non-tariff barriers in the Tokyo Round of the General Agreement on Tariffs and Trade (1973-79), which reduced most import tariffs to 10 per cent. Faced with an influx of low-cost products made in South and East Asia, low-technology labour-intensive industries in the West – such as the manufacture of garments, footwear, electrical goods, and toys – simply could not compete; some closed, others automated to save on labour costs, while a third group decentralized the labour-intensive parts of their production to low-wage peripheral regions, often as part of a new international division of labour. These changes are well known and widely discussed.[10]

Less apparent is the fact that this liberalization of world trade and investment also impacted on resource industries whose immobility and bulky products are generally thought to provide some insulation against the kind of fierce global competition seen in more footloose industries. Yet Canadian newsprint producers encountered increasing competition in their major markets from producers in Scandinavia, Brazil, Argentina, New Zealand, Indonesia, and several other countries. Moreover, the growing use of recycled newspapers created an alternative source of fibre in major cities. This competition fed back to producers in Canadian resource towns, precipitating waves of restructuring, especially during the economic recessions of 1981-83 and 1990-92.[11]

Restructuring may affect individual plants or whole companies, it may occur at the local level or at a larger regional scale, it may impact on trading relations, and it may involve an ensemble of these elements such that the whole mode of production is changed. Given this diversity, it is useful to consider the five major forms of restructuring identified by Lovering (1989):

- sectoral switches of capital;
- geographical changes of location;
- changes in the scale of production;
- changes in the labour process and the division of labour;
- technological change.

In Corner Brook, the first three of these forms were not evident. The sector of investment remained pulp and paper, the restructuring necessarily occurred *in situ*, and the scale of production remained largely unchanged. Thus, restructuring in Corner Brook focused on the labour process and on new technologies.

Equally relevant is Peck's (1992: 334-5) contribution on labour and agglomeration, in which he critiques Scott's ideas on the formation of flexible industrial agglomerations in new industrial spaces. Peck writes:

> A characteristic of flexible production is, for Scott, that it is "always some distance – socially or geographically – from the major foci of Fordist industrialization". Thus in some instances flexible production will be found outside the old manufacturing regions, and in others within it: "new" industrial spaces are sometimes located within old industrial spaces. So in some cases capital seeks out a *tabula rasa*, where flexible employment relations can be created "with a minimum of local obstruction", whereas in others it is apparently possible to reconstruct these employment relations *in situ*. . . . Unfortunately, geographers are sometimes guilty of focusing primarily or exclusively on spatial restructuring processes and relocation strategies and of ignoring *in situ* ones.

Barnes et al. (1990) call to our attention the specifics of *in situ* restructuring and the need to grasp the internal dynamics of discrete local labour markets in isolated places, such as Corner Brook. Because most resource industries need to locate close to their raw materials – for reasons of weight loss and spoilage long ago dissected by Alfred Weber (1929) – relocation is rarely an option. Nor are these industries immune to international competition, whether in the form of cheap newsprint produced in Indonesia or de-inked recycled newspapers in New York.

Structural changes are much easier to introduce when relocation takes place. Such changes may include: the installation of new technologies with increased levels of automation, higher productivity, and more flexible machines; the recruitment of a more flexible and non-unionized workforce, or a younger workforce endowed with more human capital but paid fewer social benefits; the adoption of lower staffing levels; a squeeze on real wages, the social wage, or both; a spacious site on low-cost land, which may permit the capitalization of valuable city land formerly occupied by an older plant; and the renegotiation of the linkage structure of the plant, with more outsourcing. In most instances these changes are considerably harder to achieve *in situ*, as was the case in Corner Brook.

Regulation theorists suggest that conflicts arising in society can usually be resolved by a variety of mechanisms, so that only rarely will they spill over into widespread civil disorder. Thus a myriad of social and institutional practices may act singly or in combination to overcome difficulties and stabilize a particular regime of accumulation (see Boyer, 1990; Lipietz, 1986). In some instances this approach seems somewhat mystical; indeed, Marden (1992: 756) suggests that the Paris school of regulationists tends "to emphasize the importance of economic metaimperatives at the expense of institutional practice concerning modes of regulation." He finds the Paris school's neo-Keynesian emphasis on balancing production and consumption to be particularly limiting. This emphasis on institutions is also made by Clark (1989), who sees regulation more as a social practice contingent on local norms. From a geographical perspective this interpretation is especially valuable because it suggests that there will be considerable local diversity in the way societies choose to regulate *in situ* restructuring.

Clearly, the brunt of restructuring is borne by the labour force; indeed, it is precisely to avoid the resistance of labour that restructuring often takes the form of relocation. It is unlikely that the established workforce of a plant would willingly accept the full panoply of change due to restructuring. *In situ* restructuring may therefore require the state, or an agency of government, to play an important mediating role and the courts to arbitrate legal disputes. In the case of Corner Brook, the provincial government assumed this central role, consciously excluding the local government from the main negotiations. The function of the government was threefold.

(1) On paper, the sale of the newsprint mill took place between two private corporations, Bowater and Kruger. But the activities of the mill impinged on public interests in many ways, including logging on Crown land, floating logs down the Humber River, shipping at the port of Corner Brook, complying with environmental standards, transporting inputs and outputs on public highways, labour laws, waste disposal, and the whole issue of community development in Corner Brook. In becoming a party to the negotiations, the

provincial government indicated that it would become a *facilitator* of the sale.

(2) As with many purchases, the costs stretch the resources of a buyer. Large sums of money have to be spent before they generate a cash flow. Banks normally assume this role, but the history of Newfoundland's economic development is haunted by too many skeletons for banks to enter enthusiastically into such schemes. Thus the government also intervened as a *guarantor* of public financial support at key points.

(3) It was evident from the beginning that the government would have to assume a more proactive role. If and when a "deal" was reached, one or more of the parties would feel aggrieved. At this point, the government would have to become an active *promoter* of the deal.

The Peckford government facilitated the sale of the mill to Kruger in several critical respects. It was made clear to Kruger that it would obtain the benefits held by Bowater, including access to forest limits and leases to cut timber on Crown land (Figure 3) and ownership of the Deer Lake power plant. The latter made Kruger comparable to Alcan in the Lac St. Jean region of Quebec and at Kimano in British Columbia as a private generator of low-cost electric power. The government was a guarantor of $30 million of the $80 million loan Kruger took out to purchase the mill, and in addition guaranteed to pay up to $11 million in the form of a loan for any modernization costs in excess of the anticipated $200 million.

As a promoter, the government did several things. It actively sought buyers for the mill and secured the participation of the federal government in the cost-sharing Modernization Program. After Kruger became the tentative buyer, the government passed the Kruger Act conveying to Kruger all the perquisites enjoyed by Bowater and, at the eleventh hour, when the question of liability for employees laid off by Bowater a year earlier seemed in danger of jeopardizing the whole deal, the government rapidly promoted a bill indemnifying Kruger and Bowater from any such liability.

AFTER FORDISM: TOWARDS LEAN PRODUCTION

Up to 1984, operations at the Corner Brook mill showed many Fordist traits. Production was linearly organized in a sequence of wood preparation, pulping, papermaking, winding, wrapping, and shipping. There was an elaborate division of labour with strict job demarcation spelled out in detailed labour contracts. Promotions occurred within internal career ladders. Large-scale production was matched by an entrenched union culture. The mill was fairly autonomous with its own tradesmen doing most of the required installation, repair, upgrading, and maintenance work. There was very little subcontracting.

The Kruger Corporation and the mill's employees knew that the new regime at the Corner Brook newsprint mill would have to be accompanied by extensive restructuring. The plant was old: it exceeded acceptable standards of air and water pollution; three different methods of pulping – groundwood, sulphite, and TMP – were still in place; and the paper machines used single-wire technology that produced newsprint of inferior quality (Ofori-Amoah, 1993). By then, Bowater was selling a significant proportion of the mill's output to Third World countries at below-market prices because it could not be sold competitively in the West. Kruger did not hide its intention to change mill culture and working practices, and the company was under no illusion about the difficult task it would face to modernize the mill and make it profitable. The Kruger strategy was clearly to get agreement on all the key changes before the purchase was finalized. As chance would have it, Kruger emerged as the only bidder with both the experience and the resources to implement the long-term program that the Peckford government felt was needed. Thus Kruger Corporation found itself in a strong bargaining position, which resulted not only in buying the mill at a price discount of $12 million below the highest bidder, but also in being able to set in place the general outline of the restructuring strategy before finalizing the purchase. The main elements of that strategy were:

1. A modernization program would raise paper quality. This would involve a series of long-term layoffs as each paper machine in turn was shut down and their wet-ends rebuilt with twin-wire technology.
2. Manning levels were to be reduced.
3. A wage freeze would be in place for the first two years of an exceptional four-year contract for mill workers, with a catch-up to the wage level of Kruger's Trois-Rivières mill workers during the second two-year period. (This four-year contract put Corner Brook out of phase with mills in the rest of eastern Canada, making it difficult for the Corner Brook local to follow the pattern bargaining adopted in other mills.)
4. Many of the restrictive practices included in the preceding contract were to be dropped and the crossing of trades was allowed.
5. Kruger would be allowed to contract out.

6. On the logging side, the quota of wood that could be bought from non-union subcontractors was to rise progressively, from 10 per cent at the start to 35 per cent by 1992.[12]
7. Log runs on the Humber River would be terminated and the hauling of logs to the mill contracted out to 80 individual truckers (later reduced to 48 truckers).
8. All outstanding grievances against Bowater were to be dropped. Moreover, Kruger wanted the unions to give up the right to strike and to renounce the right to file new grievances against the corporation until the five-year modernization plan was completed. (This demand was subsequently dropped by Kruger, apparently because the Newfoundland government felt it was in conflict with Canadian labour law.)

These planned changes pose a crucial question: did they point towards a crossing of the "second industrial divide" to a new flexible mode of production as envisaged by Piore and Sabel (1984) or to some other hybrid supplanting the previous Fordist regime? Since several of these changes have been associated by Scott (1988), Schoenberger (1988), Boyer (1988), and others with forms of flexibility, they might be seen to constitute a step towards a more flexible regime. But, as Gertler (1988) and Lovering (1990) ask, flexibility for whom? And does the popular term "flexibility" really capture the main thrust of the changes brought about by *in situ* restructuring in Corner Brook?

The underlying issue is whether flexibility, although evidently important to an understanding of recent changes in Canadian forest industries, provides a comprehensive explanation of the new forms of production. Hayter (2000) adopted the title *Flexible Crossroads* for his recent book on the restructuring of British Columbia's forest industries and stresses the centrality of this perspective. But Allen and Henry (1997) argue that flexibility can be better understood as a corollary to the rising level of risk inherent in the current phase of disorganized capitalism, and therefore view it as an outcome of more fundamental processes. They raise two key issues. The presentation of flexibility as an overarching package deal tends to overlook how employment relations may change in different ways, and particularly how work may become more precarious so that insecurity rather than flexibility is the most urgent characteristic for those placed in contingent forms of work. And second, Allen and Henry have reservations about the use of flexibility as a reductive category subsuming quite different aspects of flexibility such as multiple tasking, part-time work, contract and temporary work, job insecurity, and job instability.

As the outlines of the 1984 agreement in Corner Brook took shape, it became clear that elements of both rigidity and flexibility were being put in place. Broadly speaking, the workforce became more flexible while mill operations became more rigid as the balance of power shifted from labour to capital. It is important to consider why this shift of power allowed capital to extract concessions from labour that might not have been yielded in a typical plant during the Fordist period. The technological argument stressed by French regulationists does not help much since the new paper mill was to use the same 50-year-old paper machines; admittedly, they were more automated, re-equipped with twin wires, had new wet ends, presses, and calender stacks, and manning levels were reduced, but they were essentially the same machines still engaged in continuous production. The social regulation perspective provides more insights. First, it is easier to extract concessions from a dominated labour force such as is found in single-industry towns.[13] Second, neo-conservative philosophies, globally ascendant during the 1980s, sought both through legislation and political rhetoric to trim the powers of organized labour and promote laissez-faire policies. The Progressive Conservative government of Brian Peckford was broadly in support of these arguments, although mixed with a dose of the welfarism that was much needed in Canada's poorest province (Peckford, 1983). Third, the freeing of international trade provided corporations with a powerful case for restructuring the workforce: they argued that it was imperative in order to compete in a global system of production (Laxer, 1993).

The push to make the plant profitable led Kruger to demand a series of concessions from the labour force: in 1984 it was a wage freeze, simplified job demarcation, and a higher level of subcontracting. Subsequent contracts were to press further with some crossing of trades, a new shift system, and a squeeze on statutory holidays. There would also be an increase in the number of self-employed subcontractors and an expansion of a secondary labour force.

Mill operations, in contrast, would become more rigid. To improve the quality of newsprint, logs were to be used within a few weeks of being cut while they were still moist. Thus the supply of wood had to be fairly evenly paced, especially in summer, whereas previously the large inventory of logs held in the woodyard allowed considerable flexibility in the supply of wood. Logging would now continue during the coldest months; previously, many loggers went on unemployment insurance (UI) during this period.[14] The time when it is most difficult to log is during the spring thaw, but some of the new tree harvesters Kruger purchased could operate even during that difficult period, with large rubber tires that minimize environmental degradation. The result was a slow-motion just-in-time system, the aim being to keep only a small log inventory in the mill yard. This also necessitated the construction of a new wood room to debark the logs brought in by truck (logs previously run down the Humber River had most of their bark rubbed off en route).[15]

The overall effect of the takeover by Kruger was to initiate a version of *in situ* restructuring whereby the labour force was reduced, reorganized, and (in order to save the jobs of the remaining workers) required to concede various forms of flexibility to increase labour productivity and lower operating costs. This mix of workforce flexibility and process rigidity can be interpreted as a move towards lean production. The first three elements of Kruger's strategy – upgraded pulp and papermaking technology, reduced staffing levels, and a squeeze on wages – are specific elements of lean production. Given the necessity to restructure *in situ*, many Canadian newsprint producers found lean production methods were the most practicable solution. The specifics of lean production at Corner Brook are discussed in the following chapter.

CO-STABILIZATION

Peck and Tickell (1991: 5) observe that "the coupling of a mode of social regulation with an accumulation system and their temporary 'co-stabilization' is the lynchpin of the regulationist research project."[16] The principle of co-stability needs linking with that of *coherence*, a concept employed by Harvey (1989a: 122) to describe the way the various competing elements of a capitalist system, and in particular the spheres of economic production and social reproduction, work together over a period of time. The tendency towards coherence is achieved through specific acts of co-stabilization. Such acts may take a variety of forms, several of which played a part in the resolution of the problems that confronted Corner Brook in 1984. Principal among these were: contracts of various kinds, but especially contracts between unions and employers; judicial rulings by the courts; acts of parliament and local government; informal concessions of various kinds; changes in work practices; the acceptance of new technologies; and social and political pressures (some of which can only be guessed at) that influenced the stance of the purchaser and the seller, and of the provincial government, and that moulded attitudes in the community at large. Co-stabilization may also require a certain degree of coercion.

Perhaps the decisive contract in the whole restructuring process was the initial memorandum signed by Bowater and the Newfoundland government; a number of key elements in the sale of the mill flow from this document. First, it excluded the local government, which meant that local priorities (such as cancelling the mill's local tax exemption) would no longer figure prominently in the negotiations. Second, by offering short-term money at an early stage in the negotiations the provincial government had signalled its willingness to offer financial incentives and other possible forms of support. Third, this pointed to the government's intention of blocking an opportunistic takeover for asset-stripping and a desire to assure the long-term future of Corner Brook.

The other key contract set out the terms of the sale. Being a private company, Kruger was in a position to insist that this would remain confidential, and the government and Bowater acceded to this request. For this reason Bill 52, the Kruger Act, contains no factual information but refers to a document in the care of the Clerk of the Executive Council. My attempt, moreover, to obtain a copy of the volume of Hansard recording the debate was rebuffed by the Newfoundland Government Information Services with the comment: "the debates are produced primarily for the use of Members and Officers of the House and it is not their practice to distribute them." Thus Hansard, which by common practice elsewhere is viewed as the public record of the work of the very fount of democracy was, in Newfoundland, declared to be in restricted circulation.[17] Published details of that bill and of Bill 37 are discussed later in this chapter.

The courts did not play a significant direct role in the sale and restructuring of the paper mill, but indirectly, they led Kruger to insist that an Act be passed absolving that company from possible liability for $6.7 million in back wages that Bowater was assumed to owe as a result of the April 1983 layoff. Only a little beforehand, the Newfoundland Supreme Court set a direct precedent by ruling that former employees of the Wabush iron ore mines in Labrador were entitled to $750,000 in retroactive wages because they had not been given sufficient layoff notice under the then current Labour Standards Act. One assumes that Kruger had obtained legal advice that Bowater was likewise liable and that, under the existing law, the union members concerned were in a strong legal position. To head off the possibility of inheriting this liability, in November 1984 Kruger had declared its offer to purchase conditional on the government amending the Labour Standards Act, thereby invalidating outstanding claims, province-wide, of $27 million and (it was said) forestalling the closure of several companies.[18]

A Commitment to the Future

On December 21, 1984 the final agreements relating to Kruger's purchase of Bowater's assets in the Province were signed in the City of Corner Brook. **After sixteen months** of tough negotiations, the divestiture process started by the Provincial Government had come to a successful conclusion. However, in addition to much hard work, the Provincial Government has also made a **$64 million** financial commitment to Kruger's **$200 million** venture in this Province. The elements of our commitment are:

(a) **$7 million** as the Province's share of a $40 million grant from the Pulp and Paper Modernization Agreement. This is a Federal/Provincial Agreement which the Province negotiated with Ottawa to facilitate the upgrading of the paper mills at Grand Falls and Corner Brook.

(b) **$11 million** by way of a loan from the Provincial Government.

(c) **$30 million** in bankruptcy protection. In the unlikely event that Kruger's new venture in Corner Brook should go bankrupt, the Province has guaranteed the banks that it would purchase the Deer Lake power plant at a maximum price of $30 million, a price far below the actual value of that plant.

(d) **$2 million** for the construction of forest access roads.

(e) **$14 million** in sales tax relief. This is part of program announced in the last budget that exempts companies from the 12% sales tax on the purchase of manufacturing equipment.

All told, these five elements of our financial aid package to Kruger amount to **$64 million.** These millions are proof positive of the Provincial Government's commitment to the City of Corner Brook and the entire Western Region of the Province.

The Provincial Government would like to thank the workers and other residents of the West coast for their patience and responsible attitude during this long but successful process.

MERRY CHRISTMAS!

Government of Newfoundland and Labrador

Figure 7: The Agreement with Kruger printed in the *Western Star*, 22 December 1984

BILL 37
AN ACT TO PROTECT JOBS

Some are saying that your Provincial Government is hurting workers by making certain retroactive changes in the layoff provisions of the Labour Standards Act. Are we favouring companies at the expense of workers? The answer is *"No"*, and here's why:

The existing Labour Standards Act (1977) does not clearly define the difference between a "temporary" and a "permanent" layoff. As a result, the Labour Standards Tribunal has ruled that insufficient notice was given Wabush Mines to its workers for a 3 week layoff in December of 1981. Such a ruling could leave that company liable to pay $750,000 in retroactive wages. This interpretation of the Act means that a company would have to give 4 months notice for an 8 day temporary layoff! *If we apply this interpretation to what has happened at the Baie Verte Asbestos Mine, the many fish processing companies and Bowater, the retroactive wage bill jumps to a staggering $27 million!*

The recent recession left most of the companies mentioned either *bankrupt or near-bankrupt.* Retroactive wage settlements of at least $27 million could shut them down permanently and *cost the Province thousands of jobs.* In the case of Bowater, it could prevent the sale of the mill. Given this Government's current budget deficit, we can't afford to pay the $27 million either.

The retroactive provisions of Bill 37 apply *only* to the clarification of "temporary" and "permanent" layoffs. No retroactive changes are being made to the terms and conditions of employment. *Indeed, the changes in the Labour Standards Act will provide our workers with the best temporary layoff protection in all of Canada.*

Bill 37 makes the best of a bad situation. *Bill 37 helps keep companies operating and thus protects existing jobs.* If *you* had a choice between receiving some retroactive pay or saving your job, which would *you* choose?

BILL 37

THE INTELLIGENT SOLUTION TO A DIFFICULT PROBLEM

Figure 8: Revisions to the Labour Standards Act, 10 December 1984

Rather harder to identify are the more informal aspects of co-stabilization. Both the potential purchaser, Kruger, and the unions made concessions in order to reach the settlement that set in motion the restructuring of the mill. Kruger, for instance, dropped demands for the five-year suspension of the right to strike and to lodge grievances and withdrew its proposal to contract out all wood-cutting, and when it pulled out of the negotiations in early October, stating that it would return only if the unions accepted the company's terms, it was persuaded by the Premier himself to return (on the condition of a news blackout). The unions likewise made substantial concessions in accepting the final offer of 31 October. Finally, one of the most interesting informal acts of co-stabilization may be an act of omission. Had the unions challenged the constitutionality of Bill 37 in the Newfoundland Supreme Court, Kruger would probably have withdrawn its offer to purchase.[19]

THE ROLE OF THE STATE

Among researchers who view regulation above all as a social practice, Gordon Clark has most cogently made the link with administrative law. His argument is that in advanced industrialized countries, the state and state apparatus are derivative of the capitalist reproduction process, not vice versa (Clark, 1980: 235). In a series of papers, Clark (1989, 1991, 1993) has explored the regulatory powers of the state. In an earlier era, governments had assumed broad regulatory powers, with the New Deal legislation in the United States seen as the archetype. According to Sunstein (1990), however, recent legislation has created social agencies that typically administer much narrower areas of social policy. This approach parallels Harvey's (1989b) interpretation of local state activities under late capitalism, with the state moving from a regulatory role during the earlier phase, when broad interventionist policies were in favour, to a more promotional – even entrepreneurial – role in the more recent phase. The two Acts relevant to the restructuring of Corner Brook in 1984 have connections with both of these periods. The Kruger Act – in practice an update of the Bowater Act of 1938 – was apparently broad in its scope. The Labour Relations Act, in contrast, was quite narrowly focused.

The Kruger Act remains a mysterious document since only parts of it have been made public. The entire Act (Chapter 30 of the *Statutes of the Province of Newfoundland* for 1984) amounts to less than three pages, the operative paragraph reading as follows:

> 2. The Agreement executed and delivered by and between Her Majesty the Queen in right of the province as represented by the Honourable Minister of Forest Resources and Lands of the first part and Kruger Inc. of the second part and deposited with the Clerk of the Executive Council is ratified, confirmed and adopted from September 18, 1984.

Indeed, when the second reading of the bill was to be introduced by the Premier, the leader of the opposition rose on a point of order to object that he was being asked to debate when "we have not been supplied copies of the agreement."[20] The Speaker overruled the objection and, unbelievably, the debate proceeded. Subsequently, certain financial aspects of the agreement were published in a full-page announcement in the *Western Star* of 22 December 1984 (Figure 7). The key clause was the section that guaranteed the upgrading of the mill under the Pulp and Paper Modernization Agreement. Kruger would spend $200 million, of which $40 million would be contributed by the two levels of government. This announcement in itself amounted to an interesting exercise in social regulation. It consciously sought to reconcile the mill workforce and the community to a settlement that in the short run brought them both temporary and permanent layoffs, but in the longer run did promise to preserve the majority of their jobs.

Bill 37 was an amendment to An Act to Provide Uniform Minimum Standards of Conditions of Employment in the Province. The amendment amounted to a mere two pages, but it was one of the most hotly contested acts of the Peckford government, eventually forced through on a closure motion.[21] Once again, the main thrust of the bill was announced in a full-page advertisement in the *Western Star* on 10 December 1984 (Figure 8), which stressed how many jobs would be saved by this legislation. What it did was retroactively reduce the period of notice required in the case of a temporary layoff.

CONCLUSION

The full-page advertisement placed in the *Western Star* on 22 December by the Newfoundland government (Figure 7) was a political "Christmas gift" to the residents of Corner Brook. It provides an interesting synopsis of the way restructuring of the Corner Brook pulp and paper mill was regulated. The main subsidies were listed as:

1. A $40 million grant under the Pulp and Paper Modernization Agreement, of which the provincial government would provide $7 million and the federal government the remainder.
2. An $11 million loan to Kruger from the provincial government.

3. A $30 million guarantee in bankruptcy protection (secured by the Deer Lake power plant, which was valued at a much greater amount).
4. A $2 million subsidy for the construction of forest access roads.
5. Sales tax relief totalling $14 million.

Provincially, these subsidies amount to far less than meets the eye. The provincial government provided only 20 per cent of the cost of the Modernization Agreement. The $11 million loan would be paid only if modernization costs exceeded the $200 million target. The bankruptcy protection was not likely to be paid (besides, it was completely covered by collateral security). The forest access roads were needed in any case. And the sales tax relief had already been announced in the previous budget. Effectively, the new cost to the provincial government was $7 million. In addition, the Newfoundland government signed a Federal-Provincial Forestry Agreement to spend $17 million on four new water bombers and to plant 46 million seedlings on 18,400 hectares. These expenditures were needed in any case and were mostly paid for by the federal government, and they were not part of the agreement with Kruger.

The rosy image of restructuring promoted by these political announcements does not touch on the painful transition that followed. The events of 1984 set in motion the process of restructuring that has gone on since. By 1992 the workforce had shrunk to 567 hourly workers inside the mill, plus 138 in the casual pool, another 500 working in the woods, and 80 “independent” truck drivers. Kruger had completed the agreed modernization of the mill and had done other things in addition.[22] Although it cannot be described as a state-of-the-art mill, it is producing high-quality paper used, for example, in British dailies that print in colour and therefore need paper that is white, strong, and light. By 1992, recycled paper, much of it being imported from New York, was being added to the local pulp, the goal being 25 per cent recycled paper content in batches of paper sold to most U.S. markets.

The concept of lean production comes closest to describing the changes introduced at the Corner Brook mill beginning in 1984. The purchase negotiations of 1984 that laid out the blueprint for this transition proved to be difficult because they went right to the heart of what organized labour sought to protect – jobs, good pay and benefits, and solidarity with other mill workers in eastern Canada. They were brought to a conclusion in December 1984 after nearly a year of negotiation during which the provincial government urged both the mill workforce and the potential buyer, Kruger, to make concessions, and the federal and provincial governments offered substantial financial inducements to modernize the aging mill. Thus the framework for restructuring Corner Brook's pulp and paper mill was forged in 1984 by an exercise in social regulation geared, in its essentials, to the economic renewal of the mill town. The implementation of that framework for lean production in the decade 1984-94 is examined in the following chapter.

Launching Lean Production, 1984-2000 4

Industrial restructuring is far from a universal process: the form it takes varies both through time and across space. Historically, it has been concentrated in waves of vigorous and sometimes even frenetic bubble-like activity, separated by longer periods of comparative inactivity. Geographically, at any one time it is concentrated in a few localities, while passing by many other places so that economic development becomes quite uneven. Doreen Massey's *Spatial Divisions of Labour* (1995) provides a valuable analytical framework for understanding this process. Her metaphor of geological sediments is illuminating as Massey depicts investment as occurring in uneven rounds of accumulation as a particular region becomes the favoured location for new investment. Over a relatively short period, considerable new fixed capital is installed in a selected locality, normally in one or a few connected sectors, and this fixed capital then ages rather like a cohort of school graduates. Thus Coalbrookdale in England, one of the wellsprings of the Industrial Revolution, saw the emergence of a new spatial division of labour in the mid-eighteenth century as the local iron industry was first launched. A century later the Manchester region was experiencing a huge investment in the cotton industry, as did Pittsburgh in its steel and railroad industries. More recently, one thinks of California during the dot-com boom of the 1990s, with spinoffs via global supply chains to other connected regions such as the Hsinchu region in Taiwan (Hsu, 2000, 2001). So we see in the real world that restructuring takes place during localized rounds of accumulation that produce new spatial divisions of labour. As time passes by and thc fixed capital becomes old, these once booming regions become "rustbelts." Thus the global tendency to restructure takes very specific local forms.

Widespread restructuring occurred in the 1970s and 1980s as the Fordist era came to a close and the search began for new ways to establish the profitability of firms. Some firms chose to move to new locations such as "right-to-work" states in the U.S. South, the maquiladora free-trade zones in northern Mexico, and various free-trade zones in the Asia-Pacific region. Some new firms concentrated on being technologically innovative, giving rise to a series of technopoles, some located in metropolises endowed with lots of creative people and others in new industrial spaces such as England's M4 Corridor and Boston's Highway 128. Neither of these options would work for Corner Brook's pulp and paper industry, but the emerging model of lean production did offer promise to cut costs and increase profits. It seems premature to raise lean production to the status of a regime of accumulation, but it does deserve recognition as a mode of production that has been applied in a number of settings in recent years. In this chapter, the recent history of Corner Brook's restructuring is interpreted as a version of lean production.

In the previous chapter, an important qualification was added to this understanding of restructuring. The pulp and paper industry is one of a number of resource industries that commonly restructure *in situ* due to the immobility of its inputs and to classical Weberian weight-loss as the wood resource is processed. This is not invariably the case, however, even in weight-losing resource industries. In British Columbia, for instance, the centre of gravity of the forest industries has moved inland as the more accessible coastal first-growth forests have been cut over so that older forest industry facilities along the littoral have had to be downsized or even shut down due to the declining wood supply. Inland, in contrast, new mills have been opened to exploit virgin forests (Hayter, 2000). Even bigger geographical jumps have occurred in the case of new paper mills built in tropical countries and, in Canada, at Whitecourt, Alberta (Preston et al., 1997) in order to exploit local forest reserves. Newfoundland's newsprint mills in Stephenville, Corner Brook, and Grand Falls have extensive forest limits that should (with silviculture and good management) sustain them at their present locations into the foreseeable future, so changes in locations are very unlikely.[1]

When Kruger purchased the Bowater operation at Corner Brook, the company took over the mill, its workforce, and most of the existing management. However, the mill was not absorbed into Kruger's own operations. It remains a wholly owned subsidiary and is a separate profit centre, although the parent company markets newsprint for the Corner Brook mill. The implication is quite clear: following the completion of the modernization program the Corner Brook mill was expected to be self-financing and could not anticipate cross-subsidies from other parts of the Kruger Corporation.

CHANGES IN PRODUCTION OPERATIONS, 1984-2000

In order to interpret the restructuring of operations at this Kruger subsidiary after 1984, it is necessary to begin with a brief overview of the technological and operational changes introduced at the mill: four stages of production are examined (logging and wood delivery; wood preparation; pulping; papermaking, testing, and shipping), as are the disposal of waste and environmental management and, finally, mill cleaning and maintenance.[2]

Logging Operations and Wood Delivery

At the time of Kruger's purchase there were two logging seasons: a longer summer season from early June to mid-November, when up to 1,000 men worked in the woods on logging and silviculture projects (this had declined to 750 workers by 1988 and to 650 by 1994); and a shorter winter season from early January to late March, when about half the number of loggers were at work, mostly in deep snow requiring mechanized operations.[3] Fewer workers were needed in the winter season because nobody was employed in silviculture programs or in building logging roads.

Until the early 1990s, the mill built up a large inventory of logs in the woodyard during the fall to supply it through the freeze-up and spring thaw, when logging operations were suspended, and in mid-winter, when deep snow could hamper much of the low-technology logging. By Christmas, up to 100,000 cords of wood (220,000 cubic metres) would be stacked in the yard.[4] More recently, wood supply at the mill has moved to a seasonal version of the manufacturers' just-in-time delivery system. This "fresh wood" approach produces whiter newsprint. As far as possible, freshly cut wood that has not dried out is used to make paper, hence the inventory of cut logs in the forest and in the mill yard is kept to a minimum, especially in the drier summer months (damage to fibre in cut wood is much less during the cold winter months). Additional mechanical tree harvesters were purchased to allow logging at times when hand loggers find it difficult to work and to shorten the period in the fall and spring breakup season when logging is suspended. The inventory buildup in the woodyard in late fall is now much less than even 15 years ago.

At the time of the Kruger purchase, most of the logs (four feet in length) were brought to the mill in four annual log runs on the

Humber River, with some supplementary truck, rail, and water transport.[5] The company last ran logs down the Humber River in 1986. It then switched wholly to truck transportation, which presented several advantages: it eliminated the killing of fish in the Humber River and Humber Arm as a result of fibre rubbing off logs and becoming trapped in the gills of fish; it avoided the problems of logs sinking and becoming stranded on the banks and shallows to become both an eyesore and a navigational hazard; it stopped the considerable loss of wood due to logs sinking and being stolen for firewood; it allowed the sorting of logs to achieve the optimal local mix for paper of 40 per cent black spruce with 60 per cent balsam fir (floated logs are all mixed up); and, with mechanized handling, the switch to eight-foot logs (which fit exactly across a truck) halved the handling cost. A computer-programmed system now co-ordinates this logging and trucking system.

In summary, under Kruger's management logging operations have been streamlined in two significant ways. First, the mill's fresh wood delivery system supplies logs that are easier to bark, softer to chip, and make whiter paper. The goal is the continuous supply of wood, excepting spring and fall when a modest inventory backlog is needed. Second, there has been considerable mechanization and job elimination and more subcontracting.

Wood Preparation, Bark-burning, and Composting

In the days when logs were run down the Humber River to the mill, wood preparation was greatly reduced by the abrasive effect of the riverbed, which removed much of the bark from the logs before they reached the mill. Ten small drum barkers then removed residual bits of bark using a wet process that produced effluent containing particulate matter, which contaminated the waters of the Humber Arm (Figure 5 in Chapter 2 shows a plume of contaminated effluent flowing out of the mill). Kruger decided to switch from this wet process to a dry process, using trucks to transport fresh-cut logs to the mill. This decision had three consequences. First, the dry process halved the amount of suspended solids in the mill's effluent. Second, operations in the woodyard were simplified. There was no longer a need for watermen, and the log ponds covering 2.1 hectares were filled in to enlarge the mill yard (see Figure 6), where a small team of traxcavators (front-loading bulldozers with caterpillar tracks) and front-end loaders empty trucks and stack logs in piles ready to be conveyed to the wood room (this eliminated 17 jobs). Third, this change made a new wood room a high priority and a key part of the Modernization Agreement. Construction of the new wood room began in June 1986; the 10 small drums using a wet barking system for four-foot logs were replaced by three much larger drums using a dry process to remove bark from eight-foot logs. The new drum barkers produce a higher-quality product because the bark strips more cleanly from the fresh logs. The new wood also chips better. Officially opened by federal Transport Minister John Crosbie in December 1987, the new and largely automated wood room was an important step towards lean production. It is managed from a soundproof operating room equipped with computers and monitors. As a wood-room worker summarizes it: "It's an air-conditioned, soundproofed control room, so that makes it a lot better . . . it is all computers and automated in there now . . . [you are] confined there and you just watch [the wood room] on television." When problems arise, either help is summoned on a two-way radio or the operator goes down to the operating floor to fix it. About 15 jobs were eliminated by these changes, including a number of trade workers who had maintained the old wood room.

The switch from log runs to trucking in dry logs, coupled with the construction of the new wood room, presented the mill with both an opportunity and a problem. The drum barkers remove bark and about 5 per cent of the wood as the logs tumble over the cutters, thus creating a substantial amount of waste. Initially, about 40 per cent of this material was used as a low-grade fuel to make steam, while the remaining 60 per cent was composted. However, both of these activities posed environmental problems, which the Corner Brook Pulp and Paper Company (CBPP) found difficult to solve[6] (the composting problem is discussed in a later section).

As a result of burning more bark in the mill's aging steam boilers, the long-existing soot problem became sufficiently acute by July 1987 that Corner Brook residents placed a formal complaint before city council.[7] A local steering committee was formed to press the mill for improvements in atmospheric quality. At that time, the problem was scheduled to be eliminated by June 1989, though in practice this deadline was to prove unrealistic. The long-term solution, settled on in late 1988, was to build a new boiler that would burn all the waste and to cease composting. This would recycle a free resource (wood bark), create steam needed for the energy-intensive TMP process, save on burning bunker C fuel, thereby eliminating sulphur dioxide pollution of the atmosphere, and reduce airborne contaminants to low levels. But it would be costly, and the subject of a number of delays discussed below.

Pulping and Paper Recycling

At the time that Kruger purchased the mill in 1984, a ground-wood mill, a sulphite mill (producing Kraft pulp), and a thermal-mechanical pulp mill were in place (see Figure 6), although only the last two were operating.[8] The plan was to create an exclusively TMP operation, but this was preceded by a phase when the sulphite mill was periodically closed and reopened as the pulp requirements of the mill fluctuated with the cycle of closure and modernization of the paper machines. Thus in September 1985 the sulphite mill was temporarily closed, with 21 men laid off during the modernization of number 4 paper machine; these men then bumped workers with less seniority in other departments (taking pay cuts in the process), in turn forcing the bumped workers either onto the casual list or to take a temporary layoff. When the sulphite mill was reopened in May 1986, the reverse happened. In the fall of 1987 the TMP operation was expanded by adding two more TMP lines, plus two heat recovery units designed to save on fuel costs.[9]

The sulphite pulp mill continued to operate through the late 1980s, but on 9 February 1992 it was closed indefinitely, as the mill switched entirely to TMP by adding two more TMP lines to make a total of six. At the same time the four older TMP lines were upgraded and a new soundproof control room was built to permit remote control of the pulp lines from a set of computer terminals and linked monitors. There are normally eight workers per shift. The four operators in the control room on "video specs" are in two-way radio contact with the four third and fourth hands (who are lower on the promotion ladder) so they can direct these workers on the floor of the pulp mill to perform various manual operations. The sulphite mill closure led to the loss of 40 permanent positions – 24 employed in the pulping operation itself and a further 16 working in the shops on repair and maintenance of the pulping machinery. Once again, the loss of jobs in production operations was accompanied by layoffs of tradespeople, including millwrights, pipefitters, oilers, carpenters, and electricians.

New environmental regulations introduced by 14 states in the United States by May 1990 forced CBPP to rethink its approach to pulping. For a long time a small fraction of paper had been recycled at Corner Brook. Torn paper falling beneath the paper machines, waste ends from the winder, and bad paper (which is either too wet or too dry) was put in a beater and repulped. White waste from the pulp mill was also filtered and fibre recycled. But this recycled fraction fell well below U.S. requirements (20-30 per cent recycled fibre) so another solution had to be found. Given Corner Brook's remoteness from the main recycled paper markets, the high cost of even a small de-inking plant (around $30 million), and the mill's ongoing heavy capital program to modernize operations, management was reluctant to add yet another major capital project. However, since the United States accounted for up to 40 per cent of the mill's sales, it was essential that recycled paper be used. Hence, in January 1992 construction began on a plant to recycle "white waste" shipped from New York on vessels returning from making deliveries of newsprint. Costing about $6 million, the unit does not de-ink because this type of paper is relatively clean, although bleaches are added to make the paper whiter. Completed in July 1992, the unit is computerized and created only two jobs with two shifts. Repulping 130-140 tonnes a day, the operation allowed CBPP to produce batches of newsprint with the required recycled content without a huge capital outlay, and thereby to continue to sell newsprint in states that have enacted legislation requiring recycled content. In 2004 output of the recycling plant was increased to 200 tonnes a day.

Another change introduced in 1992 was to implement a steam recovery system on TMP machines 5 and 6. The steam produced by the digesters is cleaned of impurities in an evaporator and then fed to the dry ends of the paper machines. The result is to cut down on energy requirements.

Papermaking, Testing, and Shipping

The original goal of the modernization program was to rebuild paper machines 1, 2, 3, and 4. Number 4 was modernized first, in the second half of 1985, number 1 from January to June 1986, and number 2 in the following six months (see Figure 6). In each case the wet ends of the machines were rebuilt with twin wire formers replacing the previous single-wire technology, new drying presses installed to speed up the drying process, and the calender stacks upgraded. Twin-wire technology has two main advantages: it allows water to escape from both sides of the wire mat and therefore speeds up the process of turning stock (which is about 95 per cent water) into paper, which has a water content in the 6 to 8 per cent range (Ofori-Amoah, 1993); twin wires also produce good-quality printing paper on both sides.[10] New steam boxes, which are positioned at the wet end after the paper goes through the first press, have also been installed; they add moisture to dry spots to make the paper of more uniform quality. The dry ends of these three paper machines were also rebuilt with new reels and winders. Each of these three paper machines cost close to $30 million to modernize.

In July 1986, as modernization began on the third paper machine, it was announced that the last of the original machines (number 3) would not be modernized next, but instead the large number 7 machine would be rebuilt with new concrete foundations and a new wet end added to it.[11] By April of the following year the possible significance of this decision led representatives of the mill's unions to meet with local members of the Newfoundland legislative assembly to express concern that this might result in paper machine number 3 never being modernized, with an associated permanent loss of jobs. They argued that this sequence was not in accordance with the Modernization Agreement. The mill's management argued for making this change in the Agreement on the grounds that the mill's wood supply was not sufficient to supply five modernized paper machines. Because the number 7 machine had the greatest potential for papermaking, management argued, its upgrading would create more jobs in other units of the mill since more wood and pulp would be required and there would be more paper to finish for shipping. The provincial government agreed to this variation from the Agreement. A solution proposed by the unions – to use Labrador's forest resource and transport chips or pulp from Labrador to Corner Brook to keep five paper machines operating – was not taken up because it required large capital expenditures, would be expensive to operate, and was not compatible with the shift towards using fresh wood.

The first phase in the modernization of paper machine number 7 began in December 1987, following the signing of phase two of the Modernization Agreement, and was completed by the end of 1988. It consisted of new concrete foundations and a new wet end with twin wire formers and new presses, which allowed some speeding up of the machine. With this done, all of the modernized paper machines were able to produce lighter-weight white newsprint with weights from 48.8 grams per square metre down to 40 grams. A new dry end for paper machine number 7 was planned for the end of the five-year modernization period, but installation work was delayed, initially by its cost ($37 million), then by the cash-flow problems the mill suffered during the 1990-92 recession, and finally by the urgent need to address environmental problems. A major component of this upgrade – new winders and reels – was installed by April 1996.[12]

All four operating paper machines were fitted by Bowater with Measurex systems in 1978. These systems monitor paper quality, basis weight, moisture content, strength, and colour. Kruger has since upgraded these Measurex systems with a big impact on paper quality and consistency. As one paper worker summed it up: "it's better – the computer runs the paper machine." In addition, in 1993 paper machine number 2 was fitted with a void detector (an automated system that scans the newsprint for holes as it is wound onto the reel). A second one was fitted to number 4 in 1994. The detector is described by the same paper worker as "a good thing – it saves a lot of work." The detector makes it much easier to catch holes in the sheet, which are either patched, if they are small, or cut out and spliced, if they are large. However, these measuring and testing devices fitted to the paper machines have resulted in the elimination of jobs in technical services. As one former paper inspector noted:

> There were three inspectors on a shift. They eliminated the jobs on 1, 2, and 4, and one on number 7 machine. They eliminated the jobs over there. There was a lot of hassle over it. I went through arbitration and what not. . . . They won their case like they won every case when it came to arbitration.

This worker, who has since retired, suffered a double whammy as a result of his job being eliminated: he took a 20 per cent pay cut when he was forced to bump into a lower-paying position and, because his pension was based on his salary during his last five years of mill work, his pension was also significantly reduced.

The speed of each paper machine on completion of phase I of its modernization by 1990 is given in Table 1. The wet end of each paper machine was rebuilt to raise paper quality and allow some speeding up. Phase II of their modernization was completed by 1999. A new winder and reel, with a price tag of $15 million, was installed on number 7 paper machine by April 1996, and further upgrading of number 7 cost another $22 million. Phase II of the modernization of the three smaller machines with new winders and reels cost about $20 million each. For the largest paper machine (number 7), phase III of its modernization was completed by 2005 with its speed raised to 3,700-3,800 feet per minute – an increase since 1984 of over half. This raised the total capacity of the mill to close to 1,400 tonnes a day. The long-term goal is to raise the speed of the other three machines to comparable speeds, which will raise daily capacity to about 1,500 tonnes a day.

Significant technological improvements have also been achieved in the fabrics fitted to the wet ends and drying presses of the paper machines. A worker who fits these fabrics remarked that "the machine clothing is better, the fabric is stronger. It runs longer and you don't have to change it so often. The dryer felt, dryer fabric we used to put on – 70 or 80 days and they were gone – worn out – a month sometimes. Now they run for a year." These improved fabrics have greatly extended the period between which repairs have to be made, and have allowed big reductions in the size of the clothing crew responsible for these repairs.

Table 1: Performance of Paper Machines at Corner Brook (phase 1 completed 1990; phase 2 completed 2000; phase 3 in progress), 1990-2004

			Phase 1		Phase 2		Phase 3	
Machine Number	Year installed	Width (inches)	Current speed (feet/min.)	Current capacity (tonnes/day)	Proposed speed (feet/min.)	Proposed capacity (tonnes/day)	Proposed speed (feet/min.)	Proposed capacity (tonnes/day)
1	1925	234	2,000-2,100	220	3,000	280	n.a	n.a.
2	1925	234	2,000-2,100	220	3,000	280	n.a.	n.a.
4	1925	234	2,000-2,100	220	3,000	280	n.a.	n.a.
7	1948	278	2,500	310	3,000	420	3,700	525
Total Capacity				970		1,260		1,400

Source: CBPP.

When the "jumbo" rolls of paper come off the paper machines, they are wound in the reverse direction on a winder, which has a series of cores placed along it, and cut to the dimensions ordered by customers. Previously there were three shifts cutting these cores, but now just one day shift makes the set of 120 cores needed through the night by each machine. If a mistake is made, the core-cutters are called in during the night, but "that don't happen very often." These workers don't greatly resent such calls – they can usually cut the extra cores in one to two hours and receive a minimum of four hours' pay for the overtime. As the sheet of newsprint passes through the winder, holes are patched and the roll is cut to the dimensions ordered by customers. These rolls are then put on a conveyor that takes them for finishing, where they are weighed, wrapped, and have the inside and outside corrugated heads put on them to protect them. They are then stacked in the storage warehouse to await shipping.

In being moved around, a few rolls are damaged, and this creates a specific job known as the truck trimmer, who effectively performs a recycling task by repairing damaged rolls:

> You do 50 to 60 rolls a day. It comes back [from the warehouse] . . . you take a knife and cut the head off the paper, take the wrapper off and tear off what's bad, say a half inch of paper's gone bad, take it off, put a new core in it . . . send it back to the route, rewrap, and send it back to the sheds again.

Operations in the shipping department have also been automated, with a number of jobs eliminated. As one long-time employee recalls:

> When I was out there [on shipping] we got in between a truck – a 1,900-pound roll of paper on a truck – and each guy on the side gave you a hand [positioning it]. Everything was done manually. . . . It's gone from manual labour; out there it's all automation. It's not hard work any more . . . at that time, believe you me, it was physically hard work. Nobody works hard at the mill like they used to work.

Waste Disposal and Environmental Standards

In March 1987 the Corner Brook Pulp and Paper Company reached an agreement with the provincial Environment Ministry and Environment Canada on a compliance schedule to meet federal environmental standards. The 1984 Pulp and Paper Modernization Agreement had included a subsidy of $12 million towards meeting these standards, but it took a long time to negotiate the details because Kruger was still assessing a range of options. Modernization of the paper machines was a fairly straightforward decision, but wood movement, pulping, bark disposal, plant heating, and white waste recycling were more difficult problems, with several possible solutions, each of which had implications for other stages in the production process. The compliance schedule addressed three problems:

1. *Water effluent.* The problem was in meeting federal standards for suspended solids in water effluent. The switch to dry de-barking would lower the level of suspended solids, and improved screening installations to extract and recycled fibre from white waste in the pulp mill and other effluent streams would bring the mill in compliance with regulations.
2. *Air emissions.* The plan was to install pollution abatement systems on the mill's boilers, since air emissions would increase when they began to burn the vast quantity of bark that the dry wood system would generate. Heat recovery units would also be installed to reduce the mill's solid fuel requirements.
3. *Solid wastes.* At this stage this was not a major problem, but the dry barking system to be used in the new wood room (then under construction, and opened eight months later) would create large quantities of wet wood bark.

Work on implementing the schedule began at once with an evaluation of the mill's boilers; stack emission tests were conducted with a view to retrofitting scrubbers. Meanwhile, the large amount of ash settling on houses and gardens downwind of the mill led to the formation of a citizens' environmental pressure group in July 1987. In response, CBPP announced that the soot problem would be eliminated within two years, but the mill was waiting for the report of an engineering study before a start could be made. In the short run the mill tried (unsuccessfully) to minimize the problem by reducing the air supply to the combustion chambers of the existing boilers.

A year later, the chair of the citizens' group, Allan Parsons, complained that the mill was six months behind the compliance date for submitting the control designs to reduce airborne emissions. In practice this was because the engineering firm doing the design work found it difficult to solve the technical problems using existing equipment. By July 1988 CBPP was considering the alternative of installing a new bark burner at an estimated cost of $25 million, as opposed to retrofitting scrubbers to existing boilers.

The lengthy strike of August 1988 (discussed below) had two unforeseen environmental consequences. Grand Lake dam was closed and power generation at Deer Lake cut back substantially. This, coupled with normal late summer dryness, led to the lowest levels of water in the Humber River in memory and permitted a major cleanup of debris left by years of log runs. Thousands of sunken and rotting logs were pulled out of the river for firewood, and several piers presenting navigational hazards were dismantled.[13] The mill closure also permitted the collection of baseline measurements of total suspended particulate matter in the atmosphere around the mill. Subsequent tests taken three months later when the mill was operating showed a rise from 28 micro-grams per cubic metre of particulate matter to around 80 grams downwind of the mill.[14]

By early 1989 CBPP was late in reporting on its progress in meeting the environmental compliance schedule. The source of the delay was the difficulty in solving the problem of bark-burning without incurring large capital costs. In a series of meetings with the provincial Environment Department it was agreed that completion of the schedule, originally set for 1990, would be put back two years to 1992. This was done to allow the construction of a large new bark boiler to replace boilers number 1 and number 2. Two other boilers (number 3 and number 6) were to be modified by June 1990 to burn bunker C fuel with reduced sulphur dioxide emissions by fitting an acid tower to the stacks. In the short run much of the bark was trucked to the composting facility at Wild Cove set up by Genesis Organics in the fall of 1988, but this facility itself became an environmental problem producing noxious leachate.

In the fall of 1989 cost and design problems caused further delays in meeting the compliance schedule. By February 1990 a subcontractor had been selected to build the bark boiler, but the cost estimate approached $40 million and CBPP was not able to obtain the necessary financing from a bank to proceed with the project. However, in June 1990 the provincial government guaranteed a loan of up to $50 million (secured with the Deer Lake Power Plant as collateral) to allow two projects costing $37 million to proceed, namely: installing new burners on oil-fired boilers numbers 3 and 6, by December 1991; and a new bark burner, which at that point in time was planned to be operational in June 1992. By early 1991 it was clear that the new bark burner could not be completed by the agreed date, mainly because the fall in world demand for newsprint, and the resulting drop in market prices, had reduced cash flow of the mill. In April 1991 the completion deadline was pushed back a year to June 1993 by the provincial government, with work on the bark boiler continuing at a reduced rate. The shell of the building was completed by late 1992. Work on the bark burner then effectively stopped while CBPP grappled with its cash-flow problems and meeting payments on its $170 million debt. In the summer of 1994 a tripartite agreement between Kruger/CBPP, the Newfoundland government, and the mill's employees resolved this problem. In this agreement $9 million was allocated to completing the bark burner, which became operational in August 1995 at a final cost of $43 million.[15] This burner and a secondary waste treatment plant were the mill's highest-priority capital projects at that time.

New environmental standards announced in April 1990 by the federal Environment Minister, Lucien Bouchard, required secondary treatment systems to be installed at all Canadian pulp and paper mills by 1994 to reduce solid wastes. The industry was at that time estimated to be responsible for half of all the waste entering Canadian waters. The estimated cost for the industry as a whole was $5 billion, and for CBPP $35 million. With hindsight and knowledge of the severe recession that was to engulf the industry from 1991 to 1994, it is clear that 1994 was an unrealistic compliance deadline, given the scale of investment needed to upgrade older mills. Indeed, only nine months later Bouchard recognized this fact and moved the compliance date for installing secondary treatment plants ahead to December 1995. The financial package negotiated in June 1994 was intended to allow CBPP to meet this deadline. However, technical and financial difficulties set back completion dates.

In the first few days of 1996 the mill was visited by Environment Canada scientists who conducted a series of tests that resulted in charges being laid against CBPP and Kruger on 20 March 1996 under the federal Environment Act for releasing harmful toxins into the Humber Arm. This made the Corner Brook mill the first in the country to be charged under the Act. CBPP and Kruger pleaded guilty and were fined $500,000 plus $250,000 to be divided among three community action programs ($125,000 for Wilfred Grenfell College, $75,000 for West Viking College, and $50,000 for the Corner Brook Stream Development Committee). In addition, a performance bond of $500,000 was set, forfeiting $100,000 on 1 July 1996, $200,000 on 1 August, and $200,000 on 1 September if the secondary treatment plant was not completed. Unfortunately, one of the treatment plant's three concrete basins settled into the fill and cracked, thus preventing the treatment system from being opened on time;[16] it had to be rebuilt on more stable land at a cost of several million dollars.[17] Because these circumstances were unforeseen and beyond the control of CBPP, which was acting in good faith, the performance bond was not forfeited.

Cleaning and Maintenance Operations

As restructuring has progressed, mill cleaning operations have been particularly affected. The Bowater tradition was one of shining brass, neatly mown lawns, and sparkling floors. A former cleaner recalls: "Bowater's used to polish all the brass and everything. Every bit of brass was shining." Kruger, in contrast, has made production, not appearances, the top priority. Mechanized cleaning has reduced the number of cleaning jobs and almost all have been moved from shift work to day jobs. For example, the "broke" – the pieces of paper that break off as the sheet winds at speed through the paper machine – is allowed to fall in the deep pit under the paper machines and accumulate all night, ready for cleaning out by a day worker driving a bobcat. Formerly, broke was continually cleaned up, but the bearings of the rebuilt paper machines are automatically lubricated and therefore are very unlikely to overheat and cause a fire; in any case, the rebuilt machines generate much less broke.

Another example concerns a former head cleaner who saw his job eliminated, suffering a substantial pay cut as a result: "You move through the cleaner into head cleaner, and then they move you back and you take a big pay cut: you moved back from about $24 an hour to $18 an hour." Most of the mill cleaning is now done by regular day workers who work 8 a.m. to 4 p.m. five days a week. Office cleaning is done in the evening after office workers leave, a small amount of cleaning elsewhere is done in the evenings and at the weekend, but in general the costs of cleaning the mill have been cut by mechanizing, shrinking the number of cleaners, cutting out most overtime and shift work, and eliminating supervisory positions.

Similar workforce reductions have been implemented throughout the shops and maintenance operations. For example, an electrician explains:

> *Electrician*: I was a substation operator, but they done away with that job.
>
> *Interviewer*: Who looks after the substation now?
>
> *Electrician*: The maintenance men . . . now if anything goes wrong at the substation they get a buzzer down at the maintenance shop and they goes up an' checks what's wrong.

ELEMENTS OF LEAN PRODUCTION

The changes seen after 1984 at the Corner Brook newsprint mill constitute a version of lean production, along the lines described by the late Bennett Harrison and discussed in Chapter 1. Five of Harrison's six elements of lean production are found at CBPP, the exception being strategic alliances, which CBPP did not negotiate with other major firms.[18] On the other hand, a further element, linked to environmental compliance, has promoted lean production in Corner Brook. Thus, six components of lean production are in evidence at Corner Brook and will be assessed to connect the empirical details of the preceding section with the main argument.

Tightening the Co-ordination of Production with a Reduced and More Flexible Labour Force

The main thrust of restructuring at Corner Brook has been the pursuit of two related goals. In every department – from the input of logs to the wrapping of newsprint rolls – new equipment has improved the co-ordination of production; and every time this has happened, a few more jobs have been eliminated and those workers remaining have been asked to adopt more flexible work practices. Operations have also been automated so that more of the work takes place at terminals in control rooms. Most of the continuous physical shop-floor work has been eliminated in the wood room and pulping operations; papermaking and finishing still require physical work, although considerably less than 20 years ago.[19] As a result, in the period since the Kruger takeover the mill's core workforce has shrunk by around 25 per cent. This has been accompanied by changes in work practices at the mill. As one worker put it:

> [Kruger] don't like to see anyone stopped, they don't like to see anybody idle. If they can work nine hours of work in eight hours, well that's their idea of a perfect day.

As explained in the previous chapter, Kruger's purchase of the mill in 1984 involved a series of negotiations with the unions and government over work practices.[20] The unions naturally resisted these demands, but faced with the possibility of the mill being closed they reluctantly made a series of concessions: a wage freeze for two years, followed by a catch-up to wage norms at Kruger's Trois-Rivières plant; an unusual four-year contract that broke the system of pattern bargaining; the introduction of some "minor" crossing of trades; and the acceptance of more subcontracting (Labour Agreement, 1984-88).

As this first contract came to an end in late summer of 1988, it became apparent that the unions, now in a stronger bargaining position, would try to regain some of the ground they had lost in 1984. Negotiations revolved around four main issues: wage parity with other paper workers in eastern Canada; early retirement at 58; a two-year contract to bring Corner Brook's contracts back into phase with other eastern Canadian mills; and job security with less subcontracting. The two sides dug in, and on 17 August 1988 the two Canadian Paperworkers Union locals went out on strike, followed soon after by all the other unions. The employer then served a week's layoff notice on 850 loggers, so that within a week 1,600 workers in total were out of work. The two sides in the strike were not willing to compromise, and a tentative settlement reached in early September was rejected almost unanimously by members of the two trades locals. A provincial conciliator was appointed and eventually succeeded in narrowing the differences so that a settlement was reached, with the mill restarting on 29 September after a 43-day work stoppage. The settlement is interesting: the employer made several concessions, including a two-year contract, wage parity, early retirement, the granting of certain benefits to casual workers, and a switch to a 12-hour shift for most production workers. But on the important issues of job security and subcontracting, the employer did not give ground; if lean production was to be achieved, then further automation and associated job losses were to be expected.

Union-management talks about changing the shift system at the mill had begun in February 1987. The system in place was an eight-hour shift with a weekly alternation, averaging 42 hours a week. At that time the workers at Abitibi-Price's mill at Stephenville and some at Grand Falls had moved to a 12-hour shift with four days on and four days off. Most workers favoured this system as it improved social and family life. However, in April 1987 the CPU locals involved in these discussions rejected the format proposed by Corner Brook Pulp and Paper (tradespeople mainly work days and were not involved in these talks). This proposal was then shelved until September 1988 when it was formally adopted as part of the strike settlement.

The two-year contract signed in 1988 expired in late 1990, when new negotiations began. In comparison with the previous negotiations, these were relatively straightforward; negotiators agreed on a 16 per cent wage increase spread over three years (Labour Agreement, 1990-93). The move towards lean production continued in a small way, with a further squeeze on statutory holidays: as of 30 December 1990, the mill no longer closed down for Canada Day, but instead an extra day was added to the Christmas shutdown. The machinists' and electrical workers' locals rejected the initial offer, but a conciliator was able to resolve the problem without a strike occurring.

The next Labour Agreement (1993) ran from July 1993 to June 1998. It stipulated no wage increase in 1993, 1 per cent in 1994, 1.5 per cent in 1995, and for the last two years of the contract a negotiated rate based on settlements elsewhere (in practice, this was an increase of 70 cents per hour plus a signing bonus of $1,000 in each of the last two years).[21]

The greatest increases in work flexibility since 1984 have occurred in the trades, with a good illustration being provided by the comments of an electrician:

> After the substation [job was eliminated] I went back to the shop and I does maintenance as well. Now, everybody does maintenance. . . . We only got two shifts now, 8 to 4, and 4 to 12. An 8-to-4 man works down in maintenance. They gave us radios [in 1992] so they can get us anywhere in the mill now. There used to be four men [i.e., electricians] on a shift 24 hours a day. Now there's only two men during the day and one man at night – drive room operator, they call him – he looks after the whole mill 12 to 8 a.m.

The adoption of two-way radios by tradesmen to increase flexibility was clearly a contentious step. He continued:

> If the TMP [i.e., pulping control room] wants you he can call you or anyone else . . . you got a phone and if someone calls you to do a job, you goes and does that job. If you're doing that job you can't be doing another job, but with the radio they can get you anywhere. . . . I put in a grievance against that – there's too much work to do.

Employees on capital projects have been more inclined to accept flexible work practices since they face the likelihood of being laid off if they don't. Thus a welder remarked: "If I'm working with a pipefitter [on capital projects] I'm expected to do a bit more pipefitting than I did when I was in maintenance." An instrument mechanic made a similar remark: "Yes, we're doing more things in the last six or seven months we usually didn't do. Like, we're doing a bit of electrical, a bit of plumbing, a bit of pipefitting, that kind of stuff. We always had certain lines and we didn't go past it." But even production workers have seen big increases in flexibility: a wood-room operator has found himself expected to cross trades: "We get to do a lot of millwright work we never had to do before . . . if one of our chains comes off the sprocket we got to lift it back on with a chain thong, and that's millwright work. [We release] wood that gets jammed under the chains – that's another millwright job." Likewise, the clothing crew find themselves cleaning broke from the pit under the paper machines, which used to be done exclusively by cleaners. A tradesman felt that Kruger was very determined to increase labour flexibility through cross-trading: "They're pushing it without paying. We got a choice – do it or go home." And it would seem that this cross-trading is costing some tradesmen their regular jobs; thus "the millwrights are doing a lot of pipefitting in certain places that we used to do it, and now the millwrights are doing it. That's probably one of the reasons why I'm not back in the pipe shop because a lot of my work is done by a millwright."

The key area of resistance to flexibility is on the paper machines, where the line of progression is well defined in the contract and observed on the ground. A young member of Local 242 (the paper makers' local) was quite emphatic:

> The way I've been taught, you're in the mill for one reason, that's your line of progression, that's the most important thing because you don't want people jumping ahead of you. . . . You don't want to be set back for no reason.

The overall effect of more than a decade of technical innovation and the associated job elimination has been to increase the sense of uncertainty in the workforce. A worker of long standing reflects:

> A lot of people don't know from one day to the next where their job is going to be. You'll always hear somebody talk about how this job is going to be eliminated or that job is going to be eliminated. They're frightened to plan ahead, they don't know one day to the next if their job is going to be cut, or if they're going to move to another department, or if they've got seniority enough to look for another post.

Along with fishing, logging must rank among the toughest of jobs in Newfoundland. Loggers work outdoors at all seasons and the vagaries of nature are a fact of daily life, the work is physically demanding, and there are significant risks. It is hardly surprising that loggers form one of the feistiest groups in Newfoundland's labour force and have been vocal in resisting some of the changes attributed to global pressures, going back to the organized civil disobedience led by John Thompson in 1936.

There has clearly been worker resistance to these various demands for greater flexibility by the employer. This is evident in the contract negotiations, grievances, and a fairly widespread sense of resentment among older workers. It is, after all, their jobs that are on the line. But there is also some recognition of the need for change:

> The percentage of people working down there is cut in half [since 1984]. I know that had to happen anyway due to automation and whatever because if that mill's not going to be among the top five in efficiency, she's not going to run and I'm not going to have a job. I realize, and other people realize that if they don't automate and modernize, the mill is going to go downhill, and eventually we'll all be out of a job.

And:

> Well, Krugers [are] better survivors. . . . With Bowater, when I went in there first, I couldn't believe how relaxed anybody could be with a company. Little wonder why they went under. But now with Kruger, they got control.

Concentrating on Core Competencies

Of their very nature, paper mills are specialized operations that typically concentrate on producing a narrow range of products, hence there is limited scope for further specialization. The Corner Brook Pulp and Paper Company manufactures one product – newsprint – in various weights and widths. Thus the mill has concentrated on its core competencies from the beginning. But there was, in 1988, a specific instance where the company chose not to diversify despite the offer of a substantial incentive.

In November 1988 consideration was given to modifying paper machine number 4 to produce clay-filled super-calendered specialty paper. The market for this type of paper, which is used in colour supplements and magazines, was thought to be less cyclical than that for newsprint and, as a premium product, it was expected to generate higher revenue. The conversion cost was estimated to be $19.5 million, of which $5.8 million would have been provided by the Atlantic Canada Opportunities Agency (ACOA). After review, CBPP decided that this capital outlay was not warranted and the modification was never implemented. The negative decision was based on two considerations: it would have cost the company $14 million, diverting that amount from the ongoing modernization program, and it would have required additional investment in human capital and marketing. After careful consideration, the company concluded that it was best to continue concentrating on automation and better co-ordination of its core operations, so as to raise productivity and shrink the workforce.

Farming Out Ancillary Activities

Since purchasing the mill, Kruger has farmed out several important aspects of mill operations while concentrating on the core project of making newsprint. More subcontracting of the mill's wood-cutting operations was a condition of the Kruger purchase agreement in 1984; by 1992, Kruger wanted the percentage of wood-cutting subcontracted to non-union operators to rise from 10 per cent to 35 per cent, the remainder being cut by unionized loggers.[22] Until 1990 some of the unionized loggers were employed by the company itself, with the rest of the logging operations subcontracted. Since then, the entire logging operation has been subcontracted, with CBPP focusing on core papermaking operations. Prudham (2002) reports similar patterns in Oregon's logging industry. In order to subcontract all logging operations the company had to provide loans to some large subcontractors to purchase tree harvesters. This large-scale capital-intensive type of logging operation had long been unionized and seemed likely to remain so. On the other hand, much of Newfoundland's forests are made up of dense thickets of small trees (especially balsam fir) where tree harvesters and mechanical feller bunchers do not operate efficiently; jobbers working with chainsaws and forwarders (a machine similar in layout to a small earth mover but with large rubber tires is used to transport a load of logs from the woods to a tractor trailer on the nearest logging road) at piecework rates can cut this small wood and provide the mill with low-cost fibre. These small, non-unionized subcontractors pay relatively low wages for seasonal work, after which their employees go on unemployment insurance. The operation of both unionized and non-unionized loggers is closely co-ordinated by the mill's forestry department using programs designed to supply the mill with a steady flow of fresh wood on a just-in-time basis, excepting the buildup of inventory during the spring thaw and fall freeze-up.

Workers have resisted these developments. In June 1990 contract negotiations between the 700 loggers forming CPU Local 60 and the Corner Brook Pulp and Paper Company reached an impasse, and the local went out on strike. At stake were three main issues: the union wanted the proportion of wood cut by non-unionized subcontractors (set in the 1984 agreement to rise to 35 per cent) to be reduced; the union did not want the company to purchase any more tree harvesters since mechanization was putting members out of work; and the local wanted wage and benefit parity with loggers working for Abitibi-Price, Newfoundland's other major newsprint maker. After a month out, the loggers settled; they gained wage parity with Abitibi-Price loggers and an agreement to create a joint union-management committee to minimize job losses. But the union achieved no concessions on the two crucial issues relating to lean production, namely subcontracting and mechanization. There were two main reasons the company refused to make concessions on these issues. First, to make high-quality paper (especially for the European market) the mill needed a continuous flow of fresh wood cut by mechanical harvesters in periods when other less mechanized logging methods were not practicable. And second, the non-unionized subcontractors using mainly hand cutting methods could cut fir thickets on a results basis, which reduced the mill's fibre costs.[23]

Conflict between the loggers and CBPP flared up again in the early summer of 1996. In that spring the mill had decided to raise the 45 per cent limit on logs cut by mechanical harvesters. Loggers protested, and even threatened to block the roads leading to Hampden, Sop's Arm, Pollard's Point, and Jackson's Arm.[24] Following sometimes heated negotiations, a compromise was reached whereby the number of mechanical harvesters operating in the disputed forests would remain at three.[25]

At the time of the Kruger takeover most of the trucks delivering logs to the mill were owned by the company and were used in combination with other means of transporting logs to the mill. Kruger decided to subcontract all of the wood haulage, in so doing helping a number of employees set up as quasi-independent truckers. A few purchased old Kruger trucks to get started. Others were provided with a "comfort letter" and a contract to help them obtain private funding to purchase a rig. The hauling of logs to the mill is now done by 48 trucks, each set up as an owner-operated business consisting of one cab and two trailers; while one trailer loaded with eight-foot logs is being driven to the mill, the other trailer is left at the logging camp for loading. Trucking rates are based on a formula that takes into account length of haul, nature of the road surface, and topography. Operations are tightly co-ordinated by the mill to provide a steady flow of fresh wood. At the same time, this trucking system saves CBPP the headache of operating and maintaining a fleet of trucks, and creates 48 small enterprises with a vested interest in the smooth operation of the mill.

The third area in which ancillary activities are now subcontracted out is the installation of new plant and equipment and in upgrading the mill's fixed capital. In the days when Bowater operated the mill, nearly all installation and maintenance were done by the large workforce employed in the mill's shops. For instance, installation of the large number 7 paper machine in 1948-49 was done by the mill's employees. However, the reconstruction of the same paper machine's concrete foundations 40 years later was done by subcontractors. Similarly, other major projects such as the construction of the recycling plant, the bark-burning boilers, and the heat recovery units were done on a turnkey basis by their suppliers. Laid-off tradesmen resent this contracting-out of plant installation:

> I'm unemployed with 20 years seniority and there's [outside] people in there [building the bark burner]. I sort of agree with Kruger in some ways, like maybe there is specialized work, but there's [also] work being done that we have been doing and can do . . . yet tradesmen and boilermakers were [recruited] from around Newfoundland.

Moreover, such subcontracting does not always save money, as a tradesman remarked: "They had contractors in there and they didn't do the job right – plain and simple. So now I think that someone is after realizing that when we [i.e., the mill's own tradesmen] do work, we do it right. We mightn't be quite as fast as some of those guys, but we do it right."

Shrinking and Segmenting the Workforce

Table 2 records employment change in the main departments of the mill in January of each year from 1986 to 1994. The figures need interpreting with some care because they fluctuate from month to month. For example, in January 1986 paper machine number 1 was closed for modernization and the sulphite mill was also temporarily closed, so that some 100 regular workers were laid off at that time, but later rehired when the upgraded paper machine was brought back on stream. Underlying these short-term fluctuations, long-term trends are evident. Employment in management rose during the main phase of modernization but has declined steadily since then. Some 17 jobs were lost in the woodyard over the period as the fresh wood system simplified operations. The new wood room, with three large drum barkers replacing 10 small ones, resulted in the elimination of 18 jobs. The full workforce complement in pulping was about 56 until the sulphite mill closed in 1992, when the workforce dropped by 20 positions. The paper machine lines changed less, although two positions – the dispatcher and the paper inspector – were cut from each crew to make a total loss of 32 positions in 1992 (having installed Measurex sensors and void detectors, the company allocated what remained of this work to other crew members at the dry end). A similar percentage of jobs was lost in finishing and in technical services, where much of the testing work was automated by the Measurex sensors. Job attrition has also occurred in the shops where the complement of millwrights, oilers, welders, plumbers, carpenters, electricians, and so on has shrunk in small decrements, with 25 per cent of the jobs eliminated during the decade. There have been minor job losses in the steam plant and warehousing. Overall, the regular workforce has declined from about 750 at the time of the takeover to around 575, a decrease of around 23 per cent.[26] This has occurred through many small changes, including layoffs and rehirings as pulp and paper lines were shut down for modernizing and then reopened, rather than in a few major layoffs.

While this workforce shrinkage was underway, the segmentation of the labour force was consolidated. The basic segmentation into a core labour force and a casual pool has been in place since at least World War II, and therefore cannot, in this instance, be attributed to the development of flexible specialization.[27] But the role of the casual segment has changed. Prior to the 1970s, the casual list served as a place to start, as a toe in the door for young men entering the mill. In the 1980s and 1990s it has functioned more as a net for laid-off workers. To what extent it might be described as a safety net depends on where a worker stands on the casual list. The top 50 names on the list are called in regularly and, on the whole, work a full working week. When a casual replaces a worker on long-term disability or vacation, hours are predictable, but at other times hours of work may be less predictable. Workers below this position on the casual list find their hours less and less predictable, and only during peak vacation periods like the fall hunting season, Christmas, and in summer are they likely to have a full week's work. They are expected to be reachable by telephone at all times and are usually required to report in at short notice, for instance, when a regular worker phones in sick or a mechanical problem occurs at the mill. Waiting for a phone call from the mill becomes the organizing principle for the daily life of these casual employees. This casual workforce has also played a role in pressuring the core workforce to accept

Table 2: Employment Change by Major Department: Corner Brook Pulp and Paper Mill, 1985-1995

	Management	Wood Preparation, Woodyard, Mill Yard	Pulping	Paper Mill	Finishing	Technical Services	Shops (Trades)	Steam Plant	Warehousing/ Stevedoring	Total Regular	Casual/ Relief	Capital Projects	Total
1985	n.a.	n.a.	n.a.	n.a.	n.a.	n.a.	n.a.	n.a.	n.a.	750	n.a.	n.a.	*C.* 1,000
1986	70	60	29	99	27	19	230	22	66	622	125	158	905
1987	75	60	52	124	27	28	228	26	66	686	142	169	997
1988	85	47	48	133	37	27	225	32	66	700	155	159	1,014
1989	84	45	48	133	38	27	204	27	65	684	117	180	981
1990	79	45	57	127	42	31	241	26	70	718	124	42	884
1991	76	44	56	128	42	32	243	26	70	717	142	27	886
1992	67	42	47	132	32	31	192	28	63	634	138	33	805
1993	58	43	32	128	31	26	179	24	60	581	162	25	768
1994	54	43	34	132	32	24	169	24	60	572	140	24	736
1995	54	43	34	131	32	25	170	24	60	573	120	47	740

Source: CBPP.

more flexible work practices. As one tradesman observed: "The millwrights and the welders are all working together now [i.e., cross-trading] . . . we don't like it but it's happening all the time. The way they do it now, the people are on layoff status. If you refuse to do it, there's two people at the back of you willing to do it."

Segmentation is also now being used to increase the numerical flexibility of the employer. For instance:

> There was five men in the finishing room when I went there. There's still five but there's four permanent and one casual. . . . Now they're hanging on to one casual, but he's there all the time – he's getting 40 hours a week, but they call him casual.

At the same time, casuals working in this situation are not eligible for the full range of worker benefits. Segmentation has further developed since the Kruger takeover with the creation of a second non-core workforce employed on capital projects. This workforce consists mostly of laid-off tradesmen (i.e., workers who have served an apprenticeship in a trade such as pipefitting or instrumentation) who were then hired back to work on modernization projects. When the first phase of the modernization project was completed in 1990 a number of these workers were laid off, although some had 15 or more years of mill seniority, while the remainder continue to work on other "capital projects." Very little of the capital project work is done on overtime – indeed, most work 8 a.m. to 4 p.m. – but some alternate between a day shift and an evening shift from 4 p.m. to midnight.[28] Like employees on the casual list, this category has acted as a buffer providing work while an employee waits for a retirement that allows the laid-off worker with the most seniority to return to the regular workforce. Given the lack of alternative work in Corner Brook and the good pay that can be earned at the mill by a full-time worker, most laid-off workers have accepted their situation in the hope that eventually they would re-enter the regular workforce. The mill keeps exact lists of seniority, by category, so that a pipefitter, for instance, knows exactly how many workers in the same trade are above him on the casual list and the retirement age of full-time pipefitters. Casual workers can therefore forecast, with some degree of certainty, when they might return to regular work. For the employer, this system has the major advantage of making a skilled workforce available for hiring without having to invest in costly training or apprenticeship programs; this amounts to a substantial cost saving.

The work history of one tradesman illustrates how this segmentation and workforce shrinkage has worked:

1980 Hired as an apprentice.

1982 Laid off for 2½ years; during this layoff obtains his trade certificate.

1985 Hired to work on the mill modernization project (mod squad).

1989 With the first phase of modernization nearly complete, gets a permanent position.

1991 Moved to capital projects crew – once again liable to layoff.

1992 Laid off 11 weeks.

With several fellow tradesmen ahead of him on the seniority list, he felt it would be some time before he regained a permanent position: "While I was with the 'mod squad,' every six months we would get laid off for a week, and then hired back so that they would not have to pay us benefits." In practice "mod-squad" workers did receive basic benefits, but they were not eligible for the full range that included a dental plan.

The trickle of new recruits to the mill workforce also enter via these segments. Thus new recruits to mill production enter the casual pool and from there work up to a permanent position. Tradesmen now enter mainly through capital projects and hope to achieve a permanent placement by seniority when applying for a posted position. The speed at which such persons achieve permanent status depends on their qualifications (especially where testing is applied) and the demand for their particular skills. For instance, an instrument mechanic achieved permanent status in six years because there is increasing demand for such skills as the mill automates production, whereas a carpenter hired in 1978 had still not achieved a permanent position in 1994.

In her study of the northern part of Vancouver Island, Maureen Reed (2003) reminds us of another aspect of labour force shrinkage and segmentation, which may not be immediately apparent in Corner Brook because women are barely represented in the mill's labour force. This squeeze on jobs perpetuates the marginalization of women in the local labour force. In regions where good new jobs are being created, for women there is greater possibility for job mobility and movement up the career ladder. In much of Canada's hinterland, including Corner Brook, low levels of job creation severely limit the prospects for women both in the private sector and, due to financial squeezes, increasingly in the public sector. That leaves women the options of poorly paying and insecure jobs in the secondary labour market or the limited possibilities of self-employment.

Complying with Environmental Regulations To Increase Technical Efficiency

Discussions about restructuring at Canadian newsprint mills have often turned to the issue of compliance with environmental regulations. Since many of the social costs of mill pollution are externalized, the growing list of environmental regulations are seen by most companies as a cost to be borne or, in some instances, delayed. In practice, however, these regulations have acted as a major stimulus to adopting lean production, and although compliance has required large capital investments (often in competition with other mill priorities), the results have been to raise productivity, reduce labour inputs, and make better use of by-products. Indeed, in the long run, the net effect may be a saving to mill operators, and this would certainly be the case if negative externalities were factored in.

At the Corner Brook mill, solutions to environmental problems have promoted lean production on three main fronts. First, the system of wood delivery by truck, which is capital-intensive and operates on a JIT basis, put an end to a complicated, labour-intensive, multi-mode transport system that delivered wood at irregular intervals while creating considerable pollution. Second, improved screening and the recycling unit have reduced the amount of new fibre required, and qualifies the mill's product for sale in American newsprint markets that set a minimum recycled quota. And third, the steam recovery unit in the pulp mill and the new bark burner convert nuisance by-products – steam and bark – into resources. The bark is used to generate about half of the mill's steam requirements, while simultaneously reducing labour inputs and the need to burn costly bunker C fuel oil, which also produces polluted air emissions.

Co-opting the Most Valuable Workers into the Mission of the Firm

Since the 1950s worker-employee relations at Corner Brook have been regulated by a series of collective agreements specifying grievance procedures, periodic negotiations between the employer and the unions, and voting procedures to ratify new contracts put to union members.[29] Such formal relations, which create an adversarial relationship between employer and employees, are inimical to any attempts by the employer to co-opt workers. Yet recently, and in subtle ways, the mill's workforce has been co-opted by management into the mission of the firm.

Corner Brook Pulp and Paper has eliminated a number of lower management positions within the mill's operating departments in recent years, assigning some of their tasks to the foremen in the relevant departments. This has imperceptibly blurred the lines between union and management; indeed, some union members have declined promotion to foreman because they are reluctant to fulfill these management functions. Moreover, once this blurring of roles is accomplished, the employer can counter complaints by arguing that if a management position is recreated in a department, all the employees will be moved one position down the ladder, with the bottom person made redundant, a Catch-22 situation for a union member.

In 1994, the core workforce was drawn much more explicitly into the "project" of the mill when CBPP proposed that the company could solve its short-term, but pressing, financial problems in several ways, one of which involved a loan by employees of $10 million to the company (to be paid out of a 10 per cent pay cut), which the company would pay back over several years out of anticipated future profits.[30] Lengthy negotiations followed, culminating with a threat by Kruger to shut down paper machine number 4 and lay off about one-quarter of the mill's workforce. The eventual solution to the issue involved a classic example of state regulation. The provincial government agreed to purchase all of the mill's freehold forest limits while allowing the company to retain cutting rights for 99 years, paying the company $17 million (which was generally considered to be far in excess of the land's real worth). But this hidden subsidy was frozen until the workforce agreed to the package involving a 10 per cent pay cut to be loaned back to the company. Union members twice rejected this proposal, but they eventually voted, by a narrow margin, to accept a compromise after making an interesting breakthrough. Union negotiators argued that since Kruger was a private company, they had no way of assessing the true severity of CBPP's financial difficulties. The company responded that it would open its financial records to a consulting accountant to be paid for by the union, on the condition of confidentiality. The New York accountant hired for the job confirmed that CBPP really did have serious financial problems in servicing its $170 million debt, and this became an important factor in persuading the union's membership to accede to the company's proposals. After further negotiations a formula was adopted, and the employees loaned the company $9.6 million in the form of a 10 per cent pay cut from their paycheques, beginning in

July 1994 and ending in April 1996. In avoiding a major layoff, the employees were co-opted into having a direct interest in the future profitability of the enterprise, and thus were made an interested party in the project to implement lean production. As a casual worker ruefully remarked: "they're taking 10 per cent out of my salary, and to do work in the mill they'll get [outside] contractors in to do it and use my money to pay them."

CONCLUSION

The picture of *in situ* restructuring that emerges in Corner Brook is of a contested process pitting global against local forces. The corporate goal was to move towards levels of productivity comparable to the best global practices at the lowest possible cost. Mill employees also recognized the need to restructure production at the mill, but not at the cost of a big squeeze on jobs, wages, and benefits. It was not clear where the line would be drawn between these two opposing interests – this had to be determined by negotiation of specific issues.

Restructuring in Corner Brook was a piecemeal process and job losses did not occur on the scale seen at Powell River, B.C., or Gatineau, Quebec (Hayter, 1997; Rose and Villemaire, 1997). In a single-industry town, two considerations made such a gradual approach to modernization preferable. First, the local economy would have been severely disrupted if large-scale *in situ* changes such as a complete shutdown were suddenly implemented. Indeed, major upheavals in the workplace might have resulted in intervention by the provincial government. In comparison to changes at many other newsprint mills, workforce reduction at Corner Brook has occurred in a series of relatively small layoffs. There have, of course, been grievances from the unions – there was a major strike in 1988, and various lesser confrontations and a number of cases of individual hardship have occurred, but three factors have mitigated the worst effects. First, the mill virtually stopped hiring over the decade, and as the workforce aged, retirements led to natural shrinkage. This was accelerated by the early retirement package agreed to in 1988 (although not all eligible workers have taken advantage of this option). Second, many of the laid-off workers were hired on to the capital projects workforce, either directly by CBPP or by subcontractors. These workers retained their mill seniority[31] and the right to apply for posted vacancies, so that they are rehired onto the permanent workforce as positions become available. And third, the casual pool acted as a buffer. Workers in the top half of this pool are called in regularly, while those in the lower half get work less regularly. The change to a 12-hour shift system in 1988 had the effect of discouraging regular workers from working overtime and has created more work for the casual pool.

The second reason for piecemeal modernization is that it allows a firm to manage its debt load by internally financing the incremental move towards lean production. Kruger has succesfully followed this strategy of asset building in other older mills it has purchased and modernized by reinvesting profits from sales in new capital projects, together with any grants or loans that may be negotiated. Modernization at Corner Brook got off to a good start in the 1980s as the pulp and paper industry went through an extremely profitable phase (Holmes and Hayter, 1993). However, the recession from 1990 to 1993 hit the whole industry hard,[32] and like many Canadian mills, the Corner Brook mill experienced significant losses during this period. Capital projects ground to a halt, and cutbacks in the labour force were made wherever the employer felt it was feasible. Cyclical fluctuations such as this form an endemic part of the economy of single-industry towns (Bradbury, 1984; Norcliffe, 1994).

The capital costs of restructuring the mill at Corner Brook have been substantial. Phase I of the modernization program was completed in May 1989 with $245 million spent, while by June 1994 a total of $352 million had been invested in modernization. The rebuilt wood room cost a little over $20 million, with an additional smaller investment in new wood-chipping equipment. Total investment in pulping operations amounted to $92.5 million, including the installation of two heat recovery units (to recycle steam), four TMP lines, and a computerized control room, as well as upgrading of the two lines previously installed by Bowater. Over $110 million was invested in modernizing paper machines number 1, number 2, number 4, and number 7. Environmental projects (with the bark burner by far the largest item, to date) absorbed $32 million by June 1994 and double that figure by the end of 2000. Other items are listed in Table 3.

The costs to the town take the form of an absent younger generation. Unlike their parents and grandparents, few young men and women have been able to find employment locally. Despite a strong place attachment, many have had no alternative but to migrate to other parts of Canada, and elsewhere, to find work. As will be shown in Chapter 6, the age structure of the community has tilted rapidly in favour of the elderly, while average family size has declined dramatically.[33] Retirees, who have become a major element of the city's population, are also discussed in Chapter 6.

The changes made to the Corner Brook mill in the past decade not only bear the hallmark of lean production, but were the conscious objective of the mill's new owner. A pointer to this is found in a crucial new clause added to the opening section in the first Labour Agreement between the Canadian Paperworkers Union and the Corner Brook Pulp and Paper Company following the Kruger takeover in 1984, defining the "General Purpose" of the Agreement. It states:

> 2.03 The unions undertake to co-operate with the company in every reasonable way:
>
> a) to increase production,
>
> b) to reduce absenteeism.

Table 3: Capital Expenditures to Modernize the Mill, 1985-1994

	$ million
New wood room	20.7
Chip handling	0.5
TMP and heat recovery units	92.5
Paper machines 1, 2, 4, and 7	110.4
Environment (air and suspended solids, incl. bark burner)	32.4
Other environment	3
Modification from 50 to 60 cycles	3.7
Regular mill capital budget	33.6
Woods department (access roads, etc.)	29.8
Deer Lake Power Company	3.5
Miscellaneous	21.9
Total	352.0
Since 1995	
Bark burner	43.0
Phase II upgrade - paper machines 1,2, and 4	60.0
Phase II upgrade - paper machine 7	37.0
Secondary treatment plant	40.0
Co-generation project (2002)	29.0
Cumulative total	561.0

Source: CBPP.

This short section served as a blueprint for Kruger's project to move the mill closer to global standards of lean production. Step by step old equipment has been replaced, the labour force downsized, cross-skilling increased, ancillary activities farmed out, and production more tightly co-ordinated and automated. The primary workforce of the mill has shrunk by about 25 per cent as the mill has focused on its core competencies. But, as Table 1 and Table 4 show, production has risen, especially since the completion of the first round of mod-

Table 4: Corner Brook, Pulp and Paper Ltd.: Production, Employment, and Productivity

Year	Tonnes of Newsprint	Regular Employment	Tonnes per Employee
1985	256,982	750 (est.)	343 (est)
1986	226,863	622	365
1987	283,135	686	413
1988	149,292	687	411*
1989	283,213	671	422
1990	319,184	709	450
1991	304,625	709	430
1992	308,298	636	485
1993	337,803	583	579
1994	351,608	574	613
1998	405,000 (est.)	560 (est.)	723 (est.)
2004	430,000 (est.)	550 (est.)	780 (est.)

* Adjusted to account for 42-day strike.
Source: CBPP.

ernization in 1988. Labour productivity has therefore risen substantially: annual output per core employee rose from 365 tonnes per year in 1986 to 579 tonnes in 1993, a rise of 59 per cent, and this was accompanied by a major improvement in the quality of the newsprint produced. In comparative terms, Corner Brook has become home to one of the more productive mills in eastern Canada: in 1993 it took approximately 3.5 person/hours to produce a tonne of paper, compared to between 3.2 and 4.5 hours in other older mills in eastern Canada and under 2.0 hours at a state-of-the-art greenfield mill such as that at Whitecourt, Alberta.[34] In the process, two secondary labour markets – one working on modernization (the capital projects workers) and the other the casual workforce – have increased labour force segmentation. All of the logging operations, all of the trucking of logs to the mill, and some of the capital projects have been subcontracted. Finally, local resistance has been contained by CBPP's efforts to co-opt the core workforce into the mission of the firm as lean production methods have been incrementally adopted.

Patterns of Work and Family Life 5

Corner Brook's history as a company town, built with government subsidies in the 1920s to exploit local forest and hydroelectric resources, prepared it badly for the recent phase of *in situ* restructuring towards lean production. A protective corporate shell had cocooned the mill and the town for decades. The internal labour and housing markets, the expectation of jobs for life, the guarantee made to employees enlisting in World War II that they could return home to their jobs, and the confident expectation that sons would follow fathers into well-paying and secure employment were all a part of the industrial culture of this successful company town.[1] The peculiar family bond between Sir Eric Bowater and the town led to the continuation of this relationship, and the mindset that it engendered, longer than in many other comparable towns. When this protective shell was progressively stripped away after the death of Sir Eric, the town and the mill were left vulnerable to the forces of global competition. By the 1980s, the mill needed more than a massive investment of capital to re-equip every department to become competitive with state-of-the-art competitors. In comparison to the new state-of-the-art mill at Whitecourt, Alberta (Preston et al., 1997) and to other modernized mills, Corner Brook had more employees in every department, the labour productivity was substantially lower, the average age of workers was higher, they enjoyed more statutory holidays, and the end product – newsprint – was not of as high a quality. Investing new capital would therefore not be enough: from Kruger's perspective, a comprehensive restructuring of the mill was needed, shifting operations (as noted in the previous chapter) to the lean production model. This implied a substantial change in the institutions of work and the culture of production, which in turn might be expected to spill over into family life and (as we will examine in the next chapter) life in the town as a whole.

The changes that occurred in Corner Brook were experienced in magnified ways in the surrounding countryside. As already noted, logging became more mechanized, but even bigger changes were underway in fishing communities faced with a complete closure of the ground fishery due to industrialized over-fishing. Some switches to fishing lobster, crab, and other unprotected species were possible, but many outports faced an economic rupture due to resource depletion on a devastating scale (Felt and Sinclair, 1995; Sinclair et al., 1999; Newell and Ommer, 1999). As will be shown in more detail in the next chapter, the demographic consequences were profound. Between the censuses of 1991 and 2001, the population of Newfoundland Census Division 5 (excluding the city of Corner Brook) shrank by 11.1 per cent, that of Census Division 8 (the Baie Verte Peninsula) by 18.7 per cent, and that of Census Division 9 (the Northern Peninsula where Annie Proulx's *Shipping News* is set) by an astonishing 19.7 per cent.

This chapter examines patterns of work in the mill during a decade of restructuring, and then connects these patterns of work with the family life of those concerned. Two main sources of information are used in the discussion, a questionnaire survey conducted through face-to-face interviews in 1993 (n = 138)[2] and a set of more wide-ranging taped interviews recorded in 1994 (n = 29): the latter were a subsample drawn from the 1993 survey.[3] Some more recent information has been gleaned from various sources, notably the *Western Star.* Discussion of work patterns relates, necessarily, to the dates when the survey and interviews were conducted.

THE WORKFORCE

Composition and Recruitment

At the time the interviews were conducted, the mill's workforce was classified as shown in Table 5. Management, which included engineers, foresters, and accountants, formed a relatively small cadre, although a few management functions were located at the corporation's head office in Montreal. There were almost equal numbers of shift and day workers, while almost a quarter of the workforce were casuals or employed on capital projects.[4] In addition, the mill had a sizable group on company pension.

Mill employees are overwhelmingly male; indeed, only one woman was employed as a production worker at the time the interviews were conducted, and she was not hired directly into the production side

Table 5: Mill Employment by Category, May 1993

	Number	% of Non-retired
Management	54	7.3
Shift workers	264	35.7
Day workers	255	34.5
Relief pool and capital projects	167	22.5
Total working	740	100.0
Retirees on company pension	234	

Source: CBPP.

but chose to bump there when her job as an office cleaner was eliminated in 1985. The case of "Mary" draws attention to the predominantly male culture of mill work that only recently has begun to change. Mary found herself in a dilemma after her layoff in 1985: although she had 13 years' seniority and had bumping rights into the mill, neither the union representative nor the mill management felt a woman could cope with the heavy work inside the mill. Since having bumping rights meant that she was not entitled to unemployment pay, she was boxed in. She was "sort of being put off because I was a woman . . . they figured there was nothing I could do." However, with strong support from her family and advice from a former union official who suggested she ask to work in the TMP operation, she opted for the relief position in the pulping mill. After two weeks' training she began to work there, and nine years later she had risen to the position of operator, often acting as senior operator running the entire set of control panels for the mill's TMP operations. She still sensed subtle gender bias from a few employees, but there was progressive acceptance that she was one of the most skilled operators in the pulp mill. Another pulp mill operator remarked:

> We got one woman working in our union, 64, and she was part of our union, she was part of the cleaners out in the main office. She bumped back into [local] 64 and Holy Jesus, "a woman coming in here, she's not coming in here." I'd say it was rough for her. As a matter of fact she kind of bumped me out. She's good. She does her work.

At the time of Mary's retirement in 2002 two more women had been recruited into the mill, and since then several more women have been hired into both production and the trades.

Nearly two-thirds of the workers were recruited directly into a mill department or the workshops, with the remainder obtaining a regular mill position (all employees holding a position at the mill are assigned a number by which they are identified) in two steps – first by working either as a summer student or as a casual in the pool with what is locally called a "5,000 number," and subsequently by applying for a posted regular job. Those entering the mill as shift workers on the production line begin on the lowest rung of the promotion ladder in each department – for example, as relief sixth hand on the paper machines (12 of 138 respondents), block handler in the now closed ground-wood pulping mill (7 of 138), or boom man in the mill yard (4 of 138).[5] Historically, some of the tradesmen entered via apprentice programs run inside the mill by Bowater, but for the past 25 years qualified tradesmen have been recruited after completing their apprenticeship.

Figure 9, showing the dates when mill workers were recruited, reveals a clustering that corresponds with the mill's expansion phases. There was a big intake of new recruits from 1947 to 1950 as paper machine number 7 was installed and matching capacity added in all other departments (26 of 134 respondents), another bunching in 1966 when the mill switched from a six-day to seven-day operation, and a third cluster during the boom years from 1973 to 1980 (48 of 134). Interestingly, in 1989-90, when CBPP had completed the first round of modernization, there was a small wave of recruitment (12 of 134). This pattern of bunched recruitment creates age cohorts that half a lifetime later form retirement waves. For example, a welder who was laid off during part of 1993 was confident that he would soon get a regular number because a cohort of six welders was due to retire during the following five years.

Figure 9: Hiring of Mill Workers, 1941-1992

Sixty per cent of the interviewees found their jobs by applying at the mill office, a substantial minority (over 20 per cent) were tipped off about positions becoming available by friends and relatives working at the mill, while a few moved up from a summer job at the mill. Clearly, in the closely knit fabric of a mill town, having contacts inside the mill has been an advantage in obtaining these coveted jobs. It has to be said that in Corner Brook, a mill job is by far the best job in town: in 1994, even casuals earned over $18 an hour (although they may, at first, have worked only a few hours per week), while the majority of regular mill workers earned between $20 and $24 per hour. In a province with an unemployment rate sometimes exceeding 20 per cent, with most of the fisheries closed, and with many workers in the service sector paid the minimum wage, mill wages have to be considered good.

In the past few years, however, the pattern of recruitment has changed dramatically in response to the institutional changes that accompany lean production and the technological requirements that accompany it. Recruits are now required to have grade 12 (high school graduation) but many have educational qualifications well beyond that. Several have completed part of a university education or have a bachelor's degree. A student at Grenfell College who took a summer job at the mill recalls the events that led to his hiring:

> The word was out that they needed fellows. . . . I went to the superintendent and asked, "Is there any chance of staying on in the fall?" I just mentioned it to him after work one morning. He said sure, and just before that I bought a car and was a little low on money and my father said, "Well, you bought a car . . . but if you still want to go to school . . . I'll pay your way through school." So, I was home one day and the phone rang and it was the mill and they said, "There's work, come in to work," and I said "okay." . . . I was already registered [at college] and everything, and I think if they hadn't phoned me to tell me to come in to work that night I probably would have went to school.

A young paper-machine worker who had completed high school also commented on the high level of qualifications held by his contemporaries: "I've worked with a lot of young workers down at that mill, young fellows, they got degrees and degrees and degrees. They still never got nothing [i.e., a job matching their degree qualifications]." Although a number of the new recruits were registered in social sciences, technical qualifications arc seen to be very useful: "I think to get in the mill now, you have to be really highly qualified, into computers."

Even for internal recruitment within the mill, the jobs posted often require an upgrading of skills and job evaluation. Thus, promotion is no longer based simply on seniority. "They came up with this job evaluation: if you wanted to get a job posted on the board, you had to pass a test and then job-evaluate. . . . It's giving the younger people that chance to progress." In the process, many older workers with less formal education and limited knowledge of computers have been cut out of these promotion competitions.

The young men recruited (they are all male) still have their roots in Corner Brook, although some have gone away for their post-secondary education before returning to the mill for a job. This rise in educational requirements is to be expected given the changing character of work at the mill, which is becoming less physical and involves much more decision-making, including activities such as reading specifications on monitors and interpreting computer output. In short, the character of mill work has undergone a dramatic change from heavy physical work requiring dexterity, stamina, and strength to a workforce invested with much more human capital and advanced technical skills. In the trades, too, there has been a shift to recruiting workers with new skills in instrumentation, programming, working with sophisticated CNC (computerized numerical control) milling machines and high-tech welding equipment, and so on.

Recent changes in recruitment and training are indicators of the new institutional arrangements introduced in the age of lean production. Gone is the hereditary principle that sons of mill employees have first crack at posted vacancies. Sons may still be recruited into the mill workforce, but only after gaining some college education or relevant technical skills, particularly in programming, setting computer specifications, and reading technical output from the computer monitors installed in every department of the mill. Thus the workforce is increasingly required to have a range of technical skills at the point of hiring.

A revealing measure of this shift is found in the kinds of community projects that have been sponsored by the mill owners. Sir Eric Bowater gave the town a park named for his wife, Lady Margaret Bowater, where on a warm summer day citizens can picnic and, if they are really reckless, cool off in the frigid waters of the Corner Brook. Kruger was initially quite cautious about developing community links, and when the new mill owner did it was to sponsor educational programs at Sir Wilfred Grenfell College and West Viking College. Whereas recreation was important in the company town, in the age of lean production technical education has become a greater priority, with institutions of higher education the favoured target for mill-sponsored community programs.

Training

The comparatively high wages paid to the mill's workforce are attributable to a number of factors, particularly to the system of pattern bargaining used to negotiate wages in the pulp and paper industry. Almost identical wage scales are used across the industry within eastern Canada, while a different pattern applies in western Canada. In terms of human capital, these wage levels are related to the high levels of skill acquired during extensive training, without which it is not possible to produce superior newsprint. The training of tradesmen is self-evident. Each has become certified in a trade – millwright, fitter, oiler, electrician, plumber, crane driver, carpenter, etc. – by serving time as an apprentice and passing the relevant trade exams. The tradesmen are all considered to be equally qualified and are paid a standard rate, seniority being governed by date of hiring. However, the wage of production workers is determined by their position on internal promotion ladders. The most elaborate division of labour is found on the paper machines – the promotion ladder rises from relief sixth hand through sixth, fifth, fourth, and third hand to back tender and machine tender. Machine tenders are the mill's highest-paid production workers, and most have 30 years' experience in how to produce large quantities of high-quality sheet from the massive and complex paper machines. Their skills are crucial to the productivity of the mill.

Production workers recruited into the mill in the past decade have normally begun with one week of classroom training, then two weeks of formal training on the job, followed by years of informal on-the-job training interspersed (for some) with short courses to introduce specific new technologies. Workers on promotion ladders begin by learning the job at the lowest rung, for instance by relieving sixth hand on the paper machines when he takes a break. With sickness and vacations, a worker will occasionally have to fill in for the person two positions higher on the ladder, and so begins the learning of the work done by fifth hand. By this process, in due course a worker will be trained to do the tasks performed by workers two or even three positions above his own. Historically, paper workers were also educated into the mysteries of making different qualities of pulp and paper by spending up to a year in technical services working sequentially in the pulp, chemical, and paper laboratories. This taught them the basics of papermaking. They would then spend a few months on the clothing crew to gain a better understanding of how the paper machines worked.

About one-third of the workforce has undergone further training since being hired, selection for this being based mainly on seniority. More recently, however, aptitude tests have been required for many of these training programs. Outside firms that have installed new equipment in the mill such as the paper machines' void detectors, the recycling plant, the bark burner, and new instrumentation and monitors in the wood room and the pulp mill control room have also provided initial training for the operators concerned. When new winders (which were described by one worker as "pretty technical") were fitted to paper machines 1, 2, and 4, those working with them were given three weeks' training in how to operate them. Tradesmen, in particular, are very conscious of the need continually to upgrade their skills. An electrician remarked, "we have to do more technical work than we have ever done"; indeed, he was about to take a basic instrumentation course as CBPP was in the process of amalgamating the categories of electricians and instrument mechanics. He felt that skills "will keep constantly upgrading. They're setting up the training centre down there now and they're putting in lots of equipment and getting it ready."

Layoffs and Bumping

The history of most Canadian paper mills has been punctuated by layoffs of varying duration (some being permanent), triggered either by corporate insolvency related to market conditions and the buildup of inventory, or by the closure of pulp and/or paper machines for decommission, repair, or upgrading. Given the system of seniority built into mill contracts, such layoffs precipitate waves of bumping among production workers that cascade through the plant as employees with greater seniority bump those with less (tradesmen do not normally have bumping clauses in their contracts). Eventually, the most junior workers are pushed out into the casual pool or are laid off. Layoffs impact most on production workers with least seniority, while those with greater seniority may still be bumped into lower-paying positions. A tradesman moved back from a permanent job to the pool by layoffs remarked: "Well, since Kruger took over, they've cut back so much that – being in the pool made a big difference. Moneywise, I got a $5.00 cut in pay, roughly – $4.85 an hour."

The majority of mill workers at Corner Brook have suffered layoffs during their working career, mainly during their first decade of work before seniority is built up. But others, even with 20 years' seniority, have experienced layoffs. These occurred frequently in the years following the Kruger purchase due to the extensive modernization program and workforce downsizing launched in 1984. For example, each of the four operating paper machines was in turn closed down for about six months to be rebuilt. The ground-wood pulp mill was closed permanently in 1984, while the sulphite pulp mill was closed and reopened several times until its final closure in February 1992 as the mill moved entirely to TMP pulping. These layoffs at Corner Brook have mostly affected younger workers with low seniority. Such workers are particularly vulnerable, for typically they have young children and a partner who is not necessarily in the paid labour force, and they may be struggling to pay off a mortgage. One couple recalled a 10-month layoff quite a number of years ago:

> Husband: Yes, there was no money coming in. Hardly any groceries, things like that. It was terrible.
>
> *Wife*: Thirty-six dollars a week unemployment, $85 a month board. [Working] didn't enter my mind. I had enough work home with two babies.
>
> *Husband*: I accepted a part-time job at a pool hall. Well, $15 to $20 a day was a bit of money.
>
> *Wife*: That helped a lot with the groceries.

Layoffs often cause financial hardship. After six weeks, a laid-off worker receives half his severance pay, with the other half paid after six months, although this can be repaid (plus interest due in the interim) to restore an employee's position in the pension fund if he is rehired. If a layoff exceeds two years an employee loses mill seniority and has to begin contributions to the pension fund from scratch. A case in point concerns a tradesman who joined the mill in the late 1970s and, after working five years, was laid off when Bowater closed down paper machine number 7. The layoff lasted over two years so he lost his pension fund, benefits, and mill seniority.[6] Hired on again, he started as a casual and worked up once more to a permanent position, only to be laid off a second time on the completion of the modernization program. In 1990 this process began a third time, and he is now close to the top of the casual list. An almost identical work history was reported by another tradesman who stressed a key consequence: "I'll have to work to 65, there's no way to get out of that, and even then I'm not going to have a full pension. . . . I've tried to get into RRSPs but it's hard when you're only working a certain amount of time."

Another example is that of a new recruit to the mill, "Larry," who was laid off during his first few weeks working at the mill (at the time of a six-week strike) and became caught in a bureaucratic nightmare. Because he was on strike, he was not eligible to draw unemployment pay. But he hadn't worked long enough to join the union, so he wasn't eligible to receive strike pay either. Philosophically, he remarked: "It wasn't so bad because that was right after our wedding, and we had a bit of money from our wedding."

Following the completion of the first phase of the modernization program, work interruptions due to construction and repair became less frequent, so that production workers experienced fewer layoffs, although tradesmen experienced more. In the three years prior to the questionnaire survey, one worker in ten had been laid off for a month or more. Most workers had experienced only one such layoff, but one unfortunate worker had been laid off four times in three years. These layoffs affected the workers lowest on the seniority lists. However, with a trickle of retirements opening up positions, the majority of laid-off workers have eventually returned to work. With fewer interruptions to production, work patterns have become more stable so that in the three years preceding the survey, only 17 of 98 workers were bumped (although two of the 17 were bumped six times and one nine times!).

There was also a fair amount of mobility within the mill, with one in five workers reporting a transfer to another department during the previous three years. During the same period, about the same proportion of workers reported that they had been promoted. Four workers had declined promotions for various reasons, including one worker who found that the heat and humidity at the wet end of a paper machine affected his health. But the main reason workers were reticent about promotion, particularly to the position of foreman, was that it placed them in "near-management" positions that affected their relations with other workers. As one worker who had accepted a position as foreman remarked, you had:

> to deal with the people you were friends with all your life in the mill . . . like they changed towards you. . . . I probably changed a lot because I was responsible. But then the other people figured I was more or less a company man. . . . Once the job was finished I told them at the time, the superintendent, that I wouldn't do it no more because it was just too hectic.

Some workers had also declined promotion to better-paying management positions because they would lose the job security that their contract gave them.

Work Hours

The adoption of the 12-hour shift system in 1988 resulted in an immediate decline in the amount of overtime worked by production line employees; after labouring 12 hours, workers are normally too tired to continue with even longer hours. In any case, overtime has been reduced in all departments as part of a strategy to cut the wage bill. Thus a tradesman remarked: "overtime is a rare thing now." Likewise, a mill cleaner recalled that in six months he had worked overtime only five or six times, and that happened when a paper machine was running badly and there was an excessive accumulation of broke under it. With overtime much reduced, increases in the total number of hours worked have been achieved mainly by calling in more casual workers for longer hours. Only a quarter of mill employees had worked any overtime in the three months preceding the 1993 survey, and more than half of these had reported in for only one or two overtime shifts (see Table 6). The consensus among regular mill employees seems to be that mill earnings permit a good standard of living and that working overtime takes work away from employees in the casual pool, who often have difficulty getting enough hours to make a good wage. However, the reverse has become true for certain categories of tradesmen where, by eliminating jobs and doing most repair and maintenance work during regular day hours, more tradesmen are being called in for overtime during evenings and nights when operating problems occur. Such calls are paid a minimum of four hours of overtime, even when the problem is quickly fixed. Some tradesmen are required to be on call periodically (by rotation) in case of a mill emergency, and this restricts their

Table 6: Overtime Shifts Worked in Three Months Prior to the Survey (n = 98)

Number of Overtime Shifts	Frequency	%
0	72	73
1	9	9
2	6	6
3	3	3
4	1	1
5	1	1
6	4	4
10	1	1
12	1	1

Source: Questionnaire survey, 1993.

movements and family lifestyle: at such times they cannot go out of town.

One group of workers with a very specific work schedule that requires regular overtime is the clothing crew, who replace the fabrics ("clothes") on the paper machines.

> Thursday is usually repair day and it's busy. We go to work seven in the morning and probably work until after midnight some nights, or ten or eleven . . . [but I] have to get in an hour early to get ready for the maintenance, the millwrights to chop up the felt or to blow down the hoods or something like this.

For the clothing crew, Friday is a day off, having often worked 17 hours straight the previous day. With only six men trained for this work (compared to 12 when Kruger took over), a maximum of three of them can leave town at a time, so that a minimum clothing crew of three is on call in town at all times in case of an emergency. The most extreme case of overtime recorded involved a member of the clothing crew who quite a number of years ago voluntarily worked 35 hours straight, although he was entitled to go home after 17 hours. When there is a major repair job on the paper machines, tradesmen first do the mechanical repairs, and the clothing crew come in last to replace the various fabrics and cloths on the machines. Given the urgency of getting the whole production line restarted as quickly as possible and the heavy cost of downtime, there is considerable encouragement to finish the job as quickly as possible (which may mean waiving statutory rights).

Vacations

Corner Brook's mill workers typically take several vacations each year; indeed, in a very special way, it is possible that they take more short vacations than any other employed group in Canada! The immediate explanation of this is the shift system, which gives shift workers four days off after working for four days, but behind this obvious explanation there is a structural interpretation that sees this pattern of short vacations as a form of place attachment and as a way of carrying on local traditions. The varied possibilities for sports and recreation and for socializing in the hinterland of Corner Brook have fostered a custom of spending a few days at cabins beside lakes and visiting relatives living in outports or at old family homes. Thus these four-day breaks often become mini-vacations. Workers may also occasionally tag together four floating holidays (taken instead of worked statutory holidays) to bridge two blocks of days off to create a twelve-day break. In addition, long-serving mill workers are entitled to five weeks of paid vacation a year. Given the attraction of vacations during the brief summer months and the continuous production operations at the mill, workers are allowed a maximum of only two weeks' vacation during the summer, on a rotation system that gives every worker a summer break. It is during this vacation period that most casuals are able to work a full week, and often overtime, too. Workers take their remaining weeks of vacation at other times to create the following vacation pattern: about two-thirds of the day and shift workers take a one- or two-week vacation during the summer months. The majority then take a week or two during the fall hunting season, while a minority take a vacation in the late winter months, mainly because their vacation time has to be used up by the end of May each year. Some use this period for a flight to the Caribbean or Florida.

Flexibility at Work

In a small town like Corner Brook, workers do not face the commuting problems found in Toronto or Montreal, although snowstorms in winter do sometimes make commuting difficult. Nearly all journeys to work at CBPP take less than 20 minutes, including the substantial minority (about one in five) who walk to work. The great majority who drive take their own cars – only a handful share rides with co-workers or are dropped off by their partners. Thus, in contrast to workers in large cities, employees can reliably commute to work and are able to respond quite quickly if they are called in unexpectedly.

Workers reported substantial changes in their patterns of work at the mill during the three years preceding 1993 (see Table 7). The two changes mentioned most frequently can both be viewed as aspects of labour flexibility. Since 1984, labour contracts have permitted the "minor crossing of trades," with management's liberal interpretation of this phrase resulting in a number of grievances – mainly unsuccessful. This has occurred particularly in cognate trades – electricians and instrumentation engineers overlap, as do pipefitters and plumbers, and welders and millwrights. In the pursuit of lean production, management has pushed the envelope permitting the crossing of trades and has encouraged the labour force to acquire polyvalent skills. Tradesmen have reluctantly complied, preferring this to the alternative of being laid off and having the work done by subcontractors. Broadly similar patterns of flexibility and multiple-skilling have also become more common within specific departments so that workers may fill in for others during breaks, when sick or on vacation, or when a bottleneck has developed along the production line.

Table 7: Changes in Patterns of Work, 1991-1993 (n = 133)

	% reporting change
Number of different tasks asked to perform	70
Greater flexibility	59
Work schedules and hours of work	51
Way supervisors assign workers to jobs	44
Contracting out work	38
Who does quality control	34
The way workers are selected for training	27
Who does maintenance	22
Scheduling of vacations	16
Scheduling of overtime	15

Source: Questionnaire survey, 1993.

Health and Safety

Gordon Pinsent's novel, *The Rowdyman*, which is set in Grand Falls in the 1970s, tells the story of Will Cole, a wild young man whose best friend is killed in an industrial accident at the paper mill caused by Will, the "Rowdyman," fooling around. In the film version of *The Rowdyman* the visual nature of the medium reinforced the sense of newsprint mills as being dangerous places, as, indeed, they could be in the days when papermaking was a very physical process, with workers engaged with huge machines, moving equipment, logs, chemicals, and massive paper rolls. Automation and improved safety standards have dramatically changed this.

For the past two decades the Corner Brook Pulp and Paper Company has had a good safety record. Given the industrial setting, with heavy equipment and massive machines, the occasional accident has occurred, but these have been infrequent. Interest here focuses on the long-term health effects of working half a lifetime in a newsprint mill where the prevalence of certain ailments varies by department. Workers who operate machines that vibrate (such as traxcavators in the mill yard and bobcats that remove broke from under the paper machines) and the clothing crew who do maintenance on the paper machines are prone to carpel tunnel syndrome in their wrists,[7] those rolling and lifting heavy paper rolls to back problems, while some retired employees who used to work in the acid tower connected to the former sulphite pulp mill have a tendency to develop respiratory problems later in life. Another health risk faced by older workers in this and many other heavy industries was exposure to asbestos, which was formerly used on the paper machines' dryer felts. National legislation stopped the use of this hazardous substance over 30 years ago, hence its effects (if any) on older paper workers are very hard to gauge. There are, however, some health problems that are widespread among mill workers.

Pulp and paper machines make such a tremendous noise that, without exception, older and retired employees have hearing problems. During interviews with retired workers, communication was frequently made difficult by partial deafness and the reluctance of some to wear hearing aids. Blaring television sets and wives having to shout to communicate with hard-of-hearing husbands were observed on several occasions. There is an insidious consequence to this that few would admit, namely, a degree of isolation and disengagement from family and community affairs among those who have become hearing-impaired.

In recent years employees at the mill have been required to wear earplugs or ear covers, and they are tested periodically for hearing, but in the case of older workers this preventive measure was introduced too late. Besides, the heat in some work areas causes heavy sweating, which makes it difficult to wear earplugs and conform to safety guidelines. Also, tradesmen working in pairs (such as a welder and a pipefitter) have to communicate back and forth, and the wearing of earplugs disrupts such necessary communication. In recent years, soundproof operating booths have been installed near the paper machines and in the new pulp and wood room control centres so that workers are now much better insulated from deafening noise. Coupled with regular testing of hearing, younger mill workers are having much less problem with deafness than the older generation had.

A related health problem results from the heat and humidity around the paper machines, and here again the new machines installed during the modernization program have resulted in big improvements. As one older couple complained:

> *Husband*: We worked in the heat and noise all the time. It wears you down.
>
> *Wife*: He comes out cripple anyway. Everyone comes out cripple and deaf.

But later in the interview he conceded:

> *Husband*: . . . the heat is not near as bad as it used to be. I find it used to wear me down all the time. I would be fine until I got on the job for an hour, but after an hour I could feel it. . . . The heat now is not as bad. . . . That's all behind us, but the damage is done.

Some workers, particularly those working at the wet end of paper machines, find the heat and humidity trigger rheumatism and have had to switch to lower-paying jobs to escape the humidity.[8]

Others point to a more general issue of stress caused not so much by the physical conditions of work as by the tensions of a turbulent work environment, of periodic layoffs or threats thereof, of employer/employee confrontations, of incremental moves to lean production with lower manning levels, all of which put pressure on workers to do more and threaten job security. When probed on the way working in the mill for 30 years had affected his health, one worker responded, "mentally, probably a lot . . . especially in the later years." This may explain the widespread refusal of workers to discuss their work at home. In interview after interview we were told by family members, "he never said much about [work] . . . he'd tell you to leave work at work." Not surprisingly, work at the mill is similar to work in other heavy industrial operations, being both physically and psychologically demanding, but it should not be assumed that it is sheer drudgery. The number of workers, particularly single and widowed workers, who have not taken the attractive early retirement package at 58 years of age, and instead carried on working to 65, is an indication that, nowadays, work is quite tolerable and, for some, rewarding. "You got a lot of the older people that don't want to retire, and they figure that there's no life after the mill. We got a lot of people like that because there's about 30 down there now."

Today, the workforce of the Corner Brook pulp and paper mill appears to be close to the threshold of a major transformation. Most of the workers interviewed were in their forties and fifties and were recruited during the Bowater era. The new patterns of work introduced after 1984 were viewed by most of these older workers as an attack on labour practices built up and institutionalized over several decades of collective bargaining. The majority resisted the changes, only reluctantly agreeing to Kruger's terms of purchase in 1984, by striking in 1988, by grieving numerous infringements of contractual agreements, by political actions, by opposing the loan scheme proposed in 1994 until the threat of layoff became real, and by minor daily acts of resistance. This older cohort of workers has begun to retire.

The mill is now well into recruiting a very different, much younger, and highly skilled workforce. The original workforce was, for the most part, also highly skilled, but these skills were acquired during on-the-job training, by apprenticing in the mill's shops, and by many years of work. Most new employees have acquired a range of skills before being recruited, and due to the process of selection and testing they have different attitudes to work practices and they do not have personal memories of the Bowater era. Further skills are acquired on the job, more so than ever, but they tend to be technical and computer-related skills rather than the more intuitive skills learned by the earlier generation of workers.

This process of retiring older workers and selectively recruiting younger workers is making the mill's workforce quite different from that in place at the time of the Kruger takeover and more like that found in other extensively restructured Canadian mills, such as at Gatineau, Quebec (Rose and Villemaire, 1997). It seems extremely unlikely, however, that CBPP's workforce will decertify in the foreseeable future to become a non-union mill like the new "greenfield" mill at Whitecourt, Alberta (Preston et al., 1997). The town's history and culture, built up over three generations, place great value on protecting local customs and interests. Interviewees understood the mill owner's goals to increase profitability by developing, managing, and marketing the region's resources. But they were also concerned that corporate interests should not push the practice of lean production so far that it destroys local culture and lifestyles.

COMPARING SHIFT WORKERS, DAY WORKERS, AND CASUAL WORKERS

The impact of changing work practices has varied among the three main categories of workers at the mill – shift workers, day workers, and casuals. Note that these categories do not correspond exactly with production and trades workers; a few tradesmen work the shifts, but most work a regular day and are required to be on call at other specified times in case problems occur. Conversely, most production workers work shifts, but a few, such as those clearing the broke under the paper machines and preparing the cores for the finishing department, just work days. Casuals work both in paper production and in the trades. It may take 10 years for a casual production worker to gain a regular mill number, and often longer for tradesmen.

Since 1988, shift workers have worked an eight-day cycle that begins with two 12-hour day shifts from 8 a.m. to 8 p.m., then 24 hours off followed by two night shifts. They come off work at 8 a.m. on the fifth day and have the remainder of that day and the three following days off (this is called a 2-2-4 pattern). A total of four shift crews are employed at the mill, and their schedules are published a year ahead so that shift workers know their work times long in advance. Day workers likewise have a predictable work pattern, 8 a.m. to 4 p.m., but occasionally they are required to work on weekends or evenings.

The structure of casual work at Corner Brook needs explaining before the social impacts of restructuring can be understood. Two groups of workers form a secondary (contingent) workforce and do not hold regular numbers in the mill: 120 are listed as casual, and a varying number (47 in 1995) work on capital projects, installing new machinery and upgrading the fixed capital of the mill.

Unless there is some urgency with an assignment, workers on capital projects work regular hours (typically 8 a.m. to 4 p.m.), and this makes it possible to plan household and family activities. The work pattern of casual workers, in contrast, is much less predictable, especially if they are in the lower part of the casual workers' list (which is ordered by mill seniority), and this affects the ability of a family to plan social activities. Again, this varies somewhat with a worker's skills and training and the number of workers who have the same skills listed above him in the casual list. Thus, if, by chance, there were no plumbers in the top 50 by seniority, then a plumber ranked lower might be called in regularly. But normally, workers in the top half of the list can expect to be called in frequently and much of the year will get 40 hours of work per week. This is especially true between May and November, when regular employees take vacations and casuals are assigned to fill regular work slots; during the rest of the year casuals are more likely to be on call, waiting for the phone to summon them to work at short notice, more often for a night shift than a day shift. A casual may be called in to work for 8 or 12 hours, and will only know at the time of the call from the mill. For this reason, casuals were less enthusiastic about the 12-hour shift system than were regular shift workers. One remarked: "If I was permanently on a 12-hour shift I think I wouldn't have any problem with it. But I'm not so I find the 12-hour shifts harder for me." His typical workweek might include any combination of 8- and 12-hour shifts, day or night. Thus he might work an 8-hour day shift on Monday, sleep that night, sit up all day Tuesday waiting to be called in, then at suppertime receive a call to report in at 8 p.m. for a 12-hour night shift.

There are three reasons for this work pattern for casuals. First, by the law of averages there are always a number of workers sick, with some on long-term disability due to various ailments and some with flu and similar short-term illnesses. Second, workers with five years' experience are entitled to five weeks of holiday a year, plus five floaters (i.e., floating holidays that can be taken when they choose) in lieu of public holidays when the mill continues to operate; these vacations, as noted earlier, are taken mostly in summer and during the fall hunting season. And third, Kruger has cut the core workforce to a level where many departments need a casual worker much of the time to operate. Production workers on the casual list who are called in to work shifts get more than their fair share of night shifts and Saturday shifts as there is a greater likelihood of a regular employee missing these.

Although the capital project crews usually work regular shifts, they are hired for short periods and risk being laid off or moved back to the casual list at short notice. In 18 years at the mill, "Jim" has worked more time as a casual than in his trade. More than once he has been laid off, received half his severance pay after six weeks, and then been called back and had to repay his pension into the fund so that he can retire on full pension. He has enough seniority that he does get sufficient hours of work, but not knowing when those hours will come can be difficult:

> *Jim*: I'm getting 40 hours a week, but I'm on call seven days a week, 24 hours a day . . . I can't plan anything, which I was never used to because before, when I was on capital projects, I was getting a 40-hour week and weekends off.
>
> *Interviewer*: What's been the effect on your family of these layoffs periodically?
>
> *Jim*: My wife is a worrier; she worries a lot, and it bothers her a lot. And I'm sitting by the phone. I had to get a phone put in where the number comes up on it. If I go out, I got to come home and check the phone calls and see who was calling, or I got to phone in [the mill] and say I'm going to be gone for an hour or so down to the store if there is any work.
>
> *Interviewer*: If you'd planned to go to your cabin or fishing with your son, did you cancel if you got called in?
>
> *Jim*: Usually if I planned a trip to go to the cabin [with my son] and they phoned in looking for me I just wouldn't answer the phone. It would break his heart if we were going to the cabin. He enjoys fishing.
>
> *Interviewer*: How long do you think it will be before you get a regular number again?
>
> *Jim*: I'd say I'd probably be retired before I get back to the regular shops. . . . If I get a chance to get a job in another department at different work, I'd take it. It's a lot less money, but I wants a steady job.

This group of casuals is often asked to work overtime, and they rarely refuse since this is not viewed as a positive sign by the employer. Further down the casual list are workers who are called in less frequently and who may spend weeks on unemployment insurance (UI) because there is no work for them at the mill. At other times they may get only one or two shifts a week and their unemployment benefits are graduated accordingly. Workers low on the casual list get called in most frequently during the summer vacation season, the fall hunting season, and around Christmas when many regular workers are away or sick. They are most likely to be called in at nights or on the weekend. For example, one casual fairly low on the seniority list stated:

> Winter time is slack, but the summer time – it usually picks up around May when the holidays start. Then it goes on through. I get good weeks then. Sometimes during the winter you pick up a week, a good week, and then you might come back with 20 hours or 8 hours or probably 12 hours. That's it for the week . . . if they phone and you don't come in to go to work, if it's continuous that you keep turning down work . . . they'll send your name to the UIC office and you'll lose your UIC.

In practice this worker had quite a good year in 1992 despite his low seniority, and he drew only two unemployment cheques (four weeks) for the whole year. Due to the specificity of skills, another tradesman, although slightly higher on the seniority list, worked fewer hours that year:

> I went a month with nothing [this winter], and then I might get a week's work and then I'd go two. . . . Any money I make I have to report to UIC. . . . Even right now I'm on UIC. I just send in my cards.

The large casual pool at Corner Brook may seem to be anomalous – several other newsprint mills, such as the ANC mill at Whitecourt in Alberta, have no casuals; instead, regular employees work a lot of overtime. A number of factors play a role in the presence of a secondary labour force at Corner Brook. First, as the mill has shed jobs since 1984, the pool has served as a safety net for workers made redundant. Second, the mill has an aging workforce, many of whom are not anxious to work overtime (in contrast to the younger workforce at Whitecourt). Third, many workers have strong place attachments that involve family, fishing, and hunting in the environs of Corner Brook. In addition, the cost of living (especially housing) in Corner Brook is quite low so a regular employee can enjoy a satisfactory lifestyle without overtime pay, and not working overtime spreads work around in an economy short of good-paying jobs. And finally, the casual pool embodies a substantial investment in human capital possessing a great variety of skills, both in trades and in newsprint production. It is almost certainly in CBPP's best interest to retain this reserve of human capital in the casual pool: to lay off and retrain such a skilled labour force would cost a great deal.

There is a big difference in the age of casual, day, and shift workers: over 80 per cent of the day workers were born before 1950 and will come up for retirement in the next 10 years; casuals are the youngest, with 70 per cent born since 1950; in between are the shift workers, with a number born before 1939 and a bigger cluster in the 1950s, which makes them, on average, younger than the day workers but with a greater age spread. These age distributions are reflected in the average years of mill seniority of workers in the three categories, shown in Table 8.

Table 8: Years of Mill Seniority by Employment Status

	Employment Status		
	Day	Shift	Casual
Mean years of seniority	22.6	19.7	11.4
Standard deviation	7.4	9.8	6.9

Source: Questionnaire survey, 1993.

Day and shift workers have fairly similar levels of overall mill seniority, both averaging close to 20 years, but there is a greater spread in the case of shift workers. Casual workers have about half the seniority of day workers, but it is striking that they average over 11 years of seniority: mill jobs are sufficiently coveted that workers are prepared to accept the inconveniences of casual work for many years in order to obtain a regular work number. It follows that being hired on to the mill's workforce before or after 1975 is a useful demarcation point among these three categories of workers: at the time of the survey, 86 per cent of day workers were hired at the mill before 1976, 78 per cent of casuals were hired in 1975 or after, while the shift workers split almost 50-50 around this date. Since the hiring of students to work at the mill peaked during the 1970s and 1980s, it is no surprise that far more casuals (almost one-third) began working at the mill as summer students, whereas less than 15 per cent of day and shift workers (who are generally older) entered by the summer student route.

It has already been suggested that family ties are important to finding work at the mill, but this generalization needs refining because it does not apply equally to all three categories. Shift workers and casuals are similar in that two-thirds of both groups have relatives working in the mill. Day workers are the exception, having much weaker family ties for the simple reason that tradesmen dominate this category (86 per cent of day workers hold trade certificates) and they were recruited over a much larger area, including some from Scotland. Not surprisingly, the small town of Corner Brook did not have a pool of qualified tradesmen large enough for the mill's recruitment needs.

The amount of on-the-job training received by the three categories of mill workers also varies substantially. Tradesmen receive very little training on the job because it is assumed that they hold a trade ticket and are fully qualified at point of recruitment, and they are paid accordingly. In contrast, most of the shift and casual workers are recruited without training for specific mill jobs and therefore receive training after being hired. Rather different is the pattern of further training, where shift workers receive far more than the other two categories of workers. As the mill began to implement lean production methods and installed labour-saving equipment, so it became essential to provide shift workers with additional training in how to operate the new technologies, including void detectors, the upgraded Measurex machines, the new TMP pulping equipment, computer monitors, and many other items.

Patterns of bumping vary among the three categories, with day workers least affected for the evident reason that most are tradesmen and there are no bumping clauses in the contracts negotiated by their unions. Only 5 per cent of day workers had been bumped in the preceding three years, compared to 20 per cent of shift workers and 25 per cent of casuals. Not only were casuals most affected by bumping – some having been bumped out of regular jobs into the pool – but they also worked the most overtime because of their job insecurity. Forty-two per cent of casuals had worked one or more overtime shifts in the preceding three months, compared to 19 per cent of day workers and just 14 per cent of shift workers.

Average family income (including the income of wives and other working family members) varies substantially among these three categories of workers. In Table 9, workers are divided into three annual income brackets – below $40,000, from $40,000 to $60,000, and above $60,000. The average income of casual workers is lowest, partly because many do not get 40 hours of mill work a week – hence their willingness to work whatever overtime is available – but also because quite a number have young families and their wives have chosen to stay home or work part-time. Shift workers have the highest average income, with nearly half the families having a gross income exceeding $60,000. It is of interest, however, that 30 per cent of the casual workers' gross family incomes exceed $60,000, confirming the point that in the local context even a casual worker's family may have a comfortable income.

Levels of stress vary quite markedly among the three categories of mill workers. Permanent day workers have the least stress – their

Table 9: Family Income of Day, Shift, and Casual Workers (percentages)

	Day	Shift	Casual
Less than $40,000	4.8	2.9	27.5
$40,000 - $60,000	57.1	48.6	42.5
More than $60,000	38.1	48.6	30.0
Signif. = .0.15			

Source: Questionnaire survey, 1993.

work hours are regular, and most weekends are free. Shift workers have to endure two long night shifts, but they are then rewarded by four days off in which to relax. Casuals have to absorb the most stress over work hours. They may be called in for 8 or 12 hours, they are usually summoned at short notice, and they may have trouble getting their sleep patterns back to normal before being called in again. This stress may affect a spouse as much as a worker. A wife who is trying to arrange meals, children's sports activities, and other social activities finds it disruptive if her husband is called at short notice to work a 12-hour shift. It is difficult for a husband who may not know until close to suppertime whether he is going to work all night; given the possibility of such a sleepless night, many take an afternoon nap in case of that eventuality. For these casual workers, regular work is a blessed relief:

> When I'm not working and in the wintertime, my nerves are worse than when I'm working. When I'm working I feel perfect. When I'm not working I feel the difference. I guess that's natural.

Casuals suffer from another sort of stress that generally differentiates them from the permanent workers. When layoff notices are served, it is mainly to those lowest on the totem pole, which means the casuals and employees on capital projects. The wife of a casual remarked: "He's gotten so many [layoff notices] over the four years we've been married that I just ignore them. I say, 'Well, the worst thing they can do is take my house.' I really don't worry about it any more because he's gotten so many." Her husband added that he had received close to 10 layoff notices in the previous four years.

Despite the stress that goes with mill work, most workers were prepared to accept it because the job was well-paying and there are few alternative jobs in town. A younger worker whose father worked in the mill for over 40 years was unequivocal about the attractiveness of a mill job: "Well around here, in Corner Brook, it was, if a fellow got a job in the mill, he could make a good living . . . it was a good place to make a lot of money." This point was echoed by many interviewees. A tradesman who has experienced a succession of layoffs was asked why he returned to work as a casual at the mill, even though he could get a regular job in construction outside the mill. He replied: "Because of the money. The money was big money."

FAMILY LIFE

Quite clearly, the patterns of work described above have had a profound impact on family life in Corner Brook. Shift workers alternate day and night work, but according to a standard formula that includes a four-day break. Day workers have the most regular family life, although most of them are called in occasionally to work nights or weekends. It is the erratic work hours of casual workers that have the biggest impact on family life. In families where restructuring has resulted in changes in a mill employee's work, their partners have almost always had to adapt their work patterns, both in the labour force and at home, to accommodate these changes. In turn, the mill worker has also had to make changes to his activities at home so that there is a dynamic to the changes – a mutuality as both partners and often other close members of the family circle make adaptations. Global restructuring has thus had a substantial impact on gender relations within the household. Local practices and local ideologies, rooted in the traditions of sharing, of coping, and of helping neighbours and family in Newfoundland's many isolated fishing communities, have made it easier for families to accept these kinds of adjustment, and therefore for CBPP to introduce these changes in work patterns. The flexibility of women in responding to changing work patterns helps to account for the resilience of families and the community.

Slightly under half of the workers employed at the Corner Brook pulp and paper mill, including those working in the woodyard and wood room, the pulp mill, on the four paper machines, and (since October 1994) in the outward warehouse, are shift workers. As Preston et al. (2000) stress, it is nearly always women – the shift workers' partners – who have to adapt and make adjustments, although the lifestyles of children are also often affected. For example, the sleep that night-shift workers need during the day affects the activities of the whole family. Since many mill workers and their wives are the children and grandchildren of mill workers, this rhythm has permeated local lifestyles for a long time. Asked of her recollections of her father's work at the mill, one woman remembers:

> I could picture him working hard. He worked the shifts, the day shift, the 4 to 12, and the 12 to 8. There were three shifts at the time. I remember him sleeping a lot, like in the daytime.

Prior to 1988 shift workers followed a five-day cycle of eight-hour shifts – one week 8 a.m. to 4 p.m., the next week 4 p.m. to midnight, and finally the "graveyard" shift, midnight to 8 a.m. Comparable to the shifts Gibson (1992) found in some of Queensland's coal-mining communities, these relentless shifts were stressful and disrupted family life. Discussions on changing to a cycle of 12-hour shifts began in 1986, following favourable reports on their introduction at Abitibi-Price's paper mills in Stephenville and Grand Falls, and at other newsprint mills in eastern Canada. Discussions, marked by some opposition from older employees, followed, and it was not until the adoption of the 1988 contract that the 12-hour shift system was formally introduced.[9]

This new system has had a dramatic impact on the domestic life of shift workers and, with the exception of a few elderly workers who found the 12 hours exhausting, has received a very favourable response. Typical is the remark:

> That's something we should have had 30 years ago. With this 12-hour shift you have a lot more family life, a lot more free time to yourself. It's 100 per cent better. Five night shifts, they were murder, but now you only got to do two.

A casual working fairly regular shifts enthusiastically summed it up as "excellent, excellent," although many shift workers admitted to being "wiped out" the day following the last night shift.

The workers with the most disrupted family life are the casuals. Casuals ranked low on the list spend much of their days beside the phone "on call," waiting to be summoned to work at short notice – which is most likely to be for a night shift or Fridays and Saturdays.[10] Thus at suppertime, a casual may be called in to work from 8 p.m. to 8 a.m. Some choose to rest up during the day in anticipation of such a call and may use earplugs when sleeping to avoid being disturbed by daytime noises. But there is no predicting when the phone will ring. One casual recalls:

> The crew-scheduler . . . is overworked, he's got a busy job, he doesn't take into account what hours you're working. You could be working one night and you sleep all day and he'll call you to come in the next morning. When you think about it, you just worked all night, slept all day, and you're ready to go to work again but he doesn't want you to come to work that night, he wants you to come to work the next morning. So how the hell are you going to sleep that night if you just finished sleeping during the day.

Another casual finds the unpredictability of the phone calls very annoying:

> What kills me is that you phone say eight or nine in the morning and ask if there's any work and they'll say "No, there's nothing on the go," and then you turn 'round and phone one-thirty or two and "No, there's nothing on the go." And then sometimes as much as quarter to four, "I want you in the mill now for four." Bang, you got everything planned, like you're going to have a barbecue, and bang, you got to go to work.

The effects of this on family life are clear:

> You can't make plans. You're always by that phone. Just say three of us are going out for supper tonight. Say the mill called – you got to cancel out, grab your basket, and go to work. You got no social life, none at all.

This is particularly the case for wives and families with young children. Plans to visit relatives, hold a family meal, or attend a sports event may be altered at short notice by a call to work, nearly always leaving the worker's wife the choice of taking over organizing the event or cancelling it. Thus a worker bumped back into the casual pool found he could not visit the family cottage "as much as I would have liked . . . because I didn't know when I was working from week to week and month to month." One casual worker's story of an interrupted vacation reveals even greater frustration.

> I phoned down [to the mill] and asked, "Is there any work on the go?" They said "No." I said, "What about next week?" He said, "No; there's no boats going to be in until next Friday." I said, "Okay, I'm going away for a couple of days – I'll be back by at least Wednesday. The boat's not coming in until [Friday], so it's no problem." So . . . we stayed the night at my sister's, 40 miles outside of Gander. . . . The telephone rang: [and the mill] told me, "Come back, there's all kinds of work." I came back, and I phoned in: "No boy, no work," and I phoned him the next day and no work. And then Friday and Saturday I got 10 hours . . . I got 10 hours work for the whole week.

Notwithstanding their unpredictable hours of work, casuals are only paid overtime if they work a Sunday shift, or more than four 12-hour shifts in one week, or some similar combination of 8- and 12-hour shifts.[11]

Despite the greater amount of work available during summer, one casual insisted that "I'm still going to take vacations . . . yes, definitely, because you want your life to be as normal as possible . . . when you're on unemployment you're in prison." But another casual did exactly the opposite, stating that "I've never ever enjoyed a vacation, because I can't," the reason being that he felt he had to take what hours he could in summer when he was most likely to be called in. However, he was able to take fairly frequent long weekends of two to three days at the family cabin: fortunately, his wife's vacations were quite flexible so that she could take a break at short notice to match his days off.

One shift worker's wife found that the old eight-hour shift system cut her off from the community: "I had to stay home and cook and wash. There wasn't much social life for a long period of time. With your husband working night shifts and evenings, it don't give you much time to go out or do anything in the community." The 12-hour shift allows workers and their families to plan a more active social life.

Child Care

There are many older workers employed at the Corner Brook Pulp and Paper mill, so that a relatively small percentage of mill workers (39 per cent) have children under the age of 12 at home (Table 10).

Table 10: Percentage of Families with Children under 12 Years of Age

	Day		Shift		Casual	
	Number	%	Number	%	Number	%
No children	16	69.6	19	55.9	24	58.5
1 child	4	17.4	8	23.5	12	29.3
2 or more children	3	13.0	7	20.6	5	12.2
Totals	23	100	34	100	41	100

Households in Corner Brook with young children rely on their extended families for child care to a much greater extent than families in larger North American cities. The presence in 1994 of only two registered daycare centres serving a population of about 25,000 persons exemplifies this. In many cases grandparents or other close relatives looked after children while their parents were working, but there was also evidence of some parents organizing their work lives sequentially, along the lines described by Hanson and Pratt (1995), so that each parent, in turn, would care for the children while the other partner was at work. A mother remarked:

> Most of my shifts I fixed it so that I would work 4 p.m. to midnight and "Fred" would be home in the evenings. I would probably only have to drop [the children] off at my mom's for probably an hour or so, and Fred would pick them up and look after the children in the evenings. They weren't out with babysitters much . . .
>
> I never had any problem because we always had a babysitter. Fred's sister, they would come in, or my mom, so it was never [a problem].

A couple who both worked full-time made similar arrangements. When asked who cared for the children, the response was:

> *Pamela*: His mother lived just down the street.
>
> *Ken*: We had a lot of help that way.
>
> *Pamela*: With our daughter when she was, well she was the first born, his mother took care of her when we'd work, so I didn't have any worries. I had his mother when [our daughter] was small and a good friend of mine took care of [our son] when he was small. They do have daycare here, but I didn't take the kids to daycare. I prefer my own arrangements . . . [our daughter] went to her grandmother's house after school, and then when she started down there [school] at the bottom of the street, they just went to their grandmother's until we got home.

When her husband was working night shifts "he babysat, he was Mr. Mum. We shared." Several other working couples stated that their mothers had been a great help in caring for children.

Another couple, he a tradesman mostly working days, she a nurse sharing a full-time position at the Humber Memorial Hospital and often working nights, used both family and daycare: "when [their son] was younger we used daycare, but a lot of times my wife's mother – fortunately she's here." Another couple in a very similar situation, both with quite variable work hours, felt that it was an imposition to ask his mother: "like his mother is over 60 and she raised a lot of children . . . she's had enough of it . . . I don't rely on her too much because it's not fair to her." Most of the time this couple was able to dovetail their hours of work, but when this was not possible, they were lucky to find a person who was willing to be very flexible about when she minded their child.

The solution for one working couple with seven children was to take in a teenage girl from a fishing outport. She became part foster child, part home-help, and part nanny, and when she had her own child, that child was accepted as part of the family. Central to this couple's coping strategy was the need to keep their jobs, especially the well-paying mill job, so that the extended family – which reached 11 at its peak – could enjoy a satisfactory lifestyle.

For casuals employed in the pool and workers on capital projects (and therefore liable to layoff), child care can be a particular problem, not least because many of their wives work to balance the uncertainty of their husband's work. One working couple who did not have close family members living in town had employed a child-minder who came to babysit several hours per week. When the husband was laid off for an indeterminate period, they faced a dilemma since he was now available to mind the children and, moreover, with the loss of income they would have preferred to cut the expense; but if they cancelled their babysitter's job, she would probably not be available if he was rehired. In practice he was called back after 11 weeks off and the problem was solved.

Another working couple, he a casual with unpredictable hours, placed their child in a local daycare centre. His wife normally dropped the child off at the centre early, before she started work, by special arrangement with the operator. They chose this solution partly because her steady job was crucial to the stability of family income, partly because his hours at the mill were so irregular (if he was working an 8 a.m.-4 p.m. shift, he had already left for work, and if he had worked a night shift, he was trying to sleep).

The special needs of one casual's family, coupled with his unpredictable work hours, led a mother to postpone her further education at West Viking College. Initially they had employed a full-time babysitter during the day while she attended courses, but after their young child developed a long-term illness that needed constant monitoring, she gave up her course and stayed home: his work hours as a casual were too erratic, and she couldn't "depend on him being home some days to care for [the child] . . . and there was nobody that was around willing just to be there to be on call when he is on call, and babysit just when he had to go to work." For this family, unpredictable mill hours combined with their child's health problems led a wife to postpone indefinitely a planned career.

Housework

The labour force participation rates in 1996 for men and for women living in Corner Brook, in Newfoundland as a whole, and in Canada are listed in Table 11. The Corner Brook figures deviate very little from the Newfoundland averages, except that the female participation rate is slightly higher, but when compared to Canada as a whole both the men's and the women's participation rates are substantially lower. The main reason for this (as will be discussed further in Chapter 6) is the unusual age distribution of Corner Brook, with many retirees now living in town, whereas large numbers of younger persons ages 15-30 have left town to seek work elsewhere. The main issue to be examined is: who does the various domestic tasks? It might be expected a priori that women do a disproportionate amount of work in the home on the grounds that, first, Corner Brook resembles a stereotypical resource frontier town where paid work and home work are highly gendered, and second, given the high proportion of older residents, the allocation of these tasks may be along the lines operating in years gone by.

Table 11: Labour Force Participation Rates, Corner Brook, Newfoundland, and Canada, 1996

	Corner Brook	Newfoundland	Canada
Male	63.8%	63.0%	72.7%
Female	51.3%	49.7%	58.6%

Source: Statistics Canada, *Census of Canada,* 1996.

In practice, however, the division of housework between mill employees and their spouses differs little from that found in comparable situations (Preston et al., 2000: Table 3). In many interviews, and without obvious reticence, both male and female interviewees presented evidence of men making substantial contributions to work at home and often sharing tasks, although the traditional divisions between men doing outside work and mechanical tasks and women doing inside jobs were in evidence.

Table 12 indicates who performs various domestic tasks, with four possible variations listed: the spouse of the mill worker, the mill worker, both of them, and others (most frequently children living at home). A number of jobs, including mowing the lawn, shovelling snow, car repairs, and putting out the garbage, are generally done by the mill worker. His wife most commonly does the grocery shop-

Table 12: Household Division of Homework (numbers, excluding retirees)

	Spouse	Mill Worker	Both	Other
Gardening	17	18	19	2
Mowing the lawn	1	39	13	15
Shovelling snow	1	36	16	19
Minor car repairs/maintenance	1	53	0	13
Wash car	6	21	18	24
Grocery shopping	33	5	30	3
Make the shopping list	40	4	15	3
Laundry	41	2	7	12
Vacuuming	30	4	19	20
Put out garbage	3	36	21	11
Wash dishes/load dishwasher	17	3	31	22
Can/freeze producer	16	5	17	1
Can/freeze fish or game	9	18	19	3
Prepare the main meal				
– when spouse working	6	19	11	4
– when mill worker working	22	0	2	6
– when both working	11	1	16	6
– when neither working	28	3	35	5

Source: Questionnaire survey, 1993.

ping, prepares the shopping list, does the laundry and vacuuming, and prepares the main meal when her partner is working. But quite a number of tasks – gardening, washing the car, washing dishes, canning and freezing produce, fish, and game, and preparing the main meal when the spouse is working or when neither are at work – are shared fairly equally. Older children are most commonly found mowing lawns, shovelling snow, vacuuming, and washing dishes. Quite a number of families use the local car wash.

This sharing of home work was borne out in a number of interviews. For instance, one husband stated in a matter-of-fact way:

> Oh yes, I washes and hangs out the clothes – I always did . . . we shares [cooking] between us, and if two of us are off on Sundays, I cooks dinner . . . when the family all comes home, they all wants me to cook.

The reasons for this and similar instances of blurring the classic gender divisions in Corner Brook are complex. Its roots probably lie deep in Newfoundland's culture of coping on the margins. Historically, there were broad gender divisions of labour in the outports – men fished, hunted, and worked in the woods, while women tended gardens, cleaned fish, did housework, and raised children, but there were too many emergencies and tragedies for these gender divisions ever to be very rigid. As the saying goes, "the sea is made of mothers' tears." In the hard life of the outport, survival required considerable stoicism and everyone pitched in when needed.[12] But equally, the nature of contemporary work in Corner Brook must be taken into account. More than half the adult women in Corner Brook have paid work, with hours that do not correspond with those of their mill-working husbands. Both partners are therefore obliged to adapt their lifestyle and contribute to domestic work – for instance, by preparing their own meals, especially if they are shift and casual workers.

Table 13: Percentage of Itemized Homework Tasks Performed by Household Members

	Spouse	Mill Worker	Both	Other	Total
Day	37.3	22.7	22.3	17.7	100
Shift	28.6	24.2	31.8	15.4	100
Casual	26.8	28.4	24.5	15.3	100
Retired	33.7	30.3	23.3	12.7	100

Source: Questionnaire survey, 1993.

One working couple agreed that they share housework very equally: when it comes to preparing the main meal each day, they shared the task "fifty-fifty." Another working couple did the housework together during the evenings: "I was used to getting housework done at night and Ken was helping me." Another couple practised a clearer division of housework, with the husband doing "a nice bit of housework – she'll probably say not enough . . . I do cook a bit but not a lot," but he did more of the vacuuming and cleaning up. Another casual whose wife had a full-time job was quite emphatic about his contribution to housework, which included baking bread and doing the laundry. Indeed, when he was not called in to the mill he did the majority of the housework.

Some husband's skills were more limited – as one noted, he could fry up a quick dinner but "not a glamorous meal." But he made up for this by doing more of the child care and splitting the laundry duties with his wife.

There were also significant differences in the division of housework among day workers, shift workers, and casuals (Table 13). Spouses did the greatest proportion of this work in the households of day workers, their husbands did least, and they shared these jobs less. There is no obvious explanation for this, except that day workers are older, on average, than the other workers, and fewer of their wives have jobs. As Hochschild (1989) reports, younger men and women have less traditional attitudes to sharing work at home. Shift workers share home work most, presumably because there are times when he is home for several days off work, followed by four days when he spends most of his waking hours at work. Casuals do the most home work and also share a lot. This is attributed to their being obliged to stay home when on call, and because many of their spouses have jobs.

House Building and Maintenance

In much of Newfoundland, families owning smallholdings have created building plots for younger family members by severing small parcels that are sold to them for a nominal amount. This is a rarer pattern in Corner Brook where few smallholdings remain, but it does occur in the surrounding hinterland (Bates, 1997). More generally, this forms part of a pattern of self-reliance and community reliance in establishing a family home that long predates the do-it-yourself economy described by Gershuny and Miles (1983). Despite their relatively well-paying jobs, many mill workers have, with help from family and friends, built or modified their own homes following long-established local practices. For generations, outport fishermen have had the right to cut timber growing within three miles of the shore for domestic purposes, including buildings, furniture, docks, boats, and firewood (Gray, 1981). In the countryside, it is still quite common to see a circular saw attached to a gas engine operated by a group of three or four men sawing seasoned logs to make studs and planks for construction. In such a rural society, houses have a use value rather than a commodity value. Even in Corner Brook, house prices remained very low by metropolitan standards until the 1960s. In the 1970s the recruitment to Corner Brook of college professors and provincial government employees brought into town groups of people who viewed property both as a home and as an investment.[13] Since then house prices have risen somewhat closer to those found in other Canadian towns of the same size.

Such customary ways of building and repairing homes are changing, but the tradition of self-help remains. As Table 14 shows, mill workers do a great deal of home repair and maintenance themselves so that, despite the city's connection to the global economy, local customs and lifestyles live on at home. Approximately half of the interviewees have done their own roof repairs, wiring, and major plumbing; even more have done painting and decorating. A typical interview response came from a carpenter, who remarked of his house: "I built it myself, pretty well . . . well the carpentry – I had a contractor for the plumbing and a contractor for the electrical, but the carpentry part I done it." Others have purchased older houses and remodelled them. Many tradesmen at the mill have acquired a broad range of practical skills that are put to good use at home. One pipefitter remarked:

> We bought this place and I've been tearing it up and fixing it up ever since. . . . I added an upper storey, two bedrooms upstairs and extended that wall out. We tore all that out. I'm doing all my own wiring, all my own carpenter work, and plastering and painting.

Another day worker told a similar story of building his family's home:

> I built it. Well, I had a carpenter with me. The carpenter came in and framed it all up. At that time I got someone, and we took all the plaster and we gyprocked it, the two of us. When I got back, unfortunately, I had to turn around and re-plaster it myself. What you see now, everything that's done in this house, I'm after doing myself or her uncle. The kitchen cabinets are another thing. Plumbing was done by the father-in law because he was a plumber, my brother-in-law was an electrician so he came down. Ever since that I've been renovating. I hung all the doors and put all the door boxes on – I did all that. Downstairs I completed it all myself – showers,

> the wiring – but my brother-in-law came along and said it was perfect there, no problem there, and hooked it up to the box. I didn't know how to hook it up to the box.

Table 14: Home Repairs and Maintenance Since Moving into Present Home

Activity	Yes	No	Performed by Self	With Help	Paid
Minor repairs	127	6	117	4	6
Interior painting	125	8	105	17	3
Exterior painting	94	38	83	9	32
Major plumbing	73	60	51	14	8
Wiring	61	72	24	12	25
Roof replacement/repair	63	70	21	10	32
Extension to house	18	115	7	4	7

Source: Questionnaire survey, 1993.

There is also a degree of sharing among tradesmen, amounting to a form of reciprocity that is also rooted in local culture. A carpenter, plumber, or electrician at the mill may help with the building or modernization of a friend's home, and in due course the favour may be returned. We interviewed one retired couple who occupied quite a large house built by their sons, each of whom had particular skills. Such sharing of work and pooling of skills also extends to work on family cabins and fixing up old family homes located in outports. To the extent that these activities sustain locally embedded values and practices, they can be seen as a shrewd form of resistance to globalization. Elsewhere in Canada it is more common for a worker to purchase such services on the market, sometimes paying for them by working overtime.

Self-provisioning

Few Canadian industrial communities provide as much of their families' needs, or do as much of the construction and repair to family homes, as do the workers of Newfoundland. Self-provisioning and self-help are deeply ingrained in Newfoundland culture and continue to be widely practised by mill employees despite their relatively high incomes. It is quite common for interviewees to provide their family's entire meat requirements by hunting moose, caribou, and bear, in season, and small game at all seasons. Fishing, in the sea or rivers in summer, and on frozen trout ponds in winter, is equally common.

It is difficult to underestimate the significance of moose hunting in Newfoundland. Due to some inexplicable lapse in species diffusion, the moose is not indigenous to Newfoundland, but was introduced to the island by George Tipple in 1904. Ideally suited to the island's forests, the animal has since multiplied manyfold. Its niche is different from the island's other large ungulate – the indigenous caribou – which inhabits the barren uplands.[14] A bull moose weighs up to 600 kilograms, and a cow somewhat less, and roughly half that weight is edible meat. Since licences are issued to a hunter and his partner, and the meat is generally split 50-50, this implies about 250-300 pounds of meat per hunter, which is typically a one-year supply of meat for his own family and one or two close relatives. Frozen or cooked and bottled, moose is the main source of meat in many families and represents a monetary saving of $600 to $1,000 annually. The hunt is also of great cultural significance, as shown by the commonly heard challenge, "You've got to get your moose, boy." Mill workers submit their applications early to the annual hunting licence lottery and often arrange a block of vacation towards the end of the hunting season. If, by that date, they have not shot their moose during weekend hunting, then there is a greater chance of snow falling by the time of their vacation, making it much easier to spot and shoot a moose. In instances where a hunter has not shot his moose by the last few days of the season, anxiety-induced stress may necessitate sick leave while the symptoms are relieved by intensive hunting in the woods. Casuals then have to fill the hunter's place at work.

A smaller number of mill workers cut their own firewood. When the mill's contractors cut a hillside for pulp logs, they leave behind birch, which is unsuitable for pulping but has a high calorific value for heating. Workers can obtain permits from the company to cut this wood. One interviewee cuts seven cords of birch each winter for his wood furnace, which also heats his hot water. Wood is also cut for the construction of cabins, decks, and siding.

It bears repeating that there are alternatives to self-help and self-provisioning, namely, purchasing the required goods and services on the open market. A mill worker's income makes this possible, especially if some overtime is worked. In fact, Preston et al. (1997) found that mill workers at Whitecourt, Alberta, where there are no casual workers, work a great deal of overtime, spending some of the extra income on high-end consumer goods. But at Corner Brook this is less the case. Patterns of work are adapted to a lifestyle that connects with the region and its traditions. Shift workers have frequent opportunities to take short breaks out of town, day workers can do the same most weekends, while vacations taken fishing during summer and hunting during spring or fall permit workers to spend sustained periods in Newfoundland's hinterland. The 12-hour shift system at Corner Brook has been accepted with enthusiasm by most shift workers in part because it offers them the maximum opportunity to leave town and engage in hunting and fishing and other country activities. Likewise, the low interest in working overtime is related to the desire to set time aside for self-provisioning.

CONCLUSION

Restructuring of older plants has occurred in numerous communities across Canada during the past 25 years as their economies have been progressively exposed to continental and global competition. In most instances, restructuring has required greater flexibility of workers in the skills they possess, in the hours they work, in the tasks they perform, and in meeting various production schedules. For workers employed in the secondary labour market, risk – of layoff, of bumping, of going on UI, of being absent when the phone summons you to work, or of not being called in to work very often – has become a fact of life under lean production. These evolving work patterns at the mill have had a significant impact on family life, and particularly on many workers' wives who have had to make major adjustments to accommodate their partners' work patterns. The wives of many casual workers have entered the labour force to stabilize family income in case their husbands are laid off or go on UI. In the case of shift workers, wives and husbands often develop serial arrangements where he does various household tasks and activities with the children when he is off, and she does them for the four days when he does little but work and sleep.

These adjustments represent a re-scaling to the local level of global trends to increase productive efficiency. In Corner Brook, as elsewhere, they are re-scaled in a particular way to reflect local circumstances and traditions. Families in Corner Brook have long-established and unique spatial relations with the town's hinterland involving frequent visits to outports and cabins to visit extended family members, to attend a *ceilidh* or a country dance, and to engage in hunting, fishing, and other forms of self-provisioning.[15] They share household work in accordance with their own work schedules; and they make little use of formal child care because the community is rich in informal and family support systems.

Mill workers have not simply responded passively to global restructuring, even though economic necessities make compliance the norm. There has been a degree of resistance on the part of local players. Workers do not always let mill schedules take precedence over family priorities, fishing, or hunting. Phone calls from the mill are sometimes left unanswered, and vacations are scheduled to take advantage of their unusual access to rustic outports and secluded cabins for peace and tranquility in the company of family and friends. Shift and day workers generally avoid overtime. Above all, values of place, and identity with Corner Brook and its hinterland, remain a subtle counterbalance to global economic "imperatives." Thus the global and the local have played out dialectically in the way families have responded to the new patterns of work that accompanied restructuring.

Impacts of Restructuring on the Community 6

The previous chapters have examined in some detail the local contingency of the restructuring process, demonstrating that the form it has taken in Corner Brook has been much influenced by a range of factors specific to the town and to Newfoundland with its history of a strongly centralized colonial and provincial governance. These local elements began with the decision of the Newfoundland government in the years after World War I to give and to sell at very low prices the forest and power resources of the western part of the island to a well-connected British company (Armstrong Whitworth's banker was the Bank of England, no less) in order to launch the colony's second integrated pulp and paper mill.[1] As was described in Chapter 3, the Kruger purchase in 1984 was facilitated by two acts of the provincial legislature. The incremental restructuring of the 1980s and 1990s is attributable not only to Kruger's strategy of carefully managing its debt, but also to the status of Corner Brook as a single-industry town where the prosperity of the large service sector depended to a significant degree on the continuity of jobs at the mill. Had restructuring taken place on the scale seen at some other mills with major shutdowns as the whole mill was rebuilt – such as at Gatineau, Quebec (Rose and Villemaire, 1997) – the resulting disruptions in the labour market would have caused political fallout across the province that the provincial government was anxious to avoid. These and many other aspects of restructuring were played out at the local level, often due to the re-scaling of larger processes down to the provincial and more local levels in quite complicated ways. It follows that although restructuring can be seen as a dialectical process with global and local factors impacting on and responding to each other

(Harvey, 2000: 16), the post-structuralist view taken here sees the various actors not always falling neatly into two opposing camps.

It becomes apparent, when a town like Corner Brook is put under the microscope, that individual actors and community and provincial institutions have the ability to reinforce, to modify, and occasionally to resist large-scale forces emanating from *away*. Responses depend on what these groups, families, and individuals think is the most reasonable position and where their best interest lies. The deep historical roots of many Newfoundland institutions and the "inherited governance structures" account for considerable resistance to change (Tomblin, 2002). In Corner Brook, links to the land, to ancestral outports, to extended families, to the community, and to a self-provisioning lifestyle remain strong, but not universal: a number of individuals prefer a modern city-based lifestyle and advocate various strategies to connect more directly with the global economy.

The most dramatic changes to the Corner Brook community in the past 20 years have been demographic. A generation ago, Newfoundland had the highest birth rate in Canada and the largest average family size among the 10 provinces. Today, the province's birth rate is the lowest in Canada. Given the closure of the groundfish fishery and restructuring of the newsprint industry, jobs in Newfoundland's resource sector would have declined catastrophically had the offshore oil and gas industry not grown rapidly in the 1990s. But the latter is based at St. John's and has had little impact on the Corner Brook region. The result has been a relentless decline in the town's population since 1966 and, more recently, a substantial shift of population towards the older cohorts. The census of Canada for 2001 shows that of the 140 census agglomerations (CAs) in Canada, the population of 62 (or 44 per cent) has declined since 1996, so population decline has become quite widespread in Canada's CAs, and particularly in those located in the Near North. In fact, only five urban agglomerations had a faster rate of decline over the five-year period than Corner Brook's -7.9 per cent: Prince Rupert (-12.1 per cent); Elliot Lake (-12.0 per cent); Baie-Comeau (-9.0 per cent); Labrador City (-8.0 per cent); and Timmins (-8.0 per cent). Note that these are all peripheral resource communities that, like Corner Brook, have experienced restructuring crises. In all of these declining towns, younger adults have been decamping in droves for the past 10 years or more, so that as many as half of the children born there have left by the time they are in their mid-thirties. The result is a dramatic deficit of young adults in these communities when compared with the rest of Canada. Many high school graduates head out of town soon after completing their secondary education, leaving an extraordinary demographic hole and depriving the town of its more energetic, skilled, and entrepreneurial youth. In addition, very few of Canada's new immigrants have settled in these peripheral communities. In consequence, there is compelling evidence that Corner Brook will increasingly become a community of the elderly.

Implicit in this rapid rate of out-migration from Corner Brook is the existence of a low rate of new job creation, matched by a steady loss of existing jobs, as follows:

- at the newsprint mill, as noted in Chapter 4;
- in the public sector where, in the 1990s and 2000s, provincial cutbacks to balance the budget have resulted in jobs being trimmed;
- in the fishery where the Gulf of St. Lawrence groundfish fishery has been shut for a decade;
- in the service sector as it, too, has restructured, with the shrinking population demanding fewer services.

A related weakness has been the low measure of success of community economic development initiatives in the Corner Brook region, and in many other peripheral resource towns that have suffered comparable population decline. Had such initiatives created a steady flow of new jobs they might have reversed this out-migration and persuaded more young adults to stay in the community (Bates and Norcliffe, 2005). This weakness is attributed not to a lack of strong social networks but to a shortage of capital investment and, as Tomblin (2002) stresses, to the resistance of existing institutional structures to change. The result is poorly developed frameworks on which to build local economic development initiatives, and through much of Newfoundland's history the culture of centralized governance has contributed to this malaise at the local level (Cohen, 1975).[2]

The two preceding chapters have examined restructuring inside the mill and its impact on the workforce. In this chapter the discussion turns to the impact of restructuring on the community as a whole and on lifestyles within the community. Historically, these impacts have occurred not just during periods of retrenchment, but also during periods of growth. Thus if we look back into Corner Brook's history, we find that its ancestral communities – Humbermouth, Townsite, Corner Brook West, and Curling – were effectively put on the map by the original Newfoundland Power and Paper Company, and that the community has been transformed down the decades by subsequent changes to mill operations. Most notably, Bowater's post-World War II mill expansion led to in-migration, a building boom, and an increase in the town's population. As Table 15 shows, the city of Corner Brook's population grew steadily, to a peak of 27,116 in 1966, but since then has declined in every five-year census period so that by 2001 the population of 20,103 represented a loss of one-quarter since the peak.[3] The downsizing of the mill's workforce since 1984 has impacted on the evolving character of Corner Brook's service industries in two major ways. First, it has reduced the mill's total wage bill (measured in constant dollars) and therefore consumer spending. Second, the shift to higher skilling and training, the smaller size of families, the aging of the workforce, and early retirements have all contributed to changing lifestyles and, therefore, to changes in the mix of goods and services purchased. The elderly, for instance, spend more on pharmaceutical drugs and less on fashion garments and entertainment.

Table 15: Population of Corner Brook, 1921-2001

Year	Population
1921[1]	1,349
1935[1]	8,603
1951[2]	13,835
1956	23,225
1961	25,185
1966	27,116
1971	26,309
1976	25,198
1981	24,204
1986	22,719
1991	22,365
1996	21,895
2001	20,103

[1]Corner Brook + Curling + Humbermouth
[2]Corner Brook East + Corner Brook West + Curling

Sources: *Census of Newfoundland and Labrador*, 1935; *Census of Canada*, 1951, 1961, 1966, 1971, 1976, 1981, 1986, 1991, 1996

The rise of Corner Brook as the major regional service centre during the post-war period was the outcome of a conscious political decision by the Smallwood government to make Corner Brook Newfoundland's main service centre west of St. John's. There were credible rival claimants for such a status, including the railway terminus at Port-aux-Basques with its ferry link to Cape Breton Island,

Stephenville, which formerly had a large American military base, Grand Falls-Windsor, which was home of the older Anglo-Newfoundland Development newsprint mill, and Gander, with its large air base and airport. But the Bowater mill's world status during Newfoundland's post-Confederation period, plus the town's central location on the west coast, appears to have given Corner Brook a decisive edge in this competition. The provincial government used tax revenue and federal transfer payments to finance the provision of municipal services, to service new subdivisions, to build the Arts and Culture Centre, Sir Wilfred Grenfell College, the government's Squires Building, the provincial law courts, and to expand Humber Memorial Hospital. These and other public investments transformed Corner Brook from a specialized paper town into a more diversified regional service centre. A retired mill worker recalls:

> Only for old Joey Smallwood we wouldn't have what we got here now. He done all this. He put in Elizabeth Street. We were here before the roads, there were no roads when we came here. We brought all our lumber in a horse and buggy. There was no roads. But after – Joey started [the development]. Joey put the water, the roads up there, water and sewerage, lights and everything for years before they put any houses on it.

This would suggest that one interviewee's remark – "as soon as that mill closes down, this is going to be a ghost town" – must be an overstatement. Mill and mine closures such as at Schefferville in Quebec (Bradbury, 1984) have occasionally caused towns to perish, but towns represent a huge investment in sunk capital that is not easily written off (Clark and Wrigley, 1995, 1997). For instance, mill downsizing and out-migration from Port Alberni in British Columbia led to an influx of retirees from Vancouver looking for cheap retirement homes, and the town lives on. Corner Brook's regional service function would keep the town alive, but much diminished, if the mill were to close. Another interviewee's assessment seems closer to the mark:

> There's $40 million in payroll comes out of the mill, now it's not all directed towards Corner Brook . . . net take-home pay is about $400,000 a week easy, maybe I would say $500,000, that's just from the mill. You take that $500,000 away, this town I think, personally, would die or be pretty close to it . . . for every one job in this mill there are four jobs in this town that are connected to that mill . . . if this mill shut down – my home is valued at $75,000. I'd be lucky to get $30,000 for it.

The mill remains the town's biggest private employer, a major purchaser of goods and services, and an important subcontractor, and it makes a substantial grant to council in lieu of taxes. Thus, changes in mill operations due to post-1984 restructuring have had an impact on the city and region, even though that impact is more muted than it would have been in the days of the company town. This chapter seeks to describe the changes underway in Corner Brook in light of ongoing restructuring at the mill. It is at this scale that some of the most telling expressions of the local-global interplay are in evidence. Faced with what are globally driven pressures to restructure, the community has chosen to reaffirm its identity through its attachment to the local region. This theme is developed in four steps. First, demographic changes, specifically the out-migration of younger persons and the aging of the community, provide a crucial context for the other changes. Second, the vigour of recreation and outdoor life is interpreted, at least in part, as a response to the new regime at CBPP. Third, the expanding role that retirees play in Corner Brook's community life is seen as a specific response to restructuring. Finally, the sometimes belligerent attachment to place and region is seen as a form of local resistance to the economic changes imposed from the outside. The concluding remarks concern the startling implications that these trends, which are clearly evident across much of Canada's Near North, have for the survival of Canada's resource hinterland in its present form.

DEMOGRAPHICS

Newfoundland as a whole has undergone a more profound demographic change in the past 30 years than any other Canadian province. As noted previously, its birth rate, which was the highest in Canada at 32.5 per thousand in 1951, had become the lowest at 10.9 per thousand in 1995.[4] In Corner Brook, this declining birth rate was overlain by a shrinking job market for young persons and, more recently, the closure of the Gulf of St. Lawrence groundfish fishery and the bankruptcy of Lundrigan's Construction Company, which at its peak was a major employer across the province. The result has been a dramatic change in the town's population pyramid between 1961 and 35 years later in 1996 (see Figure 10). Given demographic trends in evidence elsewhere, the substantial contraction of the population aged under 15 and the percentage growth of those aged over 55 are predictable; but the other feature of the pyramid – the "bite" showing an undersized cohort of men and women aged 25-34 – is stark evidence of the out-migration of a discouraged generation. This cohort was, by definition, aged 5-14 in 1976. Tracing this cohort from 1976 to 1996 shows that its male component shrank from 2,830 to 1,415 (a loss of exactly 50 per cent), and its female component from 2,580 to 1,575 (a loss of 39 per cent). Mill restructuring and the downsizing of its workforce, coupled with the negative multiplier effect this has had on the service sector, has been a significant factor in the migration of many young men and women elsewhere in search of a job.

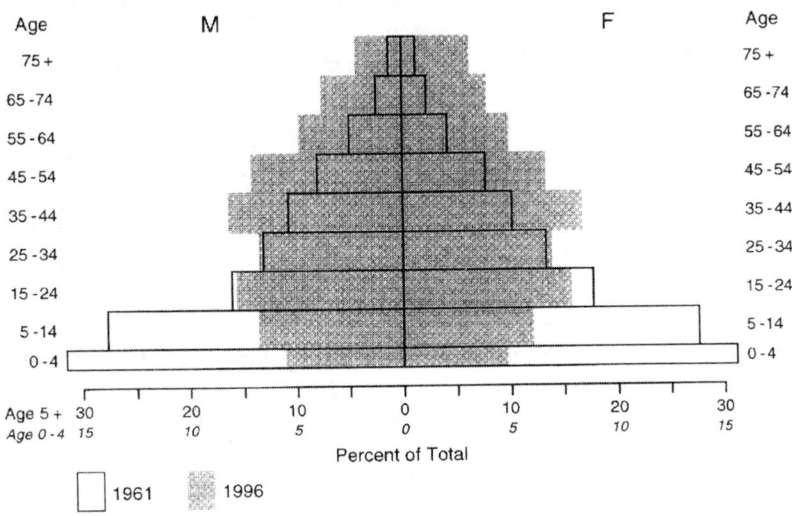

Figure 10: Demographic Profiles of Corner Brook, 1961 and 1996

An anecdote concerning the twenty-fifth class reunion that a mill worker's wife was helping to organize for her local high school provides telling evidence of the impacts of out-migration.

> The wife got a group formed just doing their twenty-fifth reunion from Herdman [High School] and there's 330 they tried to get in contact with and I don't know if it's 300 of them are from away. . . . They're all gone . . . sending back [invitations] from BC, Halifax . . .

It would be wrong to assume that this pattern of out-migration is simply the result of the loss of jobs in town. The teenage daughter of a mill worker pinpointed very clearly the issue of insecurity that has also come in the wake of restructuring. When asked whether she might encourage a future husband to work at the mill, she replied:

> I don't think so. It depends, I guess, on what type of job, like if he's secure with it – because everything I see Dad going through – and he

> went through a lot of pressure and stuff like that . . . the money isn't really [the issue], but a sense of security is.

This concern about job insecurity was widely shared by workers. During the layoff crisis of 1995, one worker in his mid-twenties summed up his prospects as follows:

> I'm 25 years old and if I lost my job here I can't see myself getting another job in this city. . . . I was moving to British Columbia. . . . They tells me there's a new mill opened up there, up at Fort Nelson.

RECREATION AND OUTDOOR LIFE

New patterns of work in the mill, with a downsized labour force, with many tradesmen working regular days, with shift workers having a four-days-on/four-days-off pattern, and with overtime work much reduced, have had an interesting impact on the life of mill workers. Excepting the casuals who are tied down by the requirement to be on call, mill workers now have the opportunity to connect more than ever before with the larger region. This is not a new trend, nor is it unique to Corner Brook. There has been a powerful attachment to the land and the sea in Newfoundland's settlements since their founding and, as Omohundro (1994, 1995) shows, living off the land is still an essential fact of life in northern Newfoundland, as it is in many other parts of the Canadian North. But the mill's new patterns of shift work and reduced overtime, when linked with road improvements and with growing disposable incomes used to purchase trucks and automobiles, snowmobiles, and all-terrain vehicles, have permitted an unprecedented reconnection to the land at all seasons. Older retirees stated in interviews that during the late 1950s they were the first mill workers to own vehicles, making it clear that the ability to return frequently to outports in Bonne Bay, on the Port au Port Peninsula, and places more distant, to build and purchase cabins, and to fish rivers, ponds, and arms of the sea further away than the Humber River and the Humber Arm, is a recent phenomenon. Prior to the 1960s, such visits were infrequent and difficult, especially in winter, and were normally made by boat or by bus, unless a destination lay close to the railway line.

The biggest changes have occurred in winter recreation patterns. Being located on the eastern shore of the Gulf of St. Lawrence has two effects on Corner Brook's winter climate: winds blowing over the open water pick up moisture that is deposited as snow when the relief of the coast triggers uplift of the saturated air, with a mechanism far more effective than the "lake effect" often remarked upon in regions surrounding the Great Lakes; and the waters also have a moderating effect on temperatures so that extremely cold air descending from Labrador is less cold after blowing across 300 or more kilometres of open sea. The Corner Brook area receives a mean monthly snowfall in winter of more than 100 centimetres, compared to 35 centimetres for Toronto, 50 centimetres for Montreal, and 60 centimetres for Quebec City and St. John's.[5] These large amounts of snow, coupled with increasing opportunities for leisure, have led residents of Corner Brook to search for new forms of winter recreation, which adds a marked seasonality to their outdoor activities. As in many other parts of Canada, new forms of winter recreation have changed lifestyles only recently. The snowmobile and all-terrain vehicle, cross-country and downhill skiing, and winterized cabins and cottages are all elements of Canada's new seasonal geography.

Quite a number of mill workers are enthusiastic about outdoor activities. One, just back from a three-day trouting trip in June, found that the hinterland of Corner Brook allowed him to enjoy a different set of activities in each season – in winter, "fishing and hunting, rabbit catching, and snowshoeing," while "early in the spring we go bear hunting . . . I shot one this month . . . two hundred pounds I guess . . . I got the skin curing to make a rug for our cabin." This was echoed by another outdoor enthusiast: "If you want to go fishing, it's just to go. It's the same thing with hunting; it's just a half-hour run and you're in a hunting area." Another cut his own logs and built his own cabin: "I ascribed them with an ascriber, cut them and fit them the old-fashioned way and put them together. Three hundred and some odd logs, and I done it all myself . . . with everything I got here, a home, a cabin, my wife, nobody wants to leave [if the mill were to shut], but if anything happened I would leave."

Corner Brookers are prepared to invest not just time, but also a significant part of their family's disposable income in these activities. Purchases of land and cabins are preferred by those who have fixed place attachments, whereas others purchase trailers and campers that permit greater mobility. One man remarked on his and his wife's new purchase: "We bought a trailer the other day and we haven't been up there yet [to the lake], but my son took it up. I love fishing . . . trout and salmon." Another told a similar story: "I got a new truck and truck camper, brand new one I had last year . . . we go off fishing . . . we got our pond, down the Sop's Arm road." Expenditures are also made on boats, snowmobiles, hunting and fishing equipment, and the many accessories and clothing that these various activities require.

Not all mill workers have equal access to Corner Brook's hinterland. Casuals, in particular, are tied to their phones, although some have arranged phone contact at family cabins so that they can return to town quickly if called in unexpectedly to work. The draw of the back country is very strong and some casuals are willing to risk missing a call from the mill for a fishing trip. Some older employees find that the outdoor activities they used to enjoy have become more strenuous and tiring, but typically they have simply substituted less demanding outdoor activities.

Table 16: Household Ownership of Means of Recreation

	Yes	No	Total
Summer cottage	33	102	135
Winterized cabin	26	109	135
Snowmobile	61	76	137
Motorboat	40	97	137
Camper/trailer	44	94	138

Source: Questionnaire survey, 1993.

Table 16 reports on the various recreation facilities owned within the interviewed households. It needs reading with care, for the numbers indicate a much higher level of involvement than might appear at first sight. Cottages, cabins, and campers are alternatives – very few households invest in more than one of these – thus the data indicate that three-quarters of the households own some form of recreational home. In addition, many of the remainder have free access to family cabins that are shared and treated as places of family reunion. In effect, only a few families do not have access to a retreat outside town. Nearly half of the households own a snowmobile, and this was in a sample where close to one-third of the interviewees were aged over 55. A quarter of the households possess a boat, and again, there are also many more households with free access to family boats. When asked how frequently they visited a cottage or cabin, only one in five said never, whereas 30 per cent went at least once a week (see Table 17). The survey revealed a high level of engagement with the country around Corner Brook.

In addition, Corner Brook is being transformed by one particular development, the Marble Mountain ski resort located beside the Trans-Canada Highway, 10 minutes north of town. Generally considered the best Canadian ski hill east of the Rockies, it remained relatively unknown until 1999 when Corner Brook hosted the Canada Winter Games. With a vertical drop of 500 metres, 27 ski runs (the longest of which is 3.6 kilometres long), over 400 centimetres of snow per year, moderate average winter temperatures of around -6°C, and a skiing season of over 100 days, the ski resort's main problems are its relative inaccessibility and the difficulty of getting publicity. Other winter sport destinations include the Blow Me Down Cross-Country Ski Park and Blomidon Cat Skiing.[6] In town, in 1997 Corner Brook opened a new Civic Centre with two ice rinks, one of which has enough seating to accommodate the spectators needed to make a junior A hockey team viable and the large audiences that watch major figure skating events. The local hope is that, in years to come, publicity surrounding the Canada Games will spur growth of the region's winter tourist industry. Meanwhile, Corner Brookers have easy access to the slopes of Marble Mountain.

Table 17: Frequency of Visits to Cottage or Cabin

	Number	%
At least once a week	40	29.9
Once a month	38	28.4
Once a year	29	21.6
Never	27	20.1
Total	134	100

Source: Interview survey, 1993.

Such an account of new winter recreation development might seem fairly routine in other parts of Canada, particularly in the West where a number of resorts have been developed over the past 25 years, including the Mount Allen Resort built for the Calgary Winter Olympics of 1988. But questions about the Marble Mountain development put to interviewees in Corner Brook provoked quite passionate responses about the importance of this development that went well beyond normal hometown boosterism. It was supported by those who were not active in winter recreation, as much as by those who were. Faced with mill restructuring, the push for mechanical logging, the closure of the Gulf groundfish fishery, the bankruptcy of Lundrigan's, the distance from developments in Hibernia and Terra Nova, the shrinkage of the local job market, and the out-migration of nearly half the preceding generation of youngsters, there was an almost defiant element in the response. The sense was that Corner Brook was not a helpless player in the global restructuring game: there were still some local strategies to be played, and most felt that winter tourism based on Marble Mountain was the best hope. It is noteworthy that Corner Brookers accepted in 1994 that they had to build a new community centre in order to host the 1999 Canada Winter Games, even though it was bound to push up local tax rates. There was, of course, some grumbling, but this was overwhelmed by the community response to being squeezed in the global game. Some action had to be taken, and the best option, both literally and metaphorically, was perceived to be in the local arena, and damn the costs.

Families often vary their recreational activity by season. Thus a couple, explain:

> *Wife*: We go fishing in the summertime and camping. Well, we did have a camper.
>
> *Husband*: [The new shift system] gives you four days. Lots of time to do something or go places.
>
> *Wife*: Well, we have a winter cabin. We go in the country in the wintertime.
>
> *Husband*: A winter cabin. Snowshoeing and skiing.

Many people see the winter as a period of opportunity. Some have developed a habit of varying their recreation by season, all the time taking advantage of the shift system and local opportunities. One couple spend a lot of time at their family's old home in Bonne Bay during summer and fall – a 90-minute drive from Corner Brook – using it for reunions with their extended family, but it is not winterized so they have to drain the pipes in fall and close up for winter. In winter they enjoy dancing in Corner Brook and neighbouring communities.

New opportunities for winter recreation are not universally welcomed; indeed, some people dread winter, while others see it as an opportunity. Various vehement remarks made by persons who dislike the winter months give some sense of the long and snowy winter that the city experiences: "you got to get used to driving in the snow and you know what to expect, and if [you] get your car home – fine, and if you don't that's fine too"; another laughs, "bring a snow blower – I don't see my neighbour because of snow"; more sombrely, another wife remarks, "I hate to see Halloween come because I know that means the snow is coming." A young wife joked, "if you are a winter person, it is wonderful. If you're not, like me, you'll have a hard time in winter. . . . Every winter I threaten to divorce [my husband] and go home to Mom because I can't take another winter here. But it is beautiful here in the summertime." Asked about life in winter, another couple suggested it was "very depressing sometimes" because "we can't get out; we can't do anything." This lament was repeated frequently: "You feel trapped in the night . . . [you] hibernate in the winter."

Those who enjoy winter recreation recognize that in some cases it can serve to divide a family. A mill worker with a teenage son was a winter devotee: "I can jump on my Ski-Doo, go up to the top of the hill, and go on right to Stephenville. I love the woods in the wintertime and skidooing. My son is the same. My wife, she'd rather stay in the house. She's not an outdoor person." Another enthusiast replied, "Winters are perfect. . . . We're gone summer and winter down to the cabin every second weekend. I don't know about other people, but I like winter." When asked at what seasons he went to his family's cabin, one outdoor activist responded: "Summer, winter, fall, it don't make any difference. As a matter of fact, winter is my best season." But he also accepted that a lot of people hibernate "like the bears do: they just use them for a summer cottage. Say October, November, when the weather turns real cold, they'll close up their cabins." The longer breaks afforded by the shift system allowed such enthusiasts to continue cottaging right through the year.[7]

This attachment to lake and forest, outport and cabin, is not unique to Newfoundland: similar patterns can be found in many places across Canada's hinterland, although here again there appear to be local differences. As Halseth (1999a) found in his study of Quesnel, Williams Lake, and 100 Mile House (all in the Cariboo region of British Columbia), coping strategies following restructuring and layoffs included widespread efforts to upgrade skills so as to reenter the labour market, reducing household expenditures, and, in a few cases, attempts to generate cash within the community, for instance, by taking in boarders. These strategies were less common in Corner Brook, probably because many of the laid-off workers were much older and less inclined to retrain, and were offered a bridging pension. Conversely, self-provisioning and reattachment to the countryside are not identified as coping strategies in these remote British Columbia towns. Also, the attachment to the backwoods found in Corner Brook is qualitatively different from the system of cottaging practised by Canada's metropolitan residents, who often recreate the city beside their lake, indulging not so much in country activities as displaced urban activities.

But in Canada's hinterland, the strength of many persons' interest in returning to the countryside and practising traditional pursuits is invested with another meaning – it amounts to a form of rejection of certain things modern, including elements of global culture. This rejection of things modern is by no means unequivocal – hunting may be done using a snowmobile, and fishing from a powerful boat using electronic fish detectors. But the bottom line is that pre-modern rights of access to common resources are kept alive, and to the extent that these are public, and not private, they represent an older way of managing the economy. That environmentalists frequently criticize these activities, ranging from seal and bear hunting to cutting peat and panning for gold, is beside the immediate point that to engage in such activities is to live outside the reach of the global economy and, therefore, to resist it.

Treating this reattachment to the land as a form of local resistance to globalization is a much debated point. Perhaps, goes the counter-argument, people do this simply because they enjoy it, just as some people enjoy baseball or euchre or quilting. A study by Mackenzie and Dalby (2003) of two super quarries planned in the Isle of Harris in Scotland and in Cape Breton, Nova Scotia, throws some light on this debate. They view this debate from the perspective of a post-structural political ecology in which the local communities have rearticulated themselves in the face of dispossession of their historical and religious traditions by larger economic forces. Just as crofting and Mi'kmaq traditions have been squeezed in Scotland and Nova Scotia, so the traditions of outport life, of hunting and fishing and hand-logging, are under siege in Newfoundland. In the face of corporate practices of industrial modernity, people in Harris and Cape Breton refused to subscribe to the separation of people from nature and of people from their community. Mackenzie and Dalby talk of "codes of community" achieved by the reassertion of older rights and identities that are beyond the reach of the international economy. Such codes were also in evidence in Corner Brook.

CORNER BROOK AS A RETIREMENT COMMUNITY

Increasing life expectancy, declining birth rates, and out-migration have turned Corner Brook into an aging community. Typical was the assessment of a tradesman who had immigrated to Newfoundland: "I think it's going to be a town of retired people." The population pyramid in Figure 10 shows that 21.3 per cent of men and 24.0 per cent of women are aged over 55 (in 1961 these percentages were 8.5 per cent and 7.8 per cent, respectively). Thus the percentage of the city's population over 55 years has increased roughly threefold in a generation. During the same period the age of retirement has declined, particularly since the early retirement package was introduced by CBPP in 1988, allowing workers to retire at 58 years.[8] The net effect has been to change quite dramatically the character of this aging community.

The stereotypical mill family of years gone by is arguably represented by the Stone family in Percy Janes's dark novel, *House of Hate*, which is set in Corner Brook. His narrative describes a mill employee working until an advanced age and then spending his brief remaining years cared for by his family.[9] Old age was a period of limited and declining activity and shrinking horizons. Such a stereotype – if it were ever true – certainly needs discarding now. Retirees, especially those retiring before 60, typically enter a phase of increasing community and social involvement and expanding horizons as they travel more and engage in new pastimes. Depending on their health and well-being, this period may last 15 years or more before physical limitations lead retirees to reduce their commitments.

One retiree, who had finished working at the mill in 1991, remarked that since retiring he had become very active, visiting his cabin at Birchy Narrows most weekends and downhill skiing at Marble Mountain frequently in winter. He remarked in 1994, "Yes, last year I skied 73 times, and one year before I skied 92, since I've retired." This is a remarkable record. Assuming that there are 100 skiing days between Christmas and early April, of which perhaps 10 per cent are marred by severe weather, then this retiree skied virtually every day the weather permitted. Skiing is often viewed as a young person's sport, yet this retiree aged close to 60 skied one of the more challenging ski slopes in Canada, snow or shine, on a daily basis throughout winter. By taking out a membership at Marble Mountain, he kept the cost of skiing down, and as for the crowds queueing for the lifts at weekends, he enjoyed that because it gave him a chance to socialize.

It might be suggested that this skier is somewhat exceptional – and as far as vigorous sports go, this is true – but if more passive sports like fishing, snowmobiling, golf, bowling, and hunting are included, then this case is quite unexceptional. Most of the retirees and their wives under the age of 70 are engaged in outside activities, including regular visits to cottages and cabins located out of town. There were some concessions to age, so that fewer were prepared to chase moose up hill and down dale in the hunting season. In two of the interviewed families, wives were more active fishing than their husbands and would go out with an ice augur to open a hole on a trout pond in winter. Good weather days at the cottage were typically devoted to doing repair and maintenance jobs, and most cabins were located close to a preferred fishing spot.

Other retirees have focused their energies in other directions, notably towards community activities, service clubs, and churches.

One senior, retired for four years, had undertaken several projects for his church:

> *Interviewer*: Has your lifestyle changed since you retired?
>
> *Walt*: Well, I thought I was going to have a lot of time on my hands, but I went over to the church and I've been working for the church ever since. It's always something to do in the church, and when you are doing it for nothing you can get all kinds of jobs. . . . We got her painted through, and then they've a little lodge down there. I've been handy with wiring so I went down and wired all the six new cabins they built down there last year. I wired them, but the electricians went to work and hooked them up.

Another retiree, who had finished working at the mill six years earlier, spent a year in New Mexico on a church mission and subsequently returned there with his wife for a long vacation. Others had used handyman skills to catch up on major projects around their home and cabin and to undertake modifications that they had never had time to do while working full-time. A few had used their skills to make such things as lawn ornaments and to tie fishing flies.

From a geographical viewpoint, the most remarkable change about the lifestyles of retirees was their mobility, at least until they reached an advanced age when physical limitations to travel had to be accepted. Many retirees had children living in towns across Canada, some at Canadian Armed Forces bases overseas, and some in the United States. Whereas in previous generations, these children would occasionally return home, the new retirees now take advantage of the opportunities to travel afforded by their pensions and by comparatively low travel costs, thus reversing the process by travelling to visit their children and grandchildren. Of course, these travels also take retirees to many other destinations. The following conversation with a retired couple who made extensive use of their mobile home is indicative of these changes:

> *Interviewer*: Do you get out much in winter?
>
> *Wife*: Yes.
>
> *Interviewer*: So you don't hibernate?
>
> *Husband*: No. Since I've been pensioned off, this is the first year yet we've been home for any length of time.
>
> *Wife*: Yes, this is the first winter we've been home.
>
> *Interviewer*: So you've travelled a lot?
>
> *Husband*: We go to Ontario. We go down to the States – Florida. And by the time we do that two or three months are gone, then, so we come back.

Another couple with two pensions enjoyed winter sun-flight vacations in such places as Arizona, Palm Springs, California, and New Mexico.

Despite the evident pleasure that many retirees take in travel, few have moved their home base. Of 233 mill retirees on pension in 1992, fully 92 per cent still lived in the Corner Brook region (defined to include Bay of Islands, the Humber Valley as far as Deer Lake, and areas to the south as far as Gallants). A further 7 per cent lived elsewhere in Newfoundland, mainly in settlements where their family has roots. Only one retiree lived outside the province (in Toronto). Taking into account the substantial exodus of seniors from big cities elsewhere in Canada, this suggests that Corner Brook's retirees have a remarkable attachment to their home turf. However, it is not just retired mill workers who have this attachment: the community at large shares these sentiments.

A SENSE OF PLACE

Time and again, interviewees revealed a powerful attachment to place and to their rights of access to the countryside and the sea. This is not unusual in small towns in rural Canada, although the special history of Corner Brook, built as a company town by its employees, may account for the exceptionally strong sense of identity. Comments such as "I'm not going to leave here. This is where I was born and this is where I will die" and "my third oldest son lives in Toronto and he'd do anything to get back here" are typical. One retiree, who had seen many parts of the world while serving in the merchant navy during World War II, made a series of affirmations for home:

> . . . I went all over the world and I never seen anything better than here in Corner Brook. . . . There's just no place like this rock. . . . Even now when I go on a trip, I go on a trip to Toronto, you've got to be looking over your shoulder instead of looking ahead where you are going, to see if someone is going to hit you. You never have to do that here. You can go and walk anywhere. You're in God's country.

Several dimensions are evident in this place attachment. First, there are the imposing natural surroundings and the recreational amenities noted above. Variations on the remark that "you can always leave here and an hour after, you're on a place where you can get a good trout" are illustrative of the proximity – even inseparability – of town and country. Second, family networks are often strongly developed in Newfoundland's geographically separated communities, which are organized partly along religious lines – Catholic and Protestant. This sense of community identity leads to remarks such as: "The people alone make [Newfoundland] special because they are friendly people and there is no way anyone is going to go hungry in Newfoundland." Third, there is a tendency to demonize large cities and to fear the entrapment apart from nature that one senses in large cities. Such a view highlights the contrasts with Corner Brook. The sentiments of the wife of a shift worker were shared by several interviewees:

> I think this is a great place to bring up children. We were in Toronto for a year and we hated it. Too fast. We lived in an apartment, there'd be fire alarms going off day and night. We just couldn't wait to get out of it. When you come here you can leave your car door open. We rarely lock our door at night.

Equally interesting was the fear of succeeding in a big city. A young couple who left the town and found good jobs in Toronto went to look at a house with a view to purchasing and settling in Ontario. This turned out to be a pivotal experience:

> I was all right when I knew I could come and leave [Toronto] any time I wanted, but then I felt that I was going to get trapped there with a house. . . . I didn't like the feeling it gave me and I got out.

In a similar vein, a paper-machine worker, very close to retirement, observed:

> Corner Brook – the most beautiful place to live in the world . . . where you can go to bed at night and feel safe, where you can still go to your cabin out in the country, leave your doors open and your windows unlocked and the same with my doors here. I don't know anywhere else in the world that you can do it . . . where your police officers still don't wear guns. . . . We have golden opportunities for your kids to grow up where you can allow them to go out and play and you don't have no worries that there are a lot of things for them to do. The opportunities are expanding all the time and it's a great place to raise a family.

Felt and Sinclair (1991) have examined this issue of "life satisfaction" in the context of the nearby Great Northern Peninsula, which stretches north from Gros Morne National Park to the Strait of Belle Isle. Despite the inhospitable climate of the region, the high unemployment rate, the low level of job creation, a relative lack of state infrastructure, and low incomes, its residents report a high level of satisfaction with their lifestyles. They like the place, blizzards, gales, and all. In seeking to explain this, Felt and Sinclair point to low levels of education and skills as an important factor, since in a large Canadian city a person without certain skills and a higher educational attainment would have difficulty finding a well-paying job but still would have a high cost of living. At home they have freedom, outdoor activities, closely knit families, virtually free land on which to build a mortgage-free home, informal labour exchange among friends and kin, and the assurance that "You'd never starve here" (i.e., country foods are readily available). So the opportunity cost of migrating elsewhere is quite high – they would have to give up many advantages found at home. The Northern Peninsula is now experiencing rapid population decline in spite of its life satisfaction, due to the effects of restructuring in the fishing and logging industries, cuts in public-sector jobs, and a squeeze on UIC (now called employment insurance, with stricter limitations on qualification). Indeed, the question might be, "Why do so many stay on?" For Felt and Sinclair, it is partly the opportunity cost of moving and the life satisfaction of staying. But current literature in the social sciences stresses that culture and institutions matter, too. Pile and Keith's *Geographies of Resistance* indicates a number of settings where assaults on local culture and identities have triggered various forms of resistance. Though the idea is controversial, an element of resistance can be seen in the way residents of Corner Brook have re-attached to the countryside in recent years – a close connection to the land was always there, but until roads were built in the 1960s and snowmobiles and trucks became widespread, the return to the country wasn't physically possible on a regular basis.

For the Corner Brook Pulp and Paper Company this attachment to place has one important repercussion. Time and again interviewees talked of the tension between the job insecurity that goes with lean production and their attraction to the place called Corner Brook. The dilemma is captured by the remark: "the last thing on our agenda is to pick up and move. We want to stay at home." From the employer's point of view, this is a great advantage because it allows a corporation to keep a reserve pool of skilled labour that can be called in when needed. In a city such as Hamilton or Calgary, or even Trois-Rivières or Sudbury, such skilled labour would eventually be lost to other firms so that an employer would have to conduct a costly program of recruiting and training to replace these workers. Restructuring and labour force downsizing in a community with such a strong place attachment, and little competition in the skilled labour market, have allowed the mill to keep a large casual labour force in place over several decades. Though it is impossible to put a dollar value on the resulting savings to the employer, it seems likely that they are substantial.

At the heart of this question of place attachment is the issue of globalization. In the post-company town of Corner Brook, workers face the global economy without the protective shell and mediating influence of a paternalistic employer. The driving force for thinking and acting globally is CBPP's need to remain competitive. Decisions by the state to deregulate international trade and finance, to form regional free trade blocs, and to permit the consolidation of firms into large multinational corporations have reinforced the argument of corporations that they have to be globally competitive. But this shift has also had an interesting effect, which has been to promote a renewed sense of local identity. The essence of the powerful place attachment among residents of Corner Brook is that it gives concrete expression to their local identity without getting into fruitless confrontation with global forces. Faced with threats of closure, layoffs, cutbacks, and job elimination to meet global competitors, people can respond by asserting an indissoluble bond between city and countryside. The most frequent expression of this bond is the recreational and social visiting that goes on, but it also finds more subtle expression. The remark that "People are learning now that they got to have other things they can depend on" is revealing, especially the use of the word "learning," for it implies that the change has come from within the community and has not been imposed from outside. This is not to deny that many younger Corner Brookers leave town to find work elsewhere, but they do so with a view to returning regularly for vacations, and quite a number plan to retire back to their hometown. It is also to stress that attitudes towards restructuring are quite complex and not easily read off like a graph. The labour unrest of the late 1980s has now largely evaporated, while Kruger has made significant steps to connect with the community, particularly in education and training. Attitudes to the events of the past 20 years are quite variable, depending on the circumstances of a family.

Maureen Reed's (2003) study of the Mount Waddington Regional District on Vancouver Island likewise builds on anti-essentialist understandings. She finds that a straightforward dialectical interpretation (pro-logging versus pro-environment) does not grasp the complexity of people's multiple-layering and social contingencies. The stance of her interviewees on the issues of logging and environmental protection varied in subtle ways depending on unique factors, and consequently their positions could not be neatly divided into two camps. Likewise in Corner Brook, the responses of interviewees to recent changes are complex and often subtle. Most people now accept the restructuring of the mill as a *fait accompli*, so that little is to be achieved on that issue at the level of the shop floor. Beyond the mill, however, is a local space in which they may assert their identities in diverse ways.

IMPLICATIONS FOR THE GREEN NORTH

Corner Brook is one of perhaps a thousand single-industry towns spread across Canada's hinterland. Various names have been applied to this vast region, but terms such as the Green North and the Near North capture the sense of its character, dependent on resources, farming, or forestry but distant from the nation's booming metropolises in which the *new economy* is flourishing. Distinct, again, is the White North or Far North, partly because birth rates in the Far North remain high and partly because the territories have been the object of considerable federal investment in the recent period as they gained territorial self-government. For Canada's Green North, the results of the 2001 Canadian census show that a dramatic decline is underway in many of its smaller census agglomerations (CAs), as well as in a few of the larger ones. As noted earlier, the population of 45 per cent of Canada's CAs and CMAs declined between 1996 and 2001. All but nine of these declining CAs were located in the Green North. Among Canada's CAs, Corner Brook had the sixth fastest rate of decline. Included in this list of declining towns are seven larger census metropolitan areas (Chicoutimi-Jonquière, Sudbury, Regina, Saint John, St. John's, Thunder Bay, and Trois-Rivières).

Implied in this eventuality is the failure of the dreams of Richard Rohmer and others who in the early 1970s envisaged that Canada's population and development would spread out from metropolitan areas into the Near North.[10] In practice, the reverse has happened. Investment, new jobs (especially in the service sector), immigrants from across the world, and migrants from within Canada have become enormously concentrated in Toronto, Vancouver, Ottawa, Montreal, Calgary, and a handful of slightly smaller metropolitan areas. The cause of decline of many of the hinterland towns is complex, and varies in detail from place to place, but an essential component in most places has been the restructuring of agriculture, fishing, and other resource industries, with lean (and capital-intensive) production leading to job elimination and, consequently, a negative multiplier in the service sector. This was compounded by the government expenditure freezes of the 1990s, which led to public-sector cutbacks

Projecting these economic and demographic trends into the future suggests that a dramatic change in the geography of Canada is underway as the life of the nation becomes heavily concentrated in a few huge metropolitan centres. The implication is that whereas the last four decades have seen hundreds of rural hamlets die, in the next decades we will also see villages and small towns begin to fall by the wayside. Given the fixed cost of maintaining services in these towns, the burden of upkeep reaches a tipping point as the population and the tax base decline, beyond which the cost becomes so heavy that the municipality becomes bankrupt. If the struggle to remain competitive in the private sector is then transferred to municipalities, higher levels of government may end up picking which towns and villages are to be supported and subsidized and which are to be left to sink. There appears to be some recognition recently of this issue at the federal level. Although the Paul Martin government announced in 2004 that it would support the development of public transport in Canada's largest metropolitan areas by returning a portion of the gas tax they paid, its rhetoric later in the year shifted to supporting all urban communities. By 2005, federal rhetoric was shifting yet again to a unified social service, which would be decentralized out of the major cities and delivered closer to the service consumers in smaller towns and rural areas. Given its size and economic base, Corner Brook will survive for a long time to come, but its population may shrink to no more than 15,000 by 2020 if there is not a substantial injection of new investment and jobs.

CONCLUSION

In Corner Brook, as in many other pulp and paper towns, the effects of restructuring have not stopped at the mill's gates. In these resource-based settlements the impacts of restructuring have flowed from the resource industry into the local community and on to the region beyond. It has often precipitated an outflow of young migrants who, despairing of finding well-paying jobs locally, move to booming parts of the resource frontier or to the large cities of the nation's heartland. It has to be stressed that mill restructuring is only one factor in the departure of discouraged workers, with job losses in fishing, in the public sector, and in the service sector also contributing to this out-migration. The demographic effects, particularly in Corner Brook, are striking, with the cohorts of young adults decimated and the birth rate in consequence dropping. The populations of resource communities are rapidly aging. By 2001, the percentage of Corner Brook's population aged 55 and over was 13 per cent higher than in Canada as a whole.

Meanwhile, the possibility of early retirement from the mill has created a group of active retirees who have filled some of the community niches that the decimated younger generation might have occupied, coaching youth sports, volunteering at hospitals and churches, and caring for children and the elderly. The majority of these retirees have active lifestyles, travel extensively, visit cabins and outports with high frequency, and fish, hunt, and pursue other sports and hobbies. Engagement with the land and the community is not, however, unique to the retirees since many mill workers on day work and shifts have also been able to take advantage of their work schedules to spend considerable amounts of time at cabins and trailers or at family homes in outports. This pattern is not unique to Corner Brook but is replicated in dozens of communities across the Green North. The connection with the land in Corner Brook is rather different from the cottaging practised by residents of Canada's big cities, which frequently involves a displacement of urban lifestyles into the countryside. In Corner Brook, the connection is to ancestral roots, to places saturated with social meaning, and to pre-modern patterns of use-value production. Such connections to the land are evidently a source of enjoyment, but they are also a subtle form of resistance to things global.

Corner Brook is not alone in facing the consequences of industrial restructuring. Across Canada in dozens of staple-based hinterland communities, global processes of restructuring have been re-scaled to find local expression in plant closures, the adoption of lean production, out-migration, and early retirements. Some communities have reinvented themselves by developing new economic roles. Chemainus painted murals on public walls and attracts day visitors from Vancouver and Victoria (Hayter et al., 1994); Elliot Lake became the retirement centre for Ontario's North Shore; and Moose Jaw went further by painting 36 large murals, rehabilitating as an underworld theme park a maze of tunnels supposedly used by Al Capone during the prohibition era, launching a Festival of Words, and crowning all this by installing Mac the (enormous) Moose. Corner Brook has not yet reinvented itself on such a scale, but there is frequent reference to the Marble Mountain ski resort, potentially a magnet as big as Whistler in British Columbia if only the accessibility problem could be overcome.

About two kilometres west of Cox's Cove – on the Middle Arm of the Bay of Islands – lies the abandoned outport of Brake's Cove. In the 1950s provincial planners had ordered this fishing hamlet closed and its inhabitants moved to new homes in Cox's Cove, where they would be less isolated and closer to schools, hospitals, and other social services. Walking to Brake's Cove along the cliff path in early summer, watching a pod of humpback whales blowing in the bay below, I was puzzled to see smoke rising from several chimneys in what I thought was a ghost hamlet. It transpired that the families of former inhabitants continue to occupy their hamlet in summer, using the former dwellings as summer cabins. The gardens are a bit overgrown, but the houses are carefully maintained, the pastures grazed by cattle and sheep, and in the neat cemetery the stones of family forebears were shown to me with unconcealed pride, together with an anecdotal story about the life of each of the deceased. The institution of the outport lives on, albeit in a modified way that takes into account the shift system at the mill and the daily rounds of local lobster fishermen. In Corner Brook and the surrounding region, place-based lifestyles and attachments have often not withered, as might be expected given the onslaught of supposedly superior modern alternatives. This tenacious attachment to place and to traditional practices is an assertion that, faced with powerful global pressures for economic change, local connections do still matter.

Conclusion 7

Do Canadian resource towns have to "shut up and dance," as Nigel Thrift (1996) puts the issue, to the tune of international capital? Are the resource industries of these towns so closely integrated into global commodity chains and financial networks that local effects are now residual? Is community resistance to global restructuring a distant memory?[1] This issue, which was posed in Chapter 1, will be re-examined here in light of the evidence presented in the intervening chapters.

THE IMPRINT OF RESTRUCTURING

The tangible results of restructuring in Corner Brook are fairly easily summarized. Kruger's goal in 1984 was to restructure the mill's operations to raise productivity in every department. In this the company has been notably successful – its targets have been achieved. The mill now produces high-quality white newsprint in large volumes, its labour productivity has risen steadily and substantially since 1984, and its workforce has slowly shrunk as mechanization has proceeded step by step. It recycles enough fibre to meet the environmental requirements of those states in the U.S. that set recycling targets, and it recycles bark as a fuel that is burned in high-tech boilers to generate steam and save on bunker C fuel oil. The installation of a secondary water treatment plant was slow, but it now almost completely eliminates the discharge of toxins into the Humber Arm. Logs are no longer transported to the mill in log tows so local streams and rivers are no longer polluted with fibres: logs are transported to the mill entirely by subcontracted truckers. The Corner Brook Pulp and Paper Company now ranks as one of the more efficient newsprint mills in eastern Canada.

The labour force has shrunk steadily but not dramatically, and their technical skills have risen significantly. There were some permanent layoffs, and some workers retired earlier than they might have wished following Kruger's takeover, but many more were moved to the casual labour force in 1984 and since then have slowly worked up the casual list to obtain regular numbers on the mill's workforce as older workers retired. The largest proportion of workers now follow a 12-hour shift system with four days on and four days off. As far as possible, tradesmen have been shifted to regular day work, with a few on evening shifts in rotation. There are two secondary labour forces, one employed as casuals who live close to the phone waiting to be called in, the other on capital projects who are laid off from time to time so that they do not qualify for the full range of benefits.

Ulrich Beck's (1992) concept of a risk society under reflexive modernity captures some important intangible consequences of restructuring for Corner Brook society. The two groups employed in the secondary labour market face job insecurity as an aspect of their life every day. When called in they earn good pay, but for those who are low on the lists, work can be erratic and stressful with more famine than feast. And when work is abundant, the unpredictable mix of day and night shifts, 8 or 12 hours long, requires a lot of adaptability. In turn, workers' families have to live with the omnipresence of income insecurity and variability of work patterns. For these workers, the immediate consequence of these work arrangements is not the flexibility that it gives the employer but the risk it imposes on them and their families (Norcliffe, 2003). Very commonly, wives have had to make substantial sacrifices to accommodate their husbands' unpredictable work patterns. Some have taken part-time or full-time jobs to cover family needs at times when there is not much work at the mill. Domestic divisions of labour have had to change, with wives taking on more activities when their husbands are working, and vice versa when they are not called in. These adaptations extend to children and close relatives, who have often helped out with child care and step in to take over various duties when the father is called in to the mill at short notice. For these families, risk and insecurity are an endemic aspect of their lives.

WHAT IS GLOBAL?

The key motor driving global industrial restructuring is capital, which, as Eric Swyngedouw (1996, 1997) reminds us, is constantly restructuring and reforming. In so doing, capital is changing its relations on many fronts. It re-scales its activities to other geographical scales; it creates new international divisions of labour; it searches out new markets; it forms powerful corporate groupings; it negotiates new political alliances; it invests in resources, utilities, industries, and services; and, according to regulationists, it occasionally shifts from one regime of accumulation to another. The current wave of globalization forms part of an ongoing shift from the integrated mass production of the post-war era (often labelled Fordism) to several locally constructed variations of post-Fordist production. In continuous process industries such as Canada's newsprint industry, lean production appears to be the emerging mode of operation. This is what Kruger has sought to introduce to Corner Brook in the years since 1984, and in this project it has been largely successful. As restructuring occurs, capital disposes of obsolete and worn-out equipment and unprofitable activities, very much along the lines of Joseph Schumpeter's *creative destruction.* Thus in the pulp and paper industry, obsolete technologies have been discarded, old equipment has been upgraded or replaced, and older imperial and continental relations are being superseded by newer international ones as corporations, marketing organizations, regulatory agencies, patterns of corporate transactions, and shareholders become increasingly global and increasingly unstable or unpredictable, forming what Lash and Urry (1987) refer to as *disorganized capital.* As noted in the introductory chapter, the term "disorganized" is taken, in this case, to denote changeable and continually renegotiated circuits of capital that are revolving at high velocity, and new forms of consumption marked by accelerating shifts in taste and fashions that, in their turn, require correspondingly greater flexibility and adaptability in the production of goods and services.

It is important to stress that the present phase of globalization has certain parallels with the free trade regime that developed in the nineteenth century and remained largely intact up to the Great Depression of the 1930s (McQuaig, 1998). From this perspective contemporary globalization is seen not as an unprecedented phase in history but as a return, in some respects, to the liberal conditions that existed in the later British imperial age. In the late nineteenth and early twentieth centuries, levels of GDP invested abroad by European industrial nations paralleled those of today, while international trade barriers were low and economies were much more open than they were by the 1930s. Both of Newfoundland's original newsprint mills were constructed during the latter part of this liberal era, so they were created under economic conditions not dissimilar from the present age. At least within the British, French,

German, and Dutch empires, capital was invested in a wide range of colonial enterprises whose products were exported to the respective imperial power.

Corner Brook was first created in the imagination of colonial administrators anxious to duplicate in western Newfoundland the success of the Harmsworth brothers' investment in a pulp and paper mill at Grand Falls. The latter mill had played an important role during World War I as a source of newsprint for British daily newspapers disseminating wartime propaganda. For Lord Northcliffe, it had proved to be a profitable venture – he had successfully harnessed the forest and hydroelectric power resources of the Exploits River valley that were given to him at a knock-down price, and he had recruited and trained a workforce. Administrators and politicians reasoned that the even larger untapped fibre resources of the forests to the west of the Exploits River watershed should also be able to attract new capital. Given the urgency of diversifying the Newfoundland economy out of its dependency on fishing and the palpable success of the Grand Falls mill, it was not difficult to mobilize the colonial system to contemplate a new newsprint venture in the Humber Valley. The realization of this imagined development depended heavily on the imperial system of investment, which, as Harold Innis demonstrated, promoted metropolitan capital investment in resource and infrastructure projects situated in remote parts of the colonial hinterland.

Pulp and paper mills in Newfoundland were little different, in a formal sense, from rubber plantations in Malaya, tea plantations in Kenya, and bauxite mines in British Guiana, except that the technical inputs were possibly greater. British capital was invested in colonial resources and infrastructure to produce raw and processed materials needed by metropolitan industry.[2] This system formed part of a regime composed, locally, of company towns, mines, and plantations, all privately owned enclaves operating, up to the 1920s, within a relatively open trading system. In the case of Corner Brook, a community of interest existed among Armstrong Whitworth, a British engineering and armaments firm urgently looking for new work in the peaceful post-World War I period, Reid Newfoundland, which had acquired large tracts of low-value forest in return for building the narrow-gauge railway across Newfoundland, and the government of the Dominion of Newfoundland, which was desperate to create jobs for soldiers returning from the war. At both Corner Brook and Grand Falls, the newsprint corporations established paternalistic company towns with internalized labour, housing, and retail markets. In many ways anticipating Eric Hobsbawm's magisterial study of *Industry and Empire*, Harold Innis saw this kind of development to form a staple economy. It was initiated by foreign capital invested in transportation and infrastructure and in the extraction of various resources for export to foreign markets. The staple economy created jobs in the host country and improved the system of transportation and communications, but much of its profits were repatriated, decisions of importance were generally made at remote head offices, and hinterland economies became "trapped" in these resource industries, thereby failing to diversify. Most of these economies were therefore caught in what Douglass North (1990) calls *path dependence*, an institutionalized arrangement that ultimately hampers economic performance.

During the Depression years of the 1930s, free trade gave way to protectionism as regulatory walls were built around national economies. The revived system of imperial preference was solidified by the Ottawa Agreement of 1933, the signatories of which – including Britain and British colonies and dominions – agreed to lower their mutual tariff walls. This placed Newfoundland's newsprint mills in a favourable trading position since the preference they were granted in the large British market was denied to newsprint producers located outside the Commonwealth. Thus a key element of the Bowater purchase of the Corner Brook mill from American interests in 1938 was that it reconnected the mill more firmly to the British trade system at a time when imperial preference and protectionism were ascendant. Indeed, due to the installation of the Commission of Government in 1934 at the height of the Depression when Newfoundland reverted to Crown colony status, the government of Newfoundland had become more colonial than it had been in the 1920s when the project was begun.

In the post-war years a permeable version of Fordism took shape in Canada, one subject to the influence and control of foreign (mainly American) capital. The concept of permeable Fordism has not achieved widespread currency in the social sciences, but it does reflect the increasingly continental orientation of the Canadian economy, particularly after 1945, at a time when the American-born C.D. Howe was Canada's Minister of Trade and Commerce (Norcliffe, 2001). During this period, an accommodation between labour and capital was worked out, private collective bargaining was institutionalized, and federal redistributive actions to promote regional equalization and nation-building were widely accepted.

More recently, capital has continued to find new ways to reconfigure its global arrangements. One part of this is the construction of newsprint mills in newly industrializing low-wage countries such as Brazil, the Philippines, and Indonesia, where cheap fibre, low-wage labour, and questionable enforcement of labour and environmental laws have attracted foreign investors. Producers continue to seek out cheap fibre in a world where few countries manage their forests on a strictly sustainable basis and even fewer extract realistic economic resource rents from their timber reserves. However, the most important event affecting capital was the ending of the system of closely regulated and protected world markets after 1970, which resulted in the institutional deregulation of capital movements, investment, trade, and corporate ownership. This led newsprint producers to press the case for making their operations internationally competitive and to introduce lean production in their pulp and paper mills, hence the difficult negotiations of 1984 described in Chapter 3. It is significant that Bowater sold the Corner Brook mill to Kruger of Montreal during this period of global deregulation and freer trade.[3] In the new global era, Bowater wished to shift its capital investments to places that, it was hoped, would increase corporate profitability. Kruger had subsidiaries in both the United States and the United Kingdom, so returning the mill to an Anglo-American alignment similar to that of the 1920s and 1930s was a logical step. In the name of this competition, pressure continues to be put on local producers to conform more and more to a global template, although not without local resistance, some forms of which are old and familiar, others new and subtle.

WHAT IS LOCAL?

Much has been written about the global economy, the global reach of transnational corporations, the huge sums involved in international capital flows, the rise of global cities that manage the global economy, and the emergence of global consumption patterns. Indeed, to insert the term "global economy" into a computer search engine is to invite a deluge of references. There is much debate, but there is also general agreement that international capital has played a central role in engineering the global economy. Less has been said about local effects; in fact, many analyses, written especially from the business school perspective, scarcely acknowledge their existence. The chronicle of Corner Brook suggests, however, that local effects are also important to community development. They appear to be connected with the notion of *embeddedness.*

As noted in Chapter 1, the concept of embeddedness can be traced back to the work of the noted anthropologist Karl Polanyi, who used the term to capture the idea that in pre-modern societies, economic relations such as buying, selling, producing, and consuming are "embedded and enmeshed" (Polanyi, 1955: 250) in social relations, in the institutions that govern a society, and (implicitly) in the historical and geographical contexts in which these social relations operate. As Veblen had already noted, such transactions may amount to forms of conspicuous consumption. In 1985 Granovetter applied the concept explicitly to the branch of institutional economics that stresses transaction costs. To oversimplify, it costs time and money to do a deal, but if deals are repeated (and become embedded) in dense and stable social networks where actors come to know and trust each other, then deals cost a lot less to negotiate. For this reason, most economic transactions become socially embedded. Granovetter's use of the term "embedded" is evidently narrower and more specific than that of Polanyi, and it puts much less emphasis on institutional structures. In the years since Granovetter's paper was published, the concept of embeddedness has been increasingly used by anthropologists, geographers, and sociologists. However, the meaning attached to the term has shifted yet again, to emphasize the way local and regional cultures influence the economies. Culture in this sense is an umbrella term that includes institutions, guilds and trade associations, networks of producers, the system that reproduces a workforce and its skills in succeeding generations, and the trading practices used to distribute products to markets.

David Harvey (1990: 418) adds an important dimension to our understanding of local culture. Space and time, he stresses, are social constructions, but they "operate with the full force of objective facts to which all individuals and institutions necessarily respond." The Corner Brook mill socializes its employees to a particular discipline of space and time. Shift workers know their schedules a year ahead, including the days when they need to be in town to work their 12-hour shifts and the blocks of time when they can spend a few days in their favourite recreational spaces. Casuals are more constrained in space and time: they need to remain in phone contact with the mill schedulers and accessible to the mill at short notice. As Tamara Hareven (1982) stresses, the pressing power of "industrial time" forces the adjustment of "family time," particularly when work schedules (such as those of the casuals) are irregular. In turn, this places local spatial constraints on the mobility of mill workers at certain times.

As was demonstrated in Chapter 2, the founding of the Corner Brook mill was embedded in Newfoundland's centralized political culture. Richard Squires, the entrepreneurial Newfoundland Premier from 1919 to 1923, was eager to create the local conditions necessary to launch his plan for a second newsprint mill. Where cheap resources, skilled low-wage labour, capital subsidies, or untapped markets are available, international capital may be persuaded to invest, provided corruption and instability do not make such an investment too risky. But the risks of creating a large newsprint mill and power facility at a location where a new labour force had to be recruited and trained, and markets for newsprint had to be found in faraway places, were clearly high. Squires had to offset these risks. Western Newfoundland offered cheap wood fibre, and Squires negotiated a bond for £10 million, issued by the British Trade Facilities Board. Even so, the Newfoundland Power and Paper Company faced a liquidity crisis within a year of the mill's opening. Subsequently, the company sold the mill to the International Power and Paper Company as international capital rapidly reconfigured the mill's ownership.

It did not take long for local interests to position themselves. They rewarded Squires politically for his swashbuckling initiatives,[4] and (notwithstanding his questionable dealings) years later transformed him into a local hero by naming the provincial building in Corner Brook after him. Workers inside the mill quickly organized and seem to have achieved some bargaining clout since, by the early thirties, their wage scales were three times those of the loggers. The loggers organized in the mid-thirties, and thereafter saw some modest improvements in their working conditions and pay scales. In subsequent decades, labour continued to confront the mill owners from time to time with strikes, grievances, and other acts of dissent, seeking to build local resistance to larger strategies. As recently as 1994 there was a prolonged faceoff between CBPP and mill employees over the proposal that employees loan $10 million to the company to see it through a financial squeeze caused by a sharp recession, an associated drop in world newsprint prices, and a need to make urgent capital expenditures tó alleviate environmental problems. The resolution of this confrontation was a compromise between essentially local and global interests.

Labour unrest is a normal form of local resistance to corporations, and it has a very long history. There are, however, more subtle forms of resistance. In Chapter 6 it was argued that there appears to be a strong attachment to place, rooted in Newfoundland's past when daily life was based on a fishing-cum-subsistence economy that required a close knowledge of the land and the inshore waters. Two generations of mill workers saw those attachments wither as the daily rhythm of mill work confined them to town much of the year and as poor land transportation made it difficult to return frequently to ancestral outports. In contrast, the present generation has seen new patterns of work (the 12-hour shift system in particular) create bigger blocks of free time, while land transportation has improved beyond recognition, in summer and in winter, both on the roads and off them. Many mill employees now revel in the pleasure of the land, and quite a few indulge in it with a passion. There is, of course, nothing unusual in heading out of town on weekends in North America, but the phenomenon in Corner Brook – and in many other resource towns across Canada's mid-North where the entry of international capital has triggered rounds of restructuring – is seen as a conscious reconnection with local culture. As Harvey (1990) notes, contestation over the use of space and allocation of time forms a part of the process of social change. Reconnecting to the land and the water in ways rooted in the culture of the resource hinterland reflects social priorities that differ markedly from corporate priorities. Harvey contends that the collapse of spatial barriers and the compression of time and space have heightened the search for local identity:

> The more global interrelations become, the more internationalized our dinner ingredients and our money flows, and the more spatial barriers disintegrate, so more rather than less of the world's population clings to place and neighbourhood or to nation, region, ethnic grouping, or religious belief as specific marks of identity. Such a quest for tangible and visible marks of identity is readily understandable in the midst of fierce time-space compression. (Harvey, 1990: 427)

In Chapter 6, in particular, evidence was presented that Karl Polanyi's concept of "embeddedness" captures many aspects of this idea of the local. The local is socially constructed, and it is learned over a long period. It cannot be fully grasped in a short time by an immigrant. It connects with local culture – in the case of Corner Brook, with fishing the bays and trout ponds, with catching lobster and crab, with cutting firewood and sawing logs and planks for construction, with hunting animals both large and small, with knitting and sewing and various handcrafts, with gathering bakeapples and partridgeberries, with mumming, and with keeping in touch with the family. All these activities require local knowledge that is first learned by children observing their mothers and fathers, and this knowledge is added to over a lifetime. Mill workers' attachment to place is a way of asserting that they have another life beyond the regimen imposed inside the mill by globalization.

In the case of Corner Brook there is an important provincial dimension to the construction of "the local." As noted in Chapter 2, the colonial tradition of strong government in St. John's and weak local government elsewhere was carried on by Premier Smallwood when Newfoundland became the newest Canadian province. Smallwood micromanaged the province's affairs for 23 years (Gwyn, 1968), and was followed by Premiers Moores, Peckford, Wells, Tobin, Grimes, and Williams, all of whom were inclined to concentrate decision-making at the provincial level.[5] In short, the municipal level of government, particularly outside the provincial capital, has been somewhat marginalized by a series of provincial governments that were unwilling to delegate much decision-making.

HOW POWERLESS IS THE LOCAL?

In her book examining the proposition that people are feeble in the face of the global economy, Linda McQuaig (1998) argues that we are not really entering uncharted waters. For a start, the current phase of globalization is not the first in history – indeed, in the heyday of the British Empire in the latter part of the nineteenth century the world economy was, in some ways, as open as it is today. At that time it suited British interests to promote free trade and foreign direct investment. More than anything it was the Wall Street crash of 1929, the ensuing Depression, and Roosevelt's New Deal that heralded an era of protectionism, regulation, and greater government intervention in the economy. This came to full flower in the age of Fordism and Keynesianism in the 1950s and 1960s when states in the West intervened, to varying degrees, in the working of both their domestic economies and the international economy. These changes over time indicate that, in the final analysis, the decision to advance or retard globalization has been a political decision (Cox, 1992). From time to time, elected governments with a mandate to promote national interests have made decisive moves to manage the international economy.[6] For instance, in the post-war period the International Monetary Fund, the World Bank, the General Agreement on Tariffs and Trade, various United Nations organizations, and many other agencies were created through conscious political decisions:

> governments around the world began to assert their power to bring footloose capital under some degree of democratic control . . . they established a new international financial system that gave governments, for the first time, considerable power over financial markets. With governments, rather than markets, flexing their muscles, the result was an agenda more geared to popular wishes, such as full employment and social programs. (McQuaig, 1998: 25)

Understandably, the private sector was critical of such interventionist moves and, as Herman and Chomsky (1988) note, tried with varying success to manufacture consent for their projects to promote enterprise.

Even when internationalism has been the main platform of international politics – as it was in Britain at the time Newfoundland's paper mills were constructed, and as it is in many industrialized countries today – regional and local governments retain jurisdiction over a range of matters. Thus local states (whether provinces, regions, or municipalities) have substantial residual powers. In a federal state such as Canada, powers are divided between federal and provincial governments, with the Constitution granting jurisdiction to the provinces over a wide range of social and economic issues. The government of Newfoundland does not have jurisdiction over international currency flows or over international trade and investment, but recent events showed that it had the ability to take a tough negotiating position – with a transnational corporation (INCO) in the development of the Voisey's Bay nickel deposit; with the Quebec government in the development of phase two of the Churchill Falls hydroelectric project; with oil companies in the development of Hibernia and Terra Nova; with the federal government over the allocation of oil revenues; and with foreign fleets in the management of the offshore fishery. And within Newfoundland, it is not an accident that Corner Brook and its politicians have played a disproportionately prominent role in provincial politics during the past half-century. This is a city with a direct interest in the global economy and a need for the local community to protect its interests from time to time.

Scott Lash and John Urry (1994: 3) pick up on the theme of community power in their fascinating book on *Economies of Signs and Space*. They write:

> the sort of economies of signs and space that became pervasive in the wake of organized capitalism do not just lead to increasing meaninglessness, homogenization, abstraction, anomie and the destruction of the subject. Another set of radically divergent processes is simultaneously taking place. The processes may open up possibilities for the recasting of meaning in work and in leisure, for the reconstitution of community and the particular, for the reconstruction of a transmogrified subjectivity, and for heterogenization and complexity of space and of everyday life.

Lash and Urry suggest that in the current age of disorganized capitalism, human behaviour is marked by greater *reflexivity*, with people questioning more and more where they stand and interrogating their own positions. Such self-questioning is inevitably set in the context of what we know of our place and our time, suggesting that the reflexive act of self-examination is an embedded process that builds on local knowledge. In Corner Brook, as has been suggested in previous chapters, self-examination has resulted in a recasting of the meaning of mill work and of leisure. Given the pressures of globalization in their work world, mill workers have countered by re-asserting their identity though place attachment in their leisure time and in local political action. For instance, the decision to bid for the 1999 Canada Winter Games in Corner Brook was a local political decision that had very wide local support.

SUBSIDIARITY AND THE NEW LOCALISM

Just as Lash and Urry (1994: 283) claim they see evidence of disorganized capital emerging in recent years, so, too, they see the emergence of the *disorganized state*. By that they mean a pluralistic political structure with all sorts of fragmented jurisdictions competing with one another, such as is found in the European Union. In practice, as the preceding chapters have shown, Newfoundland is in a similar position, with many centres of authority, including corporations, municipalities, the provincial government, organizations operating within the Atlantic provinces, the North Atlantic Fisheries Organization, the Canadian federal government, and agencies overseeing the North American Free Trade Agreement (NAFTA). Despite the historic inclination of central governments to guard their prerogatives, there has recently been a tendency towards *subsidiarity* with governments and agencies at the regional and provincial level acquiring more powers at the expense of the central state. For instance, one of the major mechanisms used by Canadian governments to reduce fiscal deficits during the 1990s was for higher levels of government to cede (i.e., "download") to lower levels the responsibility for various social programs. The federal government slashed its education and health budgets – at least until the budget of 1999 – on the grounds that these were provincial areas of jurisdiction. In turn, provinces passed on some responsibilities (roads, housing, and welfare programs) to municipalities.[7] There was a certain "beggar thy neighbour" attitude behind these developments; indeed, they were counterproductive to such a degree that as elections loomed in the late 1990s and early 2000s, and as the underfunded agencies began to experience major operating difficulties, funding levels were often restored. But the principle of subsidiarity remained intact, with some significant discretionary powers being passed down the hierarchy of government.

The net effect of this trend to subsidiarity has been to foster a "new localism" (Goetz and Clarke, 1993). Clarke (1993: 1-2) accepts that this may seem incongruous in an age of globalism, but she argues that:

> Recent evidence of intensified economic and political demands on localities and increased local development initiatives hint at a new local terrain with unexpected commonalities. Local officials the world over operate under heightened conditions of economic and political uncertainty. They now have social and economic roles and responsibilities that are often new and unanticipated. In each instance, global restructuring pressures compel local officials to reconstruct relations between the public and private sectors at the local level.

In a town like Corner Brook, which began as a sheltered company town, this has been a big transition. The company town was private, its role restricted to providing a limited range of municipal services. In the post-war years Corner Brook emerged as an integrated municipality and since then has slowly been enlarging its vision of what a municipality does. In the 1984 negotiations with Kruger, the municipality was largely out of the loop, but since then it has assumed an economic and social development role with a grander vision that includes a post-industrial dimension – and this in a municipality that was founded as an industrial company town. Of course, the Newfoundland and Labrador government retains a great deal of control over provincial affairs, following precedents that reach back far into the colonial era. But in comparison to the era when Premier Smallwood personally managed almost every detail of the province's affairs, there is now some decentralization of community development initiatives.

Simply put, Corner Brook now has a voice – it is becoming proactive and reflexive in the way it views itself. It is no longer simply a company paper town, even though a few post-colonial legacies survive. It is a regional service centre, it is an industrial town, but it is also actively constructing a post-industrial vision based on its sense of place. Visits by cruise ships are welcomed, and passengers are offered a program that highlights local culture.[8] Home-based traditional craft industries are promoted (Bates, 1997). Outfitters offer hunters and fishers a first-hand experience of the local countryside. The Blow-Me-Down Ski Centre is geared to attract outdoor enthusiasts from outside the province, as is the Marble Mountain ski hill. The Elder Hostel program at Grenfell College is designed to attract the thoughtful older tourist who will travel the extra mile to see something unusually interesting. The vigorous campaign to preserve the teaching role at Western Memorial Hospital was designed to shore up the city's status as the main medical centre in the west of the province. The city actively pursues the opportunity to host national events – conferences, the national triathlon championships, the Canada Winter Games – some big, some small, but collectively building on the idea that the place called Corner Brook has something special to offer.

AFTERWORD

In closing this chronicle of Corner Brook, we return to the lookout visited in this book's opening chapter, high over the east of the town, to contemplate the nature of this *place*. In mid-January the view westward over the town is very different from that of midsummer. Among Canadian cities, Corner Brook earns the crown for receiving the most snow. By mid-winter, Corner Brook's roads and driveways are marked out by high walls of snow that are added to almost daily by squalls coming in off the Gulf. This is good for the ski resort at Marble Mountain, but the trucks bringing logs into the mill now proceed down the Lewin Parkway with extra care to avoid jackknifing on the steeper grades. The short hours of daylight combined with the heavy cloud cover that generally prevails give a sense of greyness to the whole scene. The Corner Brook Pulp and Paper Company's newsprint mill is more visible than in summer as the steam rising from the production process creates clouds of vapour that float high into the cold air. The Humber Arm is frozen, but the grey-white mass of ice is broken by a wavy line where ice breakers have forged a watery route to the quays of the mill in order to keep the port open 12 months a year.

This time, however, we look on the scene not as an economic *space* in which newsprint production, commerce, and regional services operate; we look at Corner Brook as a *place*. Corner Brook and its region comprise a place invested with powerful meaning by its residents. Territoriality would appear to be a part of the human condition, but the strength of feeling about this place suggests that something else is compounding the territorial effect. Place attachment is a learned process, it is socially constructed – often in geopolitical terms, as evidenced by the strength of territorial feelings in Ulster, in Kosovo, and in Kurdistan. Institutions are created to sustain those feelings. But it may also be constructed in social and economic terms through debates over the political ecology of resources, environmental damage, waste disposal, factory and mine closure, jobs, and industrial restructuring. The argument made here is that place attachment and the will to exercise political power within that place give the local some countervailing authority in its dialectical dance with global capital. The local gig in Corner Brook brings out an enthusiastic crowd. This recasting of attitudes and institutions towards things local, this reassertion of the importance of community and region, this act of reflexivity gives the residents of Corner Brook some resilience when they encounter the destabilizing effects of the global economy.

The story of restructuring in the Newfoundland newsprint industry does not have an end, nor does the story of local responses to restructuring. During the summer of 2005, news has come in of Abitibi Consolidated's plans to close their newsprint mill at Stephenville due to concerns about the mill's timber supply and the high cost of energy (unlike Grand Falls and Corner Brook, the mill at Stephenville does not have a dedicated power supply). They also plan to decommission one of their paper machines at Grand Falls because readers are gleaning more of their news from the web, and less from printed paper so that demand for newsprint is falling. Not surprisingly, there was an immediate local response, with one of the mayor's insisting that "the assets can't leave the province." And so the local-global dialectic takes another turn, and the Newfoundland paper industry embarks on what may become another major round of restructuring. Once again the local arena will be where these global forces are played out.

Notes

Chapter 1

1. John Bradbury (1984, 1985) published a series of studies of Canadian resource towns that experienced extensive restructuring during this period.
2. Not all classifications include Corner Brook as a single-industry town due to the growth of its service role. In practice, one industry – pulp and paper – still completely dominates the city's manufacturing sector, and for this reason it is here considered to be a single-industry town.
3. Smallwood's intrusive personality is documented in Gwyn (1968) and Peckford (1983). In interviews, a number of elderly mill retirees remarked on how Premier Smallwood personally directed specific developments in Corner Brook.
4. For instance, in the mid-1990s Alabama and Georgia entered into a bidding war to entice a Mercedes-Benz vehicle assembly plant. Both offered around $200 million, but Mercedes then sought an additional $100 million subsidy to train a new workforce. Alabama raised its offer to $300 million and won.
5. By 2002 there was increased awareness of this local dimension. For instance, HSBC, one of the world's largest international banks, began to promote itself as "your local bank."
6. The concept of social capital, as advocated by Robert Putnam (1993) and quickly adopted into the discourse of development at the World Bank, has subsequently encountered considerable criticism, including that it commodifies social relations, ignores class and power relations, and has multiple meanings such as notions of trust that can be destroyed by the very process of exploiting social capital (see, e.g., Harris and De Renzio, 1997; and Adam and Rončevič, 2003). The argument advanced by Benjamin Chinitz (1961) in his comparison of New York (with a rich entrepreneurial base) and Pittsburgh (domi-

nated by steel and railroad oligopolies) has some affinities with the social capital approach.

7. There has been both a blunt and a subtle divergence of interests. For example, many older paper mills have ceased hiring new employees, which leaves them with aging workers who expect to spend most of their remaining life in retirement, while their children have migrated elsewhere because there no new jobs in town. This shifts a worker's balance of interest – she or he may have little interest in the company's future (being on the point of retiring), but substantial interest (as a retiree) in the quality of local lifestyles and the future of community and social services. For such a worker, higher local taxes may lower corporate profitability, but they may well raise the standard of community services.

8. It is best to view globalization discursively, with two opposing interpretations. The neo-liberal discourse sees globalization as the logical extension of economic modernity and stresses the economic gains resulting for exposing the global economy to competition. The post-structural account sees globalization as a rather chaotic process that is neither inevitable nor predetermined – it has both good and bad consequences; it has ambiguous impacts on the human condition; and it polarizes wealth at several spatial scales (see Jessop, 1999). Thrift (1996) labels the former the "Joshua discourse" – its transcendental rationality will lead us to the "promised land" – and the latter the "Genesis discourse" since the process is seen as much more heuristic.

9. Important studies include Barnes and Hayter (1992, 1994); Barnes et al. (1990); Halseth (1999a, 1999b); Hayter (1997, 2000a, 2000b); Hayter and Barnes (1997); Hayter et al. (1994); Prudham (2002, 2005); Prudham and Reed (2001); Reed (2003).

10. Antonio Gramsci (1891-1937) wrote his *Prison Notebooks* while incarcerated by the Italian fascist government in the 1930s. In later years it became the seminal document for the French School of Regulation. Essays in this collection were first translated into English only in the 1970s.

11. The critique that follows is based on a discussion paper presented by Adam Tickell at a seminar on "competitivity" at the University of Manchester, February 1997.

12. This study of restructuring in Corner Brook forms part of a larger study of selected Canadian newsprint towns published in a special issue of *Canadian Geographer* 41, 1 (Spring 1997).

13. Both regulationists (e.g., Aglietta, 1979; Boyer, 1990; Dunford, 1990; and Jessop, 1992) and neo-Schumpeterians (e.g. Freeman, 1982; Dosi et al., 1990) are in broad agreement on this point.

14. A wide range of candidates have been suggested. The discussion by Benko and Dunford (1991) of such variations as Kalmarism, Toy-

otism, and the Californian model is particularly instructive. See also Amin (1994), who discusses the variety of post-Fordist forms of production.

15. The 1984 Federal-Provincial Modernization Agreement for the Corner Brook mill included $12.5 million for environmental improvements at the mill.

Chapter 2

1. Since legislation was transmitted to Britain by the Governor with his comments, he could influence the response by the British government.
2. Hiller (1982) records that initially there was considerable hostility between the Reid Company and Premier Bond. Bond's government favoured the Harmsworth project at Grand Falls, and Reid eventually decided its best interest lay in co-operating.
3. The story of Grand Falls, and in particular the issues of gender and class in this newsprint town, are the subject of Ingrid Botting's fine-grained Ph.D. thesis (Botting, 2000).
4. There are interesting parallels between the settlement negotiated by John Cabot with Henry VII granting Cabot access to the resources of unknown lands, and the settlement negotiated by AND at Grand Falls.
5. Currently there are six generators at Grand Falls and four at Bishop's Falls.
6. Horwood (1986: 30) states that the bond was secured by a first mortgage on the mill.
7. Britain's Trade Facilities Act of 1921 authorized the British Treasury to finance loans within the Empire provided they were used to purchase British-made capital equipment. The primary aim was not to promote development in the colonies but to reduce unemployment at home (Hiller, 1990).
8. Most of the information from this section is drawn from Horwood (1986). Unfortunately, Horwood does not cite his sources.
9. These landholding arrangements became even crazier four decades later when Abitibi-Price purchased the failed linerboard mill in Stephenville, south of Corner Brook. The result was inefficient cross-hauling of logs.
10. This section draws mainly on interviews with retirees.
11. In contrast, workers without family contacts inside felt that their job prospects were limited: "No, I didn't think I'd ever get in the mill because I never had any family in there."
12. The population of the larger census agglomeration of Corner Brook, which includes settlements along the Humber Arm and up the Hum-

ber Valley, was 28,559 in 1991; this had declined to 27,945 in 1996 and to 25,747 by 2001.

13. Many of the details on the Bowater Corporation were gleaned from the annual reports of the Company.

Chapter 3

1. Statistics Canada, *The Labour Force* (Ottawa: Supply and Services, Jan. 1984), tables 1 and 3.
2. The factual base to this story of 1984 is drawn largely from the *Western Star*, published daily in Corner Brook. Only major events are cited in the notes since there were almost daily reports, rumours, and commentary on the unfolding drama.
3. From the time Newfoundland joined Canada in 1949 up until 1972, the Liberal administration led by Joseph Smallwood had engaged in a program of planned industrialization and centralization. Their philosophy was confidently *dirigiste*.
4. *Western Star*, 13 Jan. 1984.
5. Kruger Incorporated, *Annual Report* (Montreal, 1991).
6. *Western Star*, 19 Sept. 1984.
7. Other conditions included: renegotiating the Bowater Act (to grant Kruger similar concessions); reaching an agreement on forest management with the Newfoundland government; negotiating the mill's tax relations with the city council; inclusion of the Deer Lake power plant in the sale; agreeing that Bowater continue to sell a substantial amount of the mill's newsprint production for Kruger for the next two years; and approval of the sale by the Foreign Investment Review Agency.
8. *Western Star*, 2 Oct. 1984.
9. See, for example, Scott (1988); Storper and Walker (1989); Leborgne and Lipietz (1988); Peck and Tickell (1992). Note, however, that Webber and Rigby (1996) question this generalization, finding that rates of profit declined at different times in different countries during the post-war era.
10. See, for example, Donaghu and Barff (1991); Lipietz (1986); Jenkins (1987); Schoenberger (1988).
11. The context of Canadian restructuring is described by Holmes and Hayter (1993).
12. Prudham (2002) describes similar patterns of subcontracting in Oregon.
13. These issues are discussed by Sayer (1985); Clark (1980); and Norcliffe and Bartschat (1994).

14. In Newfoundland, UI was paid to a worker for a period of up to 26 weeks after layoff, provided contributions were made for 10 consecutive weeks before the layoff and a worker was "looking for work." Nicknamed "pogey," UI was a major source of income in Newfoundland, especially in fishing outports.
15. The fibrous material rubbed off the bark caused serious pollution along the river, while the finer fragments killed fish by lodging in their gills. The net result was to cause grave damage to fishing in the Humber Arm and along the Humber River system.
16. Discussions of the regulationist approach can be found in Dunford (1990); Brenner and Glick (1991); Norcliffe (1993, 1995); and Peck and Tickell (1992).
17. Verbatim Reports (Hansard) of the 39th General Assembly of Newfoundland were eventually obtained from the National Library in Ottawa.
18. *Western Star*, 10 Dec. 1984.
19. The president of Kruger, Stuart Hermon, announced on 11 December 1984 that Kruger would cancel the purchase if Bill 37 was not passed. *Western Star*, 12 Dec. 1984.
20. Verbatim Report, 6 Dec. 1984, R13.
21. The Newfoundland House sat until 4:30 a.m. on 11 December to complete the second reading. The bill was then rushed through committee and given third and final reading on 15 December.
22. These include the construction of an acid tower in December 1990; the closure of the sulphite pulping mill, resulting in 100 per cent thermo-mechanical pulping in February 1992; the installation of an infrasound combustion system in one of the bark boilers in July 1991; rebuilding number 3 and number 6 fired boilers in December 1991; and a new bark boiler begun in June 1993.

Chapter 4

1. There could be supply shortages in the medium term as recent silviculture programs will take some time to yield their full results.
2. Further details of the introduction of lean production at Corner Brook can be found in Norcliffe and Bates (1997).
3. In January 1988, 27 loggers working in the Glibe Lake area held a work stoppage because of the deep snow conditions, which made it difficult to extract eight-foot logs. They were finding it impossible to meet their daily quota of four cords. Mechanized logging can continue under such conditions.
4. This was nearly one-third of the annual wood harvest, which amounted to 675,000 cubic metres in 1986 and 930,000 cubic metres in 1990. The amount stored in the woodyard for the closed logging

seasons has been dropping so that by 1992 it was down to 174,000 cubic metres.

5. Historically, a small number of logs had been run down the Corner Brook, but this had long ceased.

6. Corner Brook Pulp and Paper Company is a wholly owned subsidiary of Kruger Corporation.

7. The soot problem seems to date back to 1982 when the mill started using wood chips for heating, but this became much more acute when the company began to burn bark.

8. Operations in the ground-wood mill ceased when paper machine number 7 was decommissioned in April 1983, and 496 "inside" employees and 250 woodsmen were laid off. The ground-wood operation was labour-intensive as logs were manually loaded into the magazines that fed the mill. The machinery was not dismantled until after the Kruger takeover.

9. The heat recovery units recycle heat from steam used in digesters to soften wood chips in the first stage of the pulping process. Previously this steam was released into the atmosphere.

10. Single-wire technology produces one "good" side, and one "bad" side, which is rougher and more likely to bleed printing inks.

11. Over the years the concrete foundation of this machine had settled unevenly so that at full speed the machine vibrated and had a tendency to tear the paper.

12. The capital equipment for the new dry end was delivered in 1992 and stored in an adjacent area awaiting a time when improved cash flow would allow the project to continue. In the meantime, the environmental compliance agreement made two other projects even more pressing – the completion of the bark-burner (which needed another $9 million), and the construction of a secondary treatment plant (at a cost of $30 million). *Western Star*, 11 Aug. 1994, 1 Aug. 1995.

13. With the mill on strike and the water in the Humber River at a low level, residents of Steady Brook called for a cleanup of the thousands of exposed rotting logs (*Western Star*, 23 Aug. 1988, 5). The press secretary for the Newfoundland Department of the Environment then announced that Kruger was responsible for the cleanup of the Humber River (*Western Star*, 24 Aug. 1988). The next day a Kruger spokesperson responded that "We didn't make the mess up there – Bowater did" and denied responsibility (*Western Star*, 25 Aug. 1988, 13). Meanwhile, hundreds of residents began to pull out logs as free firewood, and were encouraged over the next week by Kruger, the Steady Brook Council, and the local press to do so. A group of concerned citizens and boat owners then tried to organize a cleanup (*Western Star*, 31 Aug. 1988, 1). By early September, with water levels soon to rise as the water level at the Grand Lake dam was getting too high so that it had to be opened, appeals were made to residents to sal-

vage as much wood as possible, with several local committees working on the job (*Western Star*, 3 Sept. 1988, 9).

14. This is about two-thirds of the highest acceptable level of 120 micrograms of suspended particulate matter per cubic metre.

15. The bark-burner began operating on a trial basis in mid-July (*Western Star*, 15 July 1995). Ironically, the feed system caught fire (*Western Star*, 27 July 1995) and this delayed regular operation by several weeks.

16. *Western Star*, 23 July 1996, 1.

17. Ibid., 25 Sept. 1996, 1.

18. Abitibi-Price, previous owner of the newsprint mills at Grand Falls and Stephenville, owned by Abitibi-Consolidated since 1997, periodically co-operated with CBPP to reduce the costs of transporting logs to the mills.

19. Today, a soundproof control room is located at the dry end of each paper machine where the back tender monitors the specifications of the paper coming off the machine.

20. At the time of the purchase, there were three main unions. The largest union was the Canadian Paperworkers Union (CPU), which in 1992 merged with communications and energy workers to create the Communications, Energy and Paperworkers Union (CEP). CEP has five locals: Local 64, production workers excepting papermakers; Local 242, papermakers; Local 60, forestry workers; Local 57, mill guards; and Local 58, office workers. Mechanical workers employed in repair and maintenance belong to Lodge 1567 of the International Association of Machinists and Aerospace Workers, while the mill's electricians belonged to Local 404 of the International Brotherhood of Electrical Workers (this local switched affiliation to CEP in 1993).

21. *Western Star*, 16 July 1996, 3.

22. Up to 1988 loggers belonged to the United Carpenters and Joiners of America, but then voted to join the Canadian Paperworkers Union as Local 60 (which has since become the Communications, Energy, and Papermakers Union). Local 60 loggers cut wood both for the Corner Brook Pulp and Paper mill and for the Abitibi-Consolidated mill at Grand Falls.

23. The non-unionized loggers are a classic example of a dual labour force (Berger and Piore, 1980). In comparison with the unionized sector, they work a shorter season, are paid on a results basis (implying lower wages), receive no benefits, and are less mechanized.

24. *Western Star*, 29 May 1996, 3.

25. Ibid., 14 June 1996, 3.

26. This decline does not include workers moved into contingent labour markets, such as truck drivers delivering wood to the mill and subcontractors working on capital projects.

27. Atkinson (1985) associates a functionally flexible core and a numerically flexible secondary workforce with post-Fordist production. In Corner Brook, the secondary workforce existed even during the Fordist era, while only minor cross-trading is allowed in recent contracts. Hence, functionally, the core workforce remains fairly rigid.

28. For instance, an instrument mechanic reported that he worked the evening shift once every 10 weeks, by rotation with tradesmen with similar qualifications.

29. Craft unions were organized at Corner Brook as early as 1925, but they did not enter into contractual agreements until after World War II.

30. Details of these negotiations are discussed in Norcliffe (1995).

31. Laid-off workers had recall rights as follows: more than 10 years' mill seniority – 30 months on the recall list; 5-10 years seniority, 24 months; 1-5 years, 12 months; under one year, a period equal to their mill seniority.

32. The 1994 report prepared by Price Waterhouse entitled *The Canadian Pulp and Paper Industry* states that the forest industry in Canada lost $177 million in 1993, $1.4 billion in 1992, and $2.5 billion in 1991.

33. Newfoundland's provincial birth rate has gone from the highest in Canada to the lowest in two generations. From having the highest birth rate of any Canadian province of 32.5 per thousand in 1951, Newfoundland now has the lowest (10.9 per thousand in 1995 compared to a national rate of 13.2).

34. In 1990, the equivalent input was 2.2 hours in Sweden, 1.8 in the western United States, 2.5 in the U.S. South, and 4.4 in Canada as a whole (Forest Sector Advisory Council, 1991).

Chapter 5

1. Data presented by Hiller (1990) indicate that the mill was profitable throughout World War II, with net profit rising to almost $5 million in 1950. In the 10 years up to 1950, the mill made profits exceeding $20 million.

2. The questionnaire survey was conducted by Maureen McTeer and Justin Wyeth, undergraduates at Grenfell College in Corner Brook, Dr. Judy Bates, then a doctoral student at York University, and by myself. Of the mill employees we contacted, only two declined to be interviewed. This high response rate is attributed to the support of the Canadian Papermakers Union, which encouraged its members to assist with the study.

3. The interviews were conducted by the author. To preserve confidentiality names used are false names, and job descriptions are sometimes changed.
4. In practice, as noted in Chapter 4, some workers in the casual pool and assigned to capital projects have worked for long periods as day or shift workers.
5. The position of boom man disappeared in 1986 when CBPP ceased bringing in logs by water.
6. Workers receive half of their severance pay after six weeks. If they are rehired before two years, this has to be repaid in order to retain pension benefits, etc.
7. A clothing crew operator complained of "crampy hands" caused by years of pulling on "wet felts, man fashion." His hands "went to sleep" every night, and he had to pound them in the morning to wake them up. He was also prone to cracked feet as a result of working long shifts on hot concrete.
8. The senior position on a paper machine is the machine tender, who works mainly at the wet end where both heat and humidity are highest. At least one worker promoted to machine tender moved down to back tender (with an associated pay cut) to escape the heat and humidity.
9. For a long time, it has been the custom at Corner Brook for persons coming on shift to relieve workers on the previous shift early. Thus, in practice the shifts work more like 7 a.m. to 7 p.m.
10. Since Sunday shifts are paid overtime, casuals are called in less frequently on Sundays.
11. There is quite a complex formula involving 8- and 12-hour shifts. To earn overtime pay a casual worker has to exceed: four 8's and one 12; three 8's and two 12's; two 8's and three 12's; or five 8's.
12. Outport life is described in Mannion (1977).
13. These observations are based on a 1992 interview with a leading realtor in Corner Brook.
14. The great majority of hunters insist that moose meat tastes better than caribou meat.
15. Details of self-provisioning can be found in Bates (1997).

Chapter 6

1. One member of the Newfoundland legislature remarked: "The most lucky Company in the world is the Armstrong Whitworth Company, and the most generous country in the world is poor old Newfoundland" (Hiller, 1990: 17).

2. For instance, Richard Gwyn (1968) offers numerous stories of Premier Smallwood's micromanagement of the newly created province in the 1950s and 1960s.
3. The population by 2003 was almost certainly below 20,000, and if the pattern seen from 1996 to 2001 continues, the rate of out-migration and population decline will increase.
4. This compares to a national birth rate of 13.2 per thousand in 1995.
5. Various details of Corner Brook's climate are given in *The Climatic Atlas of Canada, Map Series 2: Precipitation* (Ottawa: Atmospheric Environment Service, 1984). Corner Brook also has a high number of days when snow lies on the ground – 120 days, compared to 40 for Toronto and 90 for Montreal. In the month of February there are, on average, 15 days with measurable snowfall in Corner Brook. Within Canada, only hill stations in the Rockies have comparable snowfall statistics.
6. An overview of the 1999 Canada Winter Games and winter sport facilities is provided in the *Globe and Mail*, 9 Jan. 1999, F11.
7. One interesting effect was that their children were never enrolled in summer programs in town because they were away at the cabin so much.
8. CBPP is offering early retirees a bridging pension until the Canada Pension Plan starts at 65 years. A casual worker hoping to obtain a regular number as a result of early retirements explains: "what they are doing, the company, is giving the fellow from 58 to the age of 65 with over 20 years' service, they're giving up to $200 a month on their pension to try to clear them out to let the younger men work."
9. Janes's novel, which was published in 1970 and based on the author's childhood experiences, was set in Corner Brook.
10. Richard Rohmer's book, *The Green North* (1970), was widely discussed in the 1970s.

Chapter 7

1. The possibilities for local resistance in the Atlantic Provinces are examined in Fairley et al. (1990).
2. If the Corner Brook mill was ostensibly a colonial creation, labour relations within the mill seemed to have developed along more continentalist lines, with large North American unions organized around a series of locals negotiating with the province's two large newsprint corporations. Partly for personal reasons, including a strong place attachment, Eric Bowater seems to have preserved something of a protective cloak around the mill long after worldwide changes in newsprint production should have forced restructuring. With his passing, Bowater's corporate board looked at the mill and decided it was not a priority in their evolving global production plan.

They used profits made at Corner Brook during good times mainly to finance new initiatives elsewhere.

3. Kruger has succeeded in the competitive world newsprint market by shrewdly purchasing older mills at relatively low prices and financing their modernization mainly out of cash flow and government subsidies, at the same time demanding flexibility from the labour force as part of a strategy to introduce lean production. Kruger's corporate assets were therefore built up without incurring major debt and without major borrowing (which might have forced the family company to go public).

4. In 1928 Richard Squires was elected representative for Humber (the local constituency) in the Newfoundland House of Assembly, despite an inquiry finding his practices as Premier to be unethical.

5. The tradition of strong colonial/provincial government overriding local government in Newfoundland is examined by Cohen (1975) in his study of political legitimation and the role of politics in everyday social life in the fictitious community of Focaltown.

6. In the late 1990s, for example, the federal government made moves to protect Canadian cultural industries.

7. In the 1990s, Ontario's Progressive Conservative government declassified many provincial highways, requiring regions and municipalities to maintain them. Low-income housing programs were likewise moved to municipalities.

8. The *Queen Elizabeth II* has visited Corner Brook a number of times while cruising the St. Lawrence.

Bibliography

Adam, F., and B. Rončevič. 2003. "Social capital: recent debates and research trends," *Social Science Information* 42: 155-83.

Adams, T. 1932. *Recent Advances in Town Planning.* London: J. and A. Churchill.

Aglietta, M. 1979. *A Theory of Capitalist Regulation: The American Experience.* London: New Left Books.

Albo, G. 1994. "'Competitive austerity' and the impasse of capitalist employment policy," in R. Miliband and L. Panitch, eds., *Socialist Register, 1994: Between Globalism and Nationalism.* London: Merlin Press, 144-70.

Allen, J., and N. Henry. 1997. "Ulrich Beck's risk society at work: labour and employment in the contract services industries," *Transactions of the Institute of British Geographers* 22: 180-96.

Amin, A. 1994. *Post-Fordism: A Reader.* Oxford: Blackwell.

——— and N.J. Thrift. 1994. "Globalization, institutional 'thickness' and the local economy," in P. Healy, S. Cameron, S. Davoudi, S. Graham, and A. Madinpour, eds., *Managing Cities: The New Urban Context.* Chichester: Wiley, 91-108.

Andrews, E., P. Gill, L.L. Hollett, E. Hollett, and O. Janzen. 2000. *Putting the Hum on the Humber: The First 75 Years.* Corner Brook: Corner Brook Newsprint.

Anglo-Newfoundland Development Co. 1909. *Newfoundland's New Industry: A Souvenir and a Record Issued to Commemorate the Opening of the Pulp and Paper Mills at Grand Falls, River of Exploits, Newfoundland, by Lord Northcliffe, October 9, 1909.* Grand Falls, Nfld.: Anglo-Newfoundland Development Co. (CIHM 86387).

Atkinson, J. 1985. "The changed corporation," in D. Clutterbuck, ed., *New Patterns of Work.* Aldershot, Hants: Gower.

Barnes, T.J. 1993a. "A geographical appreciation of Harold A. Innis, staple theory and local models," *Canadian Geographer* 37: 352-3.

———. 1993b. "Knowing where you stand: Harold Innis, staple theory and local models," *Canadian Geographer* 37: 357-9.

———. 1996. *Logics of Dislocation: Models, Metaphors and Meanings of Economic Space.* New York: Guildford.

———. 2001. "Retheorizing economic geography: from the quantitative revolution to the 'cultural turn'," *Annals of the Association of American Geographers* 91: 546-65.

——— and R. Hayter. 1992. "The little town that could: flexible accumulation and community change in Chemainus, B.C.," *Regional Studies* 26: 647-63.

——— and ———. 1994. "Economic restructuring, local development, and resource towns: forest communities in coastal British Columbia," *Canadian Journal of Regional Science* 17: 289-310.

———, ———, and E. Grass. 1990. "MacMillan Bloedel: corporate restructuring and employment change," in M. De Schmidt and E. Wever, eds., *The Corporate Firm in a Changing Environment.* London: Routledge, 145-65.

Bates, J. 1997. "Living Precariously: Paid Work in the Home in a Peripheral Canadian Mill Town," Ph.D. dissertation, York University.

——— and G. Norcliffe. 2005. "Community and household impacts of industrial restructuring: The case of the Corner Brook region, Newfoundland," unpublished manuscript.

Beck, U. 1992. *Risk Society: Towards a New Modernity.* London: Sage.

Benko, G., and M. Dunford, eds. 1991. *Industrial Change and Regional Development: The Transformation of New Industrial Spaces.* London: Belhaven.

Berger, S., and M.J. Piore. 1980. *Dualism and Discontinuity in Industrial Societies.* Cambridge: Cambridge University Press.

Berggren, C. 1993. "Lean production – the end of history?" *Work, Employment and Society* 7: 163-88.

Botting, I. 2000. "'Getting a Grand Falls Job': Migration, Labour Markets, and Paid Domestic Labour in the Pulp and Paper Mill Town of Grand Falls, Newfoundland, 1905-1939," Ph.D. thesis, Memorial University of Newfoundland.

———. 2003, "Labour recruitment, gender and class in the pulp and paper mill town of Grand Falls, 1905-1939," unpublished manuscript.

Boyer, R., ed. 1988. *The Search for Labour Market Flexibility.* London: New Left Books.

———. 1990. *The Regulation School: A Critical Introduction.* New York: Columbia University Press.

——— and D. Drache, eds. 1996. *States against Markets: The Limits of Globalization.* New York: Routledge.

Bradbury, J.H. 1984. "Declining single industry communities in Quebec-Labrador: 1979-1983," *Journal of Canadian Studies* 19: 125-39.

———. 1985. "International movements and crises in resource oriented companies," *Economic Geography* 61: 129-43.

——— and I. St. Martin. 1983. "Winding down in a Quebec mining town: a case study of Schefferville," *Canadian Geographer* 27: 128-44.

Brenner, N. 2004. *New State Spaces: Urban Governance and the Rescaling of Statehood.* Oxford: Oxford University Press.

______, and M. Glick. 1991. "The regulation approach: theory and history," *New Left Review* 188: 45-119.

Britton, J.N.H., ed. 1996. *Canada and the Global Economy: The Geography of Structural and Technological Change.* Montreal and Kingston: McGill-Queen's University Press.

Careless, J.M.S. 1989. *Frontier and Metropolis: Regions, Cities, and Identities in Canada before 1914.* Toronto: University of Toronto Press.

Chadwick, J. 1967. *Newfoundland: Island into Province.* Cambridge: Cambridge University Press.

Chinitz, B. 1961. "Contrasts in agglomeration: New York and Pittsburgh," *Papers and Proceedings, American Economic Review* 51: 279-89.

Clark, G.L. 1980. "Capitalism and regional equality," *Annals of the Association of American Geographers* 70: 226-37.

———. 1989. "Law and the interpretive turn in social science," *Urban Geography* 10: 209-28.

———. 1991. "Limits of statutory responses to corporate restructuring illustrated with reference to plant closing legislation," *Economic Geography* 68: 21-42.

———. 1992. "'Real regulation': the administrative state," *Environment and Planning A* 24: 615-27.

———. 1993. *Pensions and Corporate Restructuring in American Industry: A Crisis of Regulation.* Baltimore: Johns Hopkins University Press.

——— and N. Wrigley. 1995. "Sunk costs: a framework for economic geography," *Transactions of the Institute of British Geographers* new series 20: 204-23.

——— and ———. 1997. "The spatial configuration of the firm and the management of sunk costs," *Economic Geography* 73: 285-304.

Clarke, S.E. 1993. "The new localism: local politics in a global era," in Goetz and Clarke (1993): 1-21.

Cohen, A.P. 1975. *The Management of Myths: The Politics of Legitimation in a Newfoundland Community.* St. John's: ISER Books.

Cox, K. 1992, "The politics of globalization: a sceptic's view," *Political Geography* 11: 427-9.

———. 1997. *Spaces of Globalization: Reasserting the Power of the Local.* New York: Guildford.

Deyo, F.C. 1981. *Dependent Development and Industrial Order: An Asian Case Study.* New York: Praeger.

Dhesi, A.S. 2000. "Social capital and community development," *Community Development Journal* 35: 199-214.

Doeringer, P.B., and M.J. Piore. 1971. *Internal Labour Markets and Manpower Analysis.* Lexington, Mass.: Heath.

Donaghu, M.T., and R. Barff. 1991. "Nike just did it: international subcontracting and flexibility in athletic footwear production," *Regional Studies* 25: 537-52.

Dosi, G., K. Pavitt, and L. Soete. 1990. *The Economics of Technical Change and International Trade.* London: Harvester.

Drache, D. 1995. *Staples, Markets, and Cultural Change: Selected Essays of Harold Innis.* Montreal and Kingston: McGill-Queen's University Press.

Dunford, M. 1990. "Theories of regulation," *Environment and Planning D: Society and Space* 8: 297-322.

Eberts, D., and G. Norcliffe. 1998. "New forms of artisanal production in Toronto's computer animation industry," *Geographische Zeitschrift* 86: 120-33.

Fairley, B., C. Leys, J. Sacouman, and R. Williams. 1990. "Restructuring and resistance in Atlantic Canada: an introduction," in Fairley, Leys, and Sacouman, eds., *Restructuring and Resistance from Atlantic Canada.* Toronto: Garamond Press, 11-20.

Felt, L.F., and P.R. Sinclair. 1991 "Home sweet home! Dimensions and determinants of life satisfaction in an underdeveloped region," *Canadian Journal of Sociology* 16: 1-21.

——— and ———, eds. 1995. *Living on the Edge.* St. John's: ISER Books.

Flusty, S. 2004. *De-Coca-Colonization: Making the Globe from the Inside Out.* New York: Routledge.

Forsey, E.A. 1935. "The pulp and paper industry," *Canadian Journal of Economics and Political Science* 1: 501-9.

Fortier, R. 1996. "Le pouvoir de bâtir: société et aménagement de la ville industrielle au Québec 1890-1950," *Villes Industrielles Planifiées.* Québec: Les Éditions du Boréal.

Freeman, C. 1982. *The Economics of Innovation,* 2nd ed. Cambridge, Mass.: MIT Press.

Gershuny, J.I., and I.D. Miles. 1983. *The New Service Economy: The Transformation of Employment in Industrial Societies.* London: Pinter.

Gertler, M. 1988. "The limits to flexibility: comments on the post-Fordist vision of production and its geography," *Transactions, Institute of British Geographers* new series 17: 259-78.

Gibson, K. 1992. "Hewers of cake and drawers of tea: women, industrial restructuring and class processes on the coalfields of central Queensland," *Rethinking Marxism* 5, 4: 29-56.

Gillespie, B. 1986. *A Class Act: An Illustrated History of the Labour Movement in Newfoundland and Labrador.* St. John's: Newfoundland and Labrador Federation of Labour.

Goetz, E.G., and S.E. Clarke, eds. 1993. *The New Localism: Comparative Urban Politics in a Global Era.* Newbury Park, Calif.: Sage.

Graham, J., and K. St. Martin. 1990. "Resources and restructuring in the international solid wood products industry," *Geoforum* 21: 289-302.

Gramsci, A. 1971. *Prison Notebooks.* New York: International Publishers.

Granovetter, M. 1985. "Economic action and social structure: the problem of embeddedness," *American Journal of Sociology* 91: 481-510.

Gray, J.A. 1981. *The Trees behind the Shore: The Forests and Forest Industries in Newfoundland and Labrador.* Ottawa: Economic Council of Canada.

Gwyn, R. 1968. *Smallwood: The Unlikely Revolutionary.* Toronto: McClelland & Stewart.

Halseth, G. 1999a. "Resource town employment: a case study of patterns and perceptions of change in small town British Columbia," *Tijdschrift voor Economische en Sociale Geographie* 90: 196-210.

———. 1999b. "We came for the work: situating employment migration in BC's small resource-based communities," *Canadian Geographer* 43: 363-81.

Hamilton, L.C., and C.E. Seyfrit. 1994. "Resources and hopes in Newfoundland," *Society and Natural Resources* 7: 561-78.

Hanson, S., and G. Pratt. 1995. *Gender, Work and Space.* London: Routledge.

Hareven, T. 1982. *Family Time and Industrial Time.* Cambridge: Cambridge University Press.

Harris, J., and P. De Renzio. 1997. "'Missing link' or analytically missing? The concept of social capital," *Journal of International Development* 9: 919-37.

Harris, R.C. 2002. *Making Native Space: Colonialism, Resistance and Reserves in British Columbia.* Vancouver: University of British Columbia Press.

Harrison, B. 1994. *Lean and Mean: The Changing Landscape of Corporate Power in the Age of Flexibility.* New York: Basic Books.

Harvey, D. 1989a. *The Condition of Postmodernity.* Oxford: Blackwell.

———. 1989b. "From managerialism to entrepreneurialism: the transformation of urban governance in late capitalism," *Geografiska Annaler B* 71: 3-17.

———. 1990. "Between space and time: reflections on the geographical imagination," *Annals of the Association of American Geographers* 80: 418-34.

———. 2000. *Spaces of Hope*. Berkeley: University of California Press.

Hayden, D.L. 1986. *Newfoundland's Forests and Forest Industry: Statistical Information 1985 Bulletin*. Ottawa: Supply and Services Canada.

———. 1988. *The Size, Structure, and Socio-Economic Impact of the Logging Industry in Newfoundland, 1985*. Forest Resource Development Agreement Report 001. Ottawa: Ministry of Supplies and Services.

Hayter, R. 1997. "High-performance organizations and employment flexibility: a case study of in situ change at the Powell River paper mill 1980-1994," *Canadian Geographer* 41: 26-40.

———. 2000a. "Single industry resource towns," in E. Sheppard and T. Barnes, eds., *A Companion to Economic Geography*. Oxford: Blackwell, 290-307.

———. 2000b. *Flexible Crossroads: The Restructuring of British Columbia's Forest Economy*. Vancouver: University of British Columbia Press.

——— and T.J. Barnes. 1997. "The restructuring of British Columbia's coastal forest sector: flexibility perspectives," *BC Studies* 113: 7-34.

———, ———, and M.J. Bradshaw. 2003. "Relocating resource peripheries to the core of economic geography's theorizing: rationale and agenda," *Area* 35: 15-23.

———, E. Grass, and T.J. Barnes. 1994. "Labour flexibility: a tale of two mills," *Tijdschrift voor Economische en Sociale Geografie* 85: 25-38.

Head, C.G. 1976. *Eighteenth Century Newfoundland*. Toronto: McClelland & Stewart.

Henry, N., S. Pinch, and S. Russell. 1996. "In pole position? Untraded interdependencies, new industrial spaces and the British motor sport industry," *Area* 28: 25-36.

Herman, E.S., and N. Chomsky. 1988. *Manufacturing Consent: The Political Economy of the Mass Media*. New York: Pantheon.

Hiller, J. 1982. "The origins of the pulp and paper industry in Newfoundland," *Acadiensis* 11: 42-68.

———. 1990. "The politics of newsprint: the Newfoundland pulp and paper industry, 1915-1939," *Acadiensis* 19: 3-39.

——— and P. Neary, eds. 1980. *Newfoundland in the Nineteenth and Twentieth Centuries*. Toronto: University of Toronto Press.

Hobsbawm, E.J. 1969. *Industry and Empire: From 1750 to the Present Day*. Harmondsworth, Middlesex: Penguin.

Hochschild, A.R. 1989. *The Second Shift: Working Parents and the Revolution at Home*. New York: Avon.

Holmes, J. 1997. "In search of competitive efficiency: labour process flexibility in Canadian newsprint mills," *Canadian Geographer* 41: 7-25.

——— and R. Hayter. 1993. "Recent restructuring in the Canadian pulp and paper industry," Discussion Paper No. 26, Department of Geography, Simon Fraser University.

Horwood, H. 1986. *Corner Brook: A Social History of a Paper Town*. St. John's: Breakwater Press.

House, J.D. 2003. "Does community really matter in Newfoundland and Labrador? The need for supportive capacity in the new regional economic development," in R. Byron, ed., *Retrenchment and Regeneration in Rural Newfoundland*. Toronto: University of Toronto Press, 226-67.

Hsu, J.-H. 2000. "The limits of Guanxi capitalism: transnational collaboration between Taiwan and the U.S.," *Environment and Planning A* 32: 1991-2005.

———. 2001. "The Silicon Valley-Hsinchu connection: technical communities and industrial upgrading," *Industrial and Corporate Change* 10: 893-920.

Innis, H. 1954. *The Cod Fisheries: The History of an International Economy*. Toronto: University of Toronto Press.

———. 1956. "The teaching of economic history in Canada," in M.Q. Innis, ed., *Essays in Canadian Economic History*. Toronto: University of Toronto Press, 3-16.

Iverson, N., and D.R. Matthews. 1968. *Communities in Decline: An Examination of Household Resettlement in Newfoundland*. St. John's: Institute of Social and Economic Research, Newfoundland Social and Economic Studies No. 6.

Janes, P. 1970. *House of Hate*. Toronto: McClelland & Stewart.

Janes-Hodder, H., and P.R. Sinclair. 2003. *Logging the Main River Watershed: Environmental Policy and Politics in Western Newfoundland*. At: www.coastundserstress.ca/publications.php

Jenkins, R. 1987. *Transnational Corporations and Uneven Development*. London: Methuen.

Jenson, J. 1989. "'Different' but not exceptional: Canada's permeable Fordism," *Canadian Review of Sociology and Anthropology* 26: 69-94.

———. 1990. "Representations in crisis: the roots of Canada's permeable Fordism," *Canadian Journal of Political Science* 23: 653-83.

Jessop, B. 1992. "Fordism and post-Fordism: critique and reformulation," in M. Storper and A.J. Scott, eds., *Pathways to Industrialization and Regional Development*. London: Routledge, 43-65.

———. 1999. "Reflections on globalisation and its (il)logic(s)," in K. Olds, P. Dicken, P.F. Kelly, L. Kong, and Henry Wai-chung Yeung, eds., *Globalisation and the Asia-Pacific: Contested Territories*. London: Routledge.

Kelly, P.F. 2000. *Landscapes of Globalization: Human Geographies of Economic Change in the Philippines*. London: Routledge.

Kenney, M., and R. Florida. 1993. *Beyond Mass Production: The Japanese System and Its Transfer to the U.S.* New York: Oxford University Press.

Kenny, S. 2002. "Tensions and dilemmas in community development: new discourses, new Trojans," *Community Development Journal* 37: 284-99.

Labour Agreement between Bowater Newfoundland Limited and the Canadian Paperworkers' Union Local 242 and the Canadian Paperworkers' Union Local 64, 1982-1984.

Labour Agreement between Corner Brook Pulp and Paper Limited and the Canadian Paperworkers' Union Local 242 and the Canadian Paperworkers' Union Local 64, 1 June 1984 to 31 May 1988.

Labour Agreement between Corner Brook Pulp and Paper Limited and the Canadian Paperworkers' Union Local 242 and the Canadian Paperworkers' Union Local 64, 1 June 1988 to 31 May 1990.

Labour Agreement between Corner Brook Pulp and Paper Limited and the Canadian Paperworkers' Union Local 242 and the Canadian Paperworkers' Union Local 64, 1 June 1990 to 31 May 1993.

Labour Agreement between Corner Brook Pulp and Paper Limited and the Communications, Energy and Paperworkers Union of Canada Local 242 and the Communications, Energy and Paperworkers Union Local 64, 1 July 1993 to 30 June 1998.

Lang, G., and E. Mintz. 1979. "Attitudes towards public ownership of industry as a function of employment experience: employed and unemployed mill workers," unpublished manuscript, Grenfell College, Memorial University of Newfoundland.

Lash, S., and J. Urry. 1987. *The End of Organized Capital*. Cambridge: Polity Press.

——— and ———. 1994. *Economies of Signs and Space*. London: Sage.

Laxer, J. 1993. *False God: How the Globalization Myth Has Impoverished Canada*. Toronto: Lester.

Leborgne, D., and A. Lipietz. 1988. "New technologies, new modes of regulation: some spatial implications," *Environment and Planning D: Society and Space* 6: 263-80.

Lefebvre, H. 1991. *The Production of Space*. Oxford: Blackwell.

Leslie, D., and S. Reimer. 1999. "Spatializing commodity chains," *Progress in Human Geography* 23: 401-20.

Leyshon, A. 1997. "True Stories? Global dreams, global nightmares, and writing globalization," in R. Leys and J. Wills, eds., *Geographies of Economies*. London: Arnold, 133-46.

Lipietz, A. 1986. "New tendencies in the international division of labour: regimes of accumulation and modes of social regulation," in A.J. Scott and M. Storper, eds., *Production, Work, Territory: The Geographical Anatomy of Industrial Capitalism*. Boston: Allen and Unwin, 16-40.

Lovering, J. 1989. "The restructuring debate," in R. Peet and N. Thrift, eds., *New Models in Geography*, vol. 1. London: Unwin Hyman, 198-223.

———. 1990. "Fordism's unknown successor: a comment on Scott's theory of flexible accumulation and the re-emergence of regional economies," *International Journal of Urban and Regional Research* 14: 159-74.

Lucas, R.A. 1971. *Minetown, Milltown, Railtown: Life in Canadian Communities of Single Industry*. Toronto: University of Toronto Press.

Ludwig, D., R. Hilbron, and C. Waters. 1993. "Uncertainty, resource exploitation and conservation: lessons from history," *Science* 260: 17, 36.

Mackenzie, A.F.D., and S. Dalby. 2003. "Moving mountains: community and resistance in the Isle of Harris, Scotland and Cape Breton, Canada," *Antipode* 35: 309-33.

Mackenzie, S., and G. Norcliffe. 1997. "Restructuring in the Canadian newsprint industry," *Canadian Geographer* 41: 2-6.

Mannion, J.J., ed. 1977. *The Peopling of Newfoundland: Essays in Historical Geography*. St. John's: ISER Books.

Marchak, P. 1983. *Green Gold: The Forestry Industry in British Columbia*. Vancouver: University of British Columbia Press.

Marden, P. 1992. "'Real' regulation reconsidered," *Environment and Planning A* 24: 751-67.

Marshall, I. 1996. *A History and Ethnography of the Beothuk*. Montreal and Kingston: McGill-Queen's University Press.

Martin, R. 2000. "Institutional approaches in economic geography," in E. Sheppard and T.J. Barnes, eds., *A Companion to Economic Geography*. Oxford: Blackwell, 77-94.

Massey, D. 1995. *Spatial Divisions of Labor: Social Structures and the Geography of Production*, 2nd ed. New York: Routledge.

McQuaig, L.J. 1998. *The Cult of Impotence: Selling the Myth of Powerlessness in the Global Economy*. Toronto: Viking.

Neary, P. 1985. "The Bradley Report on logging operations in Newfoundland, 1934: a suppressed document," *Labour/Le Travail* 16: 195-232.

Neil, C., M. Tykkyläinen, and J. Bradbury, eds. 1992. *Coping with Closure: An International Comparison of Mine Town Experiences*. London: Routledge.

Newell, D., and R.E. Ommer, eds. 1999. *Fishing Places, Fishing People: Traditions and Issues in Canadian Small-Scale Fisheries.* Toronto: University of Toronto Press.

Norcliffe, G. 1993. "The regulation of Gerland: from mass production to flexible production in Tony Garnier's 'Cite Industrielle'," *International Journal of Urban and Regional Research* 17: 195-212.

———. 1994. "Regional labour market adjustments in a period of structural transformation: an assessment of the Canadian case," *Canadian Geographer* 38: 2-17.

———. 1995. "The regulation of restructuring: Corner Brook, 1984," *Environment and Planning C: Government and Policy* 13: 315-34.

———. 1999. "John Cabot's legacy: resource depletion and the resource cycle," *Geography* 84: 97-109.

———. 2001. "Canada in a global economy," *Canadian Geographer* 45: 14-30.

———. 2003. "Reflexive modernity, work insecurity, institutions and the new artisan," paper presented at annual meeting of the Canadian Association of Geographers, Victoria, BC.

——— and T. Bartschak. 1994. "Locational avoidance by nonmetropolitan industry," *Environment and Planning A* 26: 1123-45.

——— and J. Bates. 1997. "Implementing lean production in an old industrial space: Corner Brook, Newfoundland 1984-1994," *Canadian Geographer* 41: 41-60.

——— and D. Eberts. 1999. "The new artisan and metropolitan space," in J.-M. Fontan, J.-L. Klein, and D.-G. Tremblay, eds., *Entre la Métropolitanisation et le Village Global.* Sainte Foy: Presses de l'Université du Québec, 215-32.

North, D. 1990. *Institutions, Institutional Change and Economic Performance.* Cambridge: Cambridge University Press.

Ofori-Amoah, B. 1993. "Technology choice and diffusion in the manufacturing sector: the case of the twin-wire in the Canadian pulp and paper industry," *Geoforum* 24: 315-26.

Omohundro, J.T. 1994. *Rough Food: The Seasons of Subsistence in Northern Newfoundland.* St. John's: ISER Books.

———. 1995. "Living off the land," in Felt and Sinclair (1995: 103-27).

Osterman, P., ed. 1984. *Internal Labour Markets.* Cambridge, Mass.: MIT Press.

Parker, J. 1950. *Newfoundland: 10th Province of Canada.* London: Lincolns-Prager.

Peck, J. 1992. "Labor and agglomeration: control and flexibility in local labor markets," *Economic Geography* 68: 325-46.

———. 1996, *Work-Place: The Social Regulation of Labour Markets.* New York: Guildford.

——— and A. Tickell. 1991. "Regulation theory and the geographies of flexible accumulation: transitions in capitalism, transitions in theory," SPA WP-12, School of Geography, University of Manchester.

——— and ———. 1992. "Local modes of social regulation: regulation theory, Thatcherism, and uneven development," *Geoforum* 23: 347-63.

——— and ———.1995. "The social regulation of uneven development: 'regulatory deficit', England's South-East, and the collapse of Thatcherism," *Environment and Planning A* 27: 15-40.

Peckford, A.B. 1983. *The Past in the Present: A Personal Perspective on Newfoundland's Future.* St. John's: H. Cuff Publications.

Pile, S., and M. Keith. 1997. *Geographies of Resistance.* London: Routledge.

Pinsent, G. 1973. *The Rowdyman.* Toronto: McGraw-Hill Ryerson.

Piore, M.J., and C.F. Sabel. 1984. *The Second Industrial Divide: Possibilities for Prosperity.* New York: Basic Books.

Polanyi, K. 1955. "The economy as instituted process," in Polanyi, ed., *Trade and Market in the Early Empire.* New York: Free Press, 243-70.

———. 1957 [1944]. *The Great Transformation.* Boston: Beacon Press.

Pound, R., and G. Harmsworth. 1960. *Northcliffe.* New York: Praeger..

Power, N.G. 2005. *What Do They Call a Fisherman? Men, Gender, and Restructuring in the Newfoundland Fishery.* St. John's: ISER Books.

Preston, V., J.N. Holmes, and A. Williams. 1997. "Working with 'Wild Rose 1': Lean production in a greenfield mill," *Canadian Geographer* 41: 88-104.

———, D. Rose, G. Norcliffe, and J. Holmes. 2000. "Shift work, child care and domestic work: divisions of labour in Canadian paper mill communities," *Gender, Place and Culture* 7: 5-29.

Price Waterhouse. 1994. *The Canadian Pulp and Paper Industry: A Focus on Human Resources – Detailed Report.* Cat. no. 43-311. Ottawa: Supply and Services Canada.

Prudham, S. 2002. "Downsizing nature: managing risk and knowledge economies through production sub-contracting in the Oregon logging sector," *Environment and Planning A* 34: 145-66.

———, 2003. "Regional science, political economy, and the environment," *Canadian Journal of Regional Science* 25: 171-206.

______, 2005. *Knock on Wood: Nature as Commodity in Douglas Fir Country.* London: Routledge.

——— and M. Reed. 2001. "Looking to Oregon: comparative challenges to forest policy reform and sustainability in British Columbia and the US Pacific Northwest," *BC Studies* 130: 5-40.

Putnam, R. 1993. "The prosperous community: social capital and public life," *The American Prospect* 13: 35-42.

Raikes, P, M.F. Jensen, and S. Ponte. 2000. "Global commodity chain analysis and the French *filière* approach: comparison and critique," *Economy and Society* 29: 390-417.

Randall, J.E., and R.G. Ironside. 1996. "Communities on the edge: an economic geography of resource-dependent communities in Canada," *Canadian Geographer* 40: 17-35.

Reader, W.J. 1981. *Bowater: A History.* Cambridge: Cambridge University Press.

Reed, M.G. 2003. *Taking Stands: Gender and the Sustainability of Rural Communities.* Vancouver: University of British Columbia Press.

Roberts, S. 1995. "The world is whose oyster? The geopolitics of representing globalization," mimeo, cited in Leyshon (1997).

Robinson, I.M. 1962. *New Industrial Towns on Canada's Resource Frontier.* Chicago: University of Chicago, Department of Geography, Research Paper Number 73.

Rohmer, R. 1970. *The Green North.* Toronto: McLean Hunter.

Rose, D., and M. Villemaire. 1997. "Reshuffling paper workers: technological change and experiences of reorganization at a Quebec newsprint mill," *Canadian Geographer* 41: 61-88.

Rostow, W.W. 1960. *The Stages of Economic Growth: A Non-Communist Manifesto.* Cambridge: Cambridge University Press.

Rowe, F.W. 1980. *A History of Newfoundland and Labrador.* Toronto: McGraw-Hill Ryerson.

Saarinen, O. 1979. "The influence of Thomas Adams and the British New Town Movement in the planning of Canadian resource communities," in A.F.J. Artibise and G.A. Stetler, eds., *The Usable Urban Past: Planning and Politics in the Modern Canadian City.* Toronto: Macmillan, 268-92.

Sassen, S. 1991. *The Global City: New York, London, Tokyo.* Princeton, N.J.: Princeton University Press.

Sayer, A. 1985. "Industry and space: a sympathetic critique of radical research," *Environment and Planning D* 3: 3-29.

Schoenberger, E. 1988. "From Fordism to flexible accumulation: technology, flexible strategies and international location," *Environment and Planning D: Society and Space* 3: 3-29.

Scott, A.J. 1988. *New Industrial Spaces.* London: Pion.

———. 2000. "Economic geography: the great half century," in G.L. Clark, M.P. Feldman, and M.S. Gertler, eds., *The Oxford Handbook of Economic Geography.* Oxford: Oxford University Press, 18-44.

Setterfield, M. 1997. *Rapid Growth and Relative Decline: Modelling Macroeconomic Dynamics with Hysteresis.* London: Macmillan.

Simon, W.H. 2001. *The Community Economic Development Movement: Law, Business, and the New Social Policy.* Durham, N.C.: Duke University Press.

Sinclair, P.R., and L. Felt. 1992. "Separate worlds: gender and domestic labour in an isolated fishing region," *Canadian Review of Sociology and Anthropology* 29: 55-71.

———, H. Squires, and L. Downton. 1999. "A future without fish? Constructing social life on Newfoundland's Bonavista Peninsula after the cod moratorium," in Newell and Ommer (1999: 321-39).

Sinclair, W. 1991. "Controlling effluent discharges from Canadian pulp and paper manufacturers," *Canadian Public Policy* 17: 86-105.

Smith, F.E. (Lord Birkenhead). 1901. *The Story of Newfoundland.* London: H. Marshall.

Smith, M.R., A.C. Masi, A. van den Berg, and J. Smucker. 1995. "External flexibility in Sweden and Canada: a three industry comparison," *Work, Employment and Society* 9: 689-718.

Storper, M. 1997. "Regional economies as relational assets," in R. Lee and J. Wills, eds., *Geographies of Economies.* London: Arnold, 248-58.

——— and R. Walker. 1989. *The Capitalist Imperative: Territory, Technology, and Industrial Growth.* Oxford: Blackwell.

Sunstein, C.R. 1990. *After the Rights Revolution: Reconceiving the Regulatory State.* Cambridge, Mass.: Harvard University Press.

Swyngedouw, E. 1992. "The Mammon quest: 'Glocalisation', interspatial competition and the monetary order: the construction of new scales," in M. Dunford and G. Kafkalas, eds., *Cities and Regions in the New Europe.* London: Belhaven Press, 39-67.

———. 1996. "Producing futures: international finance as a geographical project," in P. Daniels and W. Lever, eds., *The Global Economy in Transition.* Harlow, Middlesex: Longman, 135-63.

———. 1997. "Neither local nor global: 'glocalization' and the politics of scale," in Cox (1997: 137-66).

Thrift, N.J. 1996. "Shut up and dance, or, is the world economy knowable," in P. Daniels and W. Lever, eds., *The Global Economy in Transition.* Harlow, Middlesex: Longman, 11-23.

———. 2002. "The future of geography," *Geoforum* 33: 291-8.

Tickell, A., and J. Peck. 1995. "Social regulation after Fordism: regulation theory, neo-liberalism and the global-local nexus," *Economy and Society* 24: 357-86.

Tomblin, S. 2002. "Newfoundland and Labrador at the crossroads: reform or lack of reform in a new era?" *Journal of Canadian Studies* 37: 89-108.

Watkins, M.H. 1963. "A staple theory of economic growth," *Canadian Journal of Economics and Political Science* 29: 141-58.

———. 1982. "The Innis tradition in Canadian political economy," *Canadian Journal of Political and Social Theory* 6: 12-34.

Webber, M., and D. Rigby. 1996. *The Golden Age Illusion: Rethinking Post-War Capitalism.* New York: Guildford.

Weber, A. 1929 [1909]. *Theory of the Location of Industries,* trans. C.J. Friedrich. Chicago: University of Chicago Press.

Williams, K., C. Haslam, J. Williams, T. Cutler, A. Adcroft, and S. Johal. 1992. "Against lean production," *Economy and Society* 21: 321-54.

Williams, R. 1980. *Problems in Materialism and Culture.* London: Verso.

Womack, J.D., D.J. Jones, and D. Roos. 1990. *The Machine That Changed the World.* Toronto: Collier-Macmillan Canada.

Wonders, W. 1954. "The Corner Brook area, Newfoundland," *Geographical Bulletin* 5: 29-57.

Wood, S. 1993. "The lean production model," background paper presented at conference on "The lean workplace: Labour's response to the new managerial agenda," CAW Conference Centre, Port Elgin, Ont.

Index

ISER BOOKS

Studies

70 **Global Game, Local Arena: Restructuring in Corner Brook, Newfoundland** – Glen Norcliffe
69 **What Do They Call a Fisherman?** – Nicole Gerarda Power
68 **Narratives at Work: Women, Men, Unionization, and the Fashioning of Identities** – Linda Kathleen Cullum
67 **A Way of Life That Does Not Exist: Canada and the Extinguishment of the Innu** – Colin Samson
66 **Enclosing the Commons: Individual Transferable Quotas in the Nova Scotia Fishery** – Richard Apostle, Bonnie McCay, and Knut H. Mikalsen
65 **Cows Don't Know It's Sunday: Agricultural Life in St. John's** – Hilda Chaulk Murray
64 **Place Names of the Northern Peninsula** - Edited by Robert Hollett and William J. Kirwin
63 **Remembering the Years of My Life: Journeys of a Labrador Inuit Hunter** - recounted by Paulus Maggo, edited with an Introduction by Carol Brice-Bennett
62 **Inuit Morality Play: The Emotional Education of a Three-Year-Old** - Jean Briggs
61 **The Marke of Power: Helgeland and the Politics of Omnipotence** - George Park
60 **Literacy for Living: A Study of Literacy and Cultural Context in a Rural Canadian Community** - William T. Fagan
59 **A Time of Reckoning: The Politics of Discourse in Rural Ireland** - Adrian Peace
58 **The People of Sheshatshit: In the Land of the Innu** - José Mailhot
57 **Looking Out for the Lads: Community Action and the Provision of Youth Services in an Urban Irish Parish** - Stephen A. Gaetz
56 **Making a World of Difference: Essays on Tourism, Culture and Development in Newfoundland** - James Overton
55 **Quest for Equity: Norway and the Saami Challenge** - Trond Thuen
54 **Rough Food: The Seasons of Subsistence in Northern Newfoundland** - John T. Omohundro
53 **Voices from Off Shore: Narratives of Risk and Danger in the Nova Scotian Deep-Sea Fishery** - Marian Binkley
52 **Fishing for Truth: A Sociological Analysis of Northern Cod Stock Assessments from 1977 to 1990** - Alan Christopher Finlayson
51 **Predictions Under Uncertainty: Fish Assemblage and Food Webs on the Grand Banks of Newfoundland** - Manuel Do Carmo Gomes
50 **Dangling Lines: The Fisheries Crisis and the Future of Coastal Communities: The Norwegian Experience** - Svein Jentoft

49 **Port O'Call: Memories of the Portuguese White Fleet in St. John's, Newfoundland** - Priscilla A. Doel

48 **Sanctuary Denied: Refugees from the Third Reich and Newfoundland Immigration Policy, 1906–1949** - Gerhard P. Bassler

47 **Violence and Public Anxiety: A Canadian Case** - Elliott Leyton, William O'Grady and James Overton

46 **What is the Indian 'Problem': Tutelage and Resistance in Canadian Indian Administration** - Noel Dyck

45 **Strange Terrain: The Fairy World in Newfoundland** - Barbara Rieti

44 **Midwives in Passage: The Modernisation of Maternity Care** - Cecilia Benoit

43 **Dire Straits: The Dilemmas of a Fishery, The Case of Digby Neck and the Islands** - Anthony Davis

42 **Saying Isn't Believing: Conversation, Narrative and the Discourse of Belief in a French Newfoundland Community** - Gary R. Butler

41 **A Place in the Sun: Shetland and Oil - Myths and Realities** - Jonathan Wills

40 **The Native Game: Settler Perceptions of Indian/Settler Relations in Central Labrador** - Evelyn Plaice

39 **The Northern Route: An Ethnography of Refugee Experiences** - Lisa Gilad

38 **Hostage to Fortune: Bantry Bay and the Encounter with Gulf Oil** - Chris Eipper

37 **Language and Poverty: The Persistence of Scottish Gaelic in Eastern Canada** - Gilbert Foster

36 **A Public Nuisance: A History of the Mummers Troupe** - Chris Brookes

35 **Listen While I Tell You: A Story of the Jews of St. John's, Newfoundland** - Alison Kahn

34 **Talking Violence: An Anthropological Interpretation of Conversation in the City** - Nigel Rapport

33 **"To Each His Own": William Coaker and the Fishermen's Protective Union in Newfoundland Politics, 1908–1925** - Ian D.H. McDonald, edited by J.K Hiller

32 **Sea Change: A Shetland Society, 1970–79** - Reginald Byron

31 **From Traps to Draggers: Domestic Commodity Production in Northwest Newfoundland, 1850–1982** - Peter Sinclair

30 **The Challenge of Oil: Newfoundland's Quest for Controlled Development** - J.D. House

28 **Blood and Nerves: An Ethnographic Focus on Menopause** - Dona Lee Davis

27 **Holding the Line: Ethnic Boundaries in a Northern Labrador Community** - John Kennedy

26 **'Power Begins at the Cod End': The Newfoundland Trawlermen's Strike, 1974–75** - David Macdonald

25 **Terranova: The Ethos and Luck of Deep-Sea Fishermen** - Joseba Zulaika
24 **"Bloody Decks and a Bumper Crop": The Rhetoric of Sealing Counter-Protest** - Cynthia Lamson
23 **Bringing Home Animals: Religious Ideology and Mode of Production of the Mistassini Cree Hunters** - Adrian Tanner
22 **Bureaucracy and World View: Studies in the Logic of Official Interpretation** - Don Handelman and Elliott Leyton
20 **You Never Know What They Might Do: Mental Illness in Outport Newfoundland** - Paul S. Dinham
19 **The Decay of Trade: An Economic History of the Newfoundland Saltfish Trade, 1935–1965** - David Alexander
18 **Manpower and Educational Development in Newfoundland** - S.S. Mensinkai and M.Q. Dalvi
17 **Ancient People of Port au Choix: The Excavation of an Archaic Indian Cemetery in Newfoundland** - James A. Tuck
16 **Cain's Land Revisited: Culture Change in Central Labrador, 1775–1972** - David Zimmerly
15 **The One Blood: Kinship and Class in an Irish Village** - Elliott Leyton
14 **The Management of Myths: The Politics of Legitimation in a Newfoundland Community** - A.P. Cohen
12 **Hunters in the Barrens: The Naskapi on the Edge of the White Man's World** - Georg Henriksen
11 **Now, Whose Fault is That? The Struggle for Self-Esteem in the Face of Chronic Unemployment** - Cato Wadel
10 **Craftsman-Client Contracts: Interpersonal Relations in a Newfoundland Fishing Community** - Louis Chiaramonte
9 **Newfoundland Fishermen in the Age of Industry: A Sociology of Economic Dualism** - Ottar Brox
8 **Public Policy and Community Protest: The Fogo Case** - Robert L. DeWitt
7 **Marginal Adaptations and Modernization in Newfoundland: A Study of Strategies and Implications of Resettlement and Redevelopment of Outport Fishing Communities** - Cato Wadel
6 **Communities in Decline: An Examination of Household Resettlement in Newfoundland** - N. Iverson and D. Ralph Matthews
5 **Brothers and Rivals: Patrilocality in Savage Cove** - Melvin Firestone
4 **Makkovik: Eskimos and Settlers in a Labrador Community** - Shmuel Ben-Dor
3 **Cat Harbour: A Newfoundland Fishing Settlement** - James C. Faris
2 **Private Cultures and Public Imagery: Interpersonal Relations in a Newfoundland Peasant Society** - John F. Szwed
1 **Fisherman, Logger, Merchant, Miner: Social Change and Industrialism in Three Newfoundland Communities** - Tom Philbrook

Papers

25 **The Resilient Outport: Ecology, Economy, and Society in Rural Newfoundland** – Edited by Rosemary E, Ommer
24 **Finding Our Sea Legs: Linking Fishery People and Their Knowledge with Science and Management** - Edited by Barbara Neis and Lawrence Felt
23 **Just Fish: Ethics and Canadian Marine Fisheries** - Harold Coward, Rosemary Ommer, and Tony Pitcher (eds.)
22 **Labour and Working-Class History in Atlantic Canada: A Reader** - David Frank and Gregory S. Kealey (eds.)
21 **Living on the Edge: The Great Northern Peninsula of Newfoundland** - Lawrence F. Felt and Peter R. Sinclair (eds.)
20 **Pursuing Equality: Historical Perspectives on Women in Newfoundland and Labrador** - Linda Kealey (ed.)
19 **Living in a Material World: Canadian and American Approaches to Material Culture** - Gerald L. Pocius (ed.)
18 **To Work and to Weep: Women in Fishing Economies** - Jane Nadel-Klein and Dona Lee Davis (eds.)
17 **A Question of Survival: The Fisheries and Newfoundland Society** - Peter R. Sinclair (ed.)
16 **Fish Versus Oil: Resources and Rural Development in North Atlantic Societies** - J.D. House (ed.)
15 **Advocacy and Anthropology: First Encounters** - Robert Paine (ed.)
14 **Indigenous Peoples and the Nation-State: Fourth World Politics in Canada, Australia and Norway** - Noel Dyck (ed.)
13 **Minorities and Mother Country Imagery** - Gerald Gold (ed.)
12 **The Politics of Indianness: Case Studies of Native Ethnopolitics in Canada** - Adrian Tanner (ed.)
11 **Belonging: Identity and Social Organisation in British Rural Cultures** - Anthony P. Cohen (ed.)
10 **Politically Speaking: Cross-Cultural Studies of Rhetoric** - Robert Paine (ed.)
9 **A House Divided? Anthropological Studies of Factionalism** - M. Silverman and R.F. Salisbury (eds.)
8 **The Peopling of Newfoundland: Essays in Historical Geography** - John J. Mannion (ed.)
7 **The White Arctic: Anthropological Essays on Tutelage and Ethnicity** - Robert Paine (ed.)
6 **Consequences of Offshore Oil and Gas - Norway, Scotland and Newfoundland** - M.J. Scarlett (ed.)
5 **North Atlantic Fishermen: Anthropological Essays on Modern Fishing** - Raoul Andersen and Cato Wadel (eds.)
3 **The Compact: Selected Dimensions of Friendship** - Elliott Leyton (ed.)
2 **Patrons and Brokers in the East Arctic** - Robert Paine (ed.)
1 **Viewpoints on Communities in Crisis** - Michael L. Skolnik (ed.)

Mailing address:

ISER Books
Memorial University of Newfoundland
St. John's, Newfoundland
A1C 5S7

Telephone: (709) 737-7474
FAX : (709) 737-7560
email: iser-books@mun.ca
WEB site: http://www.mun.ca/iser/

Quebec, Canada
2005